Denying the Spoils of War

DENYING THE SPOILS OF WAR

The Politics of Invasion and Nonrecognition

JOSEPH O'MAHONEY

EDINBURGH
University Press

Edinburgh University Press is one of the leading university presses in the UK. We publish academic books and journals in our selected subject areas across the humanities and social sciences, combining cutting-edge scholarship with high editorial and production values to produce academic works of lasting importance. For more information visit our website: edinburghuniversitypress.com

Edinburgh University Press Ltd
The Tun – Holyrood Road,
12(2f) Jackson's Entry,
Edinburgh EH8 8PJ

Typeset in 10.5/12.5 Adobe Sabon by
IDSUK (DataConnection) Ltd

A CIP record for this book is available from the British Library

ISBN 978 1 4744 3443 0 (hardback)
ISBN 978 1 4744 3444 7 (webready PDF)
ISBN 978 1 4744 3445 4 (epub)
ISBN 978 1 4744 5219 9 (paperback)

Contents

List of figures and tables

Acknowledgements

This book began as a simple question I had when I was in grad school: how does the international community react when states break the rule against aggression? That the answer appeared to be, 'nonrecognition, sometimes', only generated more questions. As I have come to realise while writing the book, nonrecognition is unfortunately underappreciated both as an object of study and as a force driving important international political outcomes. I hope I have begun to change that situation with this book.

I have been very lucky in the process of writing the various papers, articles and dissertation that finally produced this book because I have had the help and support of so many people and institutions. Martha Finnemore has been an unstinting critic of underdeveloped notions, unclear concepts and unelucidated logic. Henry Farrell provided many of the building blocks of my thinking on institutions and rules and introduced me to literature that I would otherwise never have been exposed to. Susan Sell has been an unflagging source of encouragement throughout my career. Robert Adcock is a beacon of intellectual integrity in every sense of the term. In numerous ways, Robert has been a source of enthusiasm for the life of the mind and of practical help and advice.

For funding and other assistance, I am grateful to The George Washington University (GWU) Department of Political Science, the Loughran Foundation, the Josephine De Karman Fellowship Trust, the Seton Hall University School of Diplomacy and International Relations, the Seton Hall University Research Council, the Stanton Foundation and the Security Studies Program at the Massachusetts Institute of Technology (MIT).

For making their collections open to me and helping me to access materials, I am grateful to the Gelman Library at GWU, the Library of Congress in Washington DC, the Bodleian Library at Oxford University, the National Archives at Kew, Seton Hall University Libraries, the Dewey Library at MIT, the Boston Athenaeum and the Boston Public Library.

At Seton Hall, I would like to thank Nabeela Alam, Margarita Balmaceda, Assefaw Bariagaber, Andrea Bartoli, Martin Edwards, Yinan He, Yanzhong Huang, Ben Goldfrank, Omer Gokcekus, Susan Malcolm, Fredline M'Cormack-Hale, Sara Moller, Philip Moreman, Ann Marie Murphy, Brian Muzas, Courtney Smith and Zheng Wang.

Thanks for discussion, commentary and other help to Samuel Barkin, Dina Bishara, Bridget Coggins, Mikulas Fabry, Eric Grynaviski, Enze Han, Allison Beth Hodgkins, Patrick Thaddeus Jackson, Michelle Jurkovich, Allison Kaufman, Paul Kowert, Ronald Krebs, Eric Lawrence, Julia MacDonald, Daniel Nexon, Chad Rector, Chana Solomon-Schwartz and Tristan Volpe. Ryan Triche and L'Dwayne Carruthers provided excellent research assistance. Thanks also to Jenny Daly, for believing in the project.

Particular mention must go to Davy Banks, who has indirectly made this book possible. Whether they be the intricacies of constructivism, the history of warfare or board games, Davy makes things fun.

Most of all, I would like to thank my family. My parents for being encouraging throughout and my brother Tom for making me laugh. Nancy, Addy and Cam, you are the lights of my life.

List of acronyms and abbreviations

AHI-PAC	American Hellenic Institute Public Affairs Committee
DBFP	Documents on British Foreign Policy
DBPO	Documents on British Policy Overseas
DNSA	Digital National Security Archive
DRVN	Democratic Republic of Vietnam
EU	European Union
FCO	Foreign and Commonwealth Office
FDR	Franklin Delano Roosevelt
FRUS	Foreign Relations of the United States
HC Deb	House of Commons Debates
HL Deb	House of Lords Debates
IR	International Relations
LNOJ	League of Nations Official Journal
LNOJ SS	League of Nations Official Journal Special Supplement
MP	Member of Parliament
NATO	North Atlantic Treaty Organization
NSC	National Security Council
PRC	People's Republic of China
PREM	Premier's Archives
RVN	Republic of Vietnam
SADR	Sahrawi Arab Democratic Republic
SBA	Sovereign Base Area
S/PV	United Nations Security Council Official Record
SRV	Socialist Republic of Vietnam
TFSC	Turkish Federated State of Cyprus
TRNC	Turkish Republic of Northern Cyprus
UAE	United Arab Emirates
UDI	Unilateral Declaration of Independence
UK	United Kingdom of Great Britain and Northern Ireland

UN	United Nations
UNCIP	United Nations Commission for India and Pakistan
UNFICYP	United Nations Peacekeeping Force in Cyprus
UNGA	United Nations General Assembly
UNSC	United Nations Security Council
UPU	Universal Postal Union
US	United States of America
US CRH	US Congressional Record, House of Representatives
US CRS	US Congressional Record, Senate
USSR	Union of Soviet Socialist Republics
WO	War Office and Ministry of Defence Archives
WSAG	Washington Special Action Group

Introduction

Law is not necessarily disintegrated by impotence; but it is destroyed by unqualified submission to the lawlessness of force. (Lauterpacht 1947: 435)

The island of Cyprus in the Eastern Mediterranean Sea is home to two groups. One defines itself as ethnically Greek, the other as ethnically Turkish. Each group has a territory and an administration that claims to represent a state as a member of the international community. However, despite this situation having existed for almost forty years, the international community does not acknowledge the claim of the Turkish-Cypriots as legitimate. No state or international organisation in the world, except for Turkey, recognises the Turkish Republic of Northern Cyprus (TRNC) as a state, despite its decades-long de facto existence. One of the most interesting features of this legal limbo is the nominal basis for the international community's rejection of the Turkish-Cypriot claim; their state is illegitimate because it is the result of aggression.

It seems natural in today's world that victory in a war of aggression does not mean that the victor should be able to do as it pleases with the property, territory, population and political institutions of the defeated state. However, in the nineteenth century, exploiting your victory in war to impose terms on your victim was seen as the normal and legitimate thing to do. One example of many is the outcome of the Franco-Prussian War fought from 1870 to 1871. At the end of that war, the victorious German Empire demanded, among other concessions, most of Alsace-Lorraine and five billion francs from France. Other powers treated these concessions as a normal and acceptable part of war-making and respected Germany's new borders. When other states did contest concessions wrung from a victim, it was not on the basis that these were a crime against peace. Often the proposed alternative was to divide the spoils among themselves. Russia, Germany and France opposed China's cession of the Liaodong peninsula to Japan in the 1895 Treaty of Shimonoseki.

1

After Japan agreed to take a large financial indemnity in place of the territory, the other colonial powers occupied the peninsula, seizing the valuable port cities for themselves (Mutsu 1982). Even as recently as 1923, at the Lausanne Conference, the official position of the British delegation on the status of some territory in Iraq was 'as the British armies defeated the Turkish armies during the great war and conquered Mosul and the whole of Irak, England can claim the possession of these countries by right of conquest' (Korman 1996: 156–7).

Such sentiments are no longer given as justifications. Instead, the reverse is true. Now states accept the principle that they cannot legally obtain territory or other advantages through the use or threat of force. Instead of 'to the victor go the spoils', where imposed concessions were considered valid, there is now a rule of 'nonrecognition of aggressive gain' (hereafter 'nonrecognition' as a shorthand). In addition to the nonrecognition of the TRNC on Cyprus, recent developments have demonstrated that the question of nonrecognition of the spoils of war is a vitally important one. The international community greeted Russia's recent annexation of the Crimean Peninsula with condemnations in the United Nations (UN)[1] and in the press,[2] and Russia still remains in de facto control of the territory. There is near-unanimous nonrecognition of the Republic of South Ossetia, which repeated its calls for recognition of its independence from Georgia after a war between Georgia and Russia in 2008. It is recognised only by Russia and five other states. David Miliband, then British foreign secretary, condemned Russia for its 'aggression',[3] and Richard Cheney, then US Vice-President, for its 'illegitimate, unilateral attempt to change [its] borders by force that has been universally condemned by the free world'.[4] Other examples include the widespread nonrecognition of the state of Manchukuo after Japan's conquest of Manchuria in 1932, Italy's conquest of Ethiopia in 1935, Israel's territorial gains in the 1967 war, Morocco's seizure of the Spanish Sahara in 1975, Indonesia's annexation of East Timor in 1975, South Africa's occupation of Namibia from 1966 to 1989, and the Nagorno-Karabakh Republic announced in 1992 during a war between Armenia and Azerbaijan.

Why do states not recognise the spoils of war? Why are states who gain advantages through the use of force not treated as the rightful owners of those advantages? Why do states condemn the outcome of certain wars when it is unclear that it will have any positive effect? Why, after the seeming failure of nonrecognition to achieve any results, do states continue to engage in it? In brief, *why do states engage in nonrecognition?*

Nonrecognition is defined in this study as the refusal by states to recognise, that is, admit the legality or legitimacy of, concessions obtained via the use or threat of force. This is not the only possible use of the word nonrecognition. States throughout history have chosen to not recognise various situations, including new states, for various reasons (Peterson 1982; Fabry 2010). However, for ease of expression, in this book I use the term nonrecognition to refer only to nonrecognition of political concessions obtained by the illegitimate use of force. Again for ease of expression, I will use the word 'aggression' as a shorthand for the illegitimate use of force.[5]

Sometimes the object of nonrecognition is territorial gain, such as Indonesia's incorporation of East Timor into the Indonesian state as its twenty-seventh province, or the territories occupied by Israel after the war in 1967. Other times nonrecognition is aimed at the creation of a new state, like Manchukuo or South Ossetia. The objects of nonrecognition are sites of intense political contestation. Nonrecognition is not merely an absence of action; it is a highly visible, provocative act. The act is a particular type of speech act that, rather than describing or referring to a state of the world, creates a state of the world. In the same way that saying, 'I promise to do X' does not describe a promise but *is* a promise, a declaration of nonrecognition, or recognition, creates what Searle (1995, 2010) calls an 'institutional fact'. Nonrecognition can be an explicit declaration or an absence of recognition when recognition is requested or expected. Collective nonrecognition is nonrecognition by the international community.[6] An important conceptual step I make is to see such nonrecognition as a *sanction* against a norm violation. Specifically, the norm against using force to gain political advantage, that is, that the spoils of war are illegitimate.

The phrase 'spoils of war' conjures up an image of piles of treasure, looted and plundered. The British and French sack of the Summer Palace of the Emperor of China at the end of the Second Opium War in 1860 saw scenes of soldiers literally carrying off bags and carts laden with gold, jades, furs, silks and porcelain, among other treasures (Swinhoe 1861: 306–11). But the primary goals of many wars are political. As Clausewitz reminds us, the aim of war is 'to compel our enemy to do our will' (1976: 75). The real fruits of victory are the ability to use your newly won dominance to change the political situation to your liking. In this sense, the very idea of 'spoils of war' is under threat. The changing norms of international politics have meant that those attempting to seize advantage by force try to justify their actions or the outcome of the fighting in ways other than 'the right of conquest'. What would have been claimed as spoils in a previous era, for example the annexation of territory or the establishment of a client state, is now framed and justified in other ways, like self-determination or 'liberation'. Have states become

3

convinced that their own use of force for political ends is wrong? This seems implausible, or at least highly contested. But do states, and the people running them, work under the assumption that there are benefits to a system where industrial war is not an accepted way of pursuing the resolution of political differences? There are strong indications that this is becoming true in large parts of the world (Mueller 2004; Pinker 2011; Goldstein 2011). Nonrecognition of aggressive gain seems an integral part of this wider phenomenon; the normative delegitimation of aggression and war for profit. Closely related more specific ideas include that conquest (Korman 1996), plunder (Sandholtz 2007) and treaties imposed by force (Malawer 1977) are illegitimate, as well as the norm of territorial integrity, that is, a proscription that force should not be used to alter interstate boundaries (Zacher 2001). When the creation of new states is also involved, ideas about self-determination, sovereignty, decolonisation, secession and irredentism are also potentially relevant. Even though we as scholars can articulate a rule or norm precisely, historical actors may have a different understanding, which may be vaguer with more or fewer or different connotations. The crucial question is how these norms have been interpreted in concrete historical cases where nonrecognition is at stake.

A BRIEF HISTORY OF NONRECOGNITION

Nonrecognition is often referred to as the Stimson Doctrine, after US Secretary of State Henry Stimson. Existing studies of the doctrine agree that it has become a central part of the rules of international behavior. For example, Korman argues that

> Ever since the proclamation of the Stimson Doctrine (in 1932) on the non-recognition of the results of conquest, states have sought to apply the *ex injuria jus non oritur* [illegal acts cannot create law] principle by not recognizing the legality of territorial acquisitions obtained by force. (Korman 1996: 234)

During the nineteenth century, treaties signed at the end of wars were seen as the natural way to end hostilities and the terms of these treaties were to be observed under the rule of *pacta sunt servanda*. Western writers 'of the nineteenth century . . . viewed all imposed treaties as valid and did not discuss the topic further' (Malawer 1977: 18). The idea that military conquest of territory was followed by recognised rights of sovereignty was endemic up to the end of the nineteenth century, both for relations between developed Western states and their colonies and relations between states comprising international society (Korman

1996). Thus, before the rise of nonrecognition there was a rule of 'to the victor go the spoils'. This pre-World War I normative acceptance of war fitted well with the procedures for dealing with the ends of any wars that broke out. However, after the war, aggression and conquest were becoming delegitimated. The Bolshevik Revolution and their ensuing call for the renunciation of annexation and indemnity was echoed by Woodrow Wilson in his Four Principles Speech and became standard rhetoric for the Allied side during the peace negotiations and afterwards (Korman 1996: 134–78). The Covenant of the League of Nations contained Article 10, which stigmatised war that was not prosecuted in self-defence.[7] The Kellogg-Briand Pact (Pact of Paris) in 1928 further asserted the principle that 'the solution of international controversies' should no longer be sought through 'recourse to war'.[8]

Japan's attack on Manchuria in 1931 constituted a crisis in the international arena as there was a dearth of clear expectations about what would happen and what should be done when a powerful state engaged in such a use of force (O'Mahoney 2014). While not the first time the idea of nonrecognition had been used in international relations (Brownlie 1963: 410–11), in January 1932 Secretary of State Henry Stimson unilaterally declared that the US would not recognise an imposed treaty in this case. This declaration was followed by a League of Nations Assembly Resolution on Forced Treaties in March 1932. This declared

> that it is incumbent upon the Members of the League of Nations not to recognise any situation, treaty or agreement, which may be brought about by means contrary to the Covenant of the League of Nation or to the Pact of Paris. (LNOJ SS 101 1932: 8)[9]

Other international instruments in the following years explicitly used nonrecognition as a means of preventing war. These included the Chaco Declaration of the Bolivia–Paraguay war of 1932, a League Council announcement on the Leticia dispute between Peru and Columbia in 1933, the Saavadra Lamas Anti-War Treaty of 1933 (for which Lamas was awarded the Nobel Peace Prize) and the Convention of the Montevideo Conference 1933 (Langer 1947). These declarations did not immediately bring practice in line with rhetoric, as the de facto attitudes towards Italy's annexation of Ethiopia and Germany's annexation of Austria and Czechoslovakia prior to World War II demonstrated, although *de jure* recognition was not always forthcoming in these cases (Brownlie 1963: 413–16).

After the outbreak of World War II, the Allies (initially the United Kingdom [UK] and France, but later joined by the Union of Soviet

Socialist Republics [USSR]) took steps to reverse their previous recognition of these situations. On 3 July 1940, the British government announced that that it no longer recognised the Italian King as Emperor of Ethiopia. In the Moscow Declaration of 1943, the Allies declared that the annexation of Austria by Germany was null and void. A provisional Czechoslovakian government was set up in London, with all Allies treating it throughout the war as the legitimate government of Czechoslovakia. Austria was also reinstated after the war (Langer 1947).

After World War II the UN was created in part 'to save succeeding generations from the scourge of war'.[10] However, initially there was no formal UN promulgation of nonrecognition. The UN General Assembly (UNGA) did pass a resolution (375) noting a Draft Declaration on Rights and Duties of States in which Article 11 stated, 'Every State has the duty to refrain from recognizing any territorial acquisition by another State acting in violation of Article 9.' However, it was not until 1969, two decades later, that a conference produced the Vienna Convention on the Law of Treaties. During the conference, there was heated debate lasting several days over what was to become Article 52: 'A treaty is void if its conclusion has been procured by the threat or use of force in violation of the principles of international law embodied in the Charter of the United Nations.' The main disagreement was on whether 'force' meant military force or economic and political coercion as well. While the meaning of Article 52 was unanimously agreed to include military force, those pushing for condemnation of economic and political coercion had to settle for a Declaration in an appendix to the Convention (Rosenne 1970). The Convention entered into force in 1980 and 114 states are currently parties to it.[11] Nonrecognition was also formalised in the UNGA's 1970 Declaration on Principles of International Law[12] and in the 1974 Declaration on Defining Aggression.[13] Since then nonrecognition has become institutionalised, both in terms of international legal instruments and in terms of state practice:

> In many of the worst crises that have confronted the international community in recent years, a statement refusing to recognise the legality of any consequences of the aggressor party's actions has often been one of the first reactions of the UN Security Council. (Turns 2003: 107)

WHY DO STATES ENGAGE IN NONRECOGNITION?

My pursuit of an answer to the question of why states engage in nonrecognition involves investigating what decision makers were thinking and saying about why nonrecognition was worth doing. The purpose of nonrecognition is not immediately apparent. It is not easily explainable as a coercive tool or deterrent against aggression as it seems not to roll back aggression nor does it seem to be a costly and hence credible signal of intent. Why would you use a sanction against a norm violator that is so weak that it is probably not going to work? Worse, nonrecognition can create situations of intense political contestation, resulting in violence and hardship for decades, as the Cyprus and Israeli–Palestinian cases demonstrate.

One inchoate intuition is you cannot just do nothing when someone breaks a rule. You have to at least refuse to celebrate the infraction, or not only would the perpetrator get away with it but suddenly people would think that anything goes. How can we understand the ideas behind this intuition more precisely? And does this thinking drive international policy?

I argue that nonrecognition is a means of creating common knowledge of what the rules of international behaviour are in the face of a lack of coercive enforcement action. Nonrecognition is thus intended to *maintain the rule* against aggression. If a rule is broken and other actors in the community do not engage in material or highly costly sanctions against the rule violator, there is uncertainty as to whether the rule still exists, has changed or has been abandoned altogether. In order that the community of actors jointly knows that the rule still exists, the rule is collectively reaffirmed. This collective public declaration of principles asserts that the rule judged to have been broken is still held to be the rule by the members of the community. This use of symbolic sanctions can be understood as consciously adopted rule or norm reproduction. Actors declaring principles are aware that future interpretations of potential violations will involve consideration of previous incidents and action taken now will influence those future interpretations by providing a clear indication of appropriate action. As decentralised rule enforcement actions often pose a coordination problem (I will contribute to punishment but only if everyone else does too), rule maintenance actions, like nonrecognition, can help actors coordinate on future sanctions.

The argument in this book contributes to our understanding of recognition and nonrecognition. The politics of international recognition, despite a small surge of recent work,[14] remains underexamined. Despite a long-standing but largely unproductive debate in international law between the constitutive and declaratory schools,[15] the political underpinnings and motivations behind formal recognition have not been adequately subjected to theoretically informed investigation.

7

The social science literature on the recognition of states generally deals with recognition without qualifying by the reason or basis for the decision. There is also little emphasis on the distinction between nonrecognition as a sanction and nonrecognition with an alternative illocutionary status.[16] So, for example, the US switched recognition between the Republic of China (Taiwan) and the People's Republic of China (PRC) in 1979 but not on the basis that Taiwan had violated an international norm. There are many other possible types of acts constituted by nonrecognition. For example, recognition could be withheld in order to be bestowed as a reward for services rendered, similar to the way that small states switch recognition between Taiwan and the PRC. Nonrecognition might also be performed to express disapproval of the nature of the entity (rather than the behaviour of a state), such as US nonrecognition of communist governments in Russia, China and the Baltic states, or the recent trend towards arguing that democracy is a requirement for recognition. Acts of nonrecognition might also be merely factual statements, such as a declaration that some conditions have been objectively fulfilled.

Surveys of large numbers of cases of recognition qua recognition (like Fabry 2010, Caspersen and Stansfield 2011, Caspersen 2012 and Coggins 2016) are valuable but do not focus intensively on decision making in particular situations. In contrast, Ker-Lindsay (2012) analyses a subclass of recognition situations: the foreign policy of counter-secession with a focus on why states resist the secession of parts of their own territory. The sheer variety of cases where recognition is at stake, from fully de facto states like Taiwan to attempted secessions like Katanga or Biafra, to territorial conquests like the Occupied Territories, Goa and East Timor, suggests that more fine-grained analysis is a crucial part of adequately dealing with the complexity of the phenomenon of non-recognition. This book addresses the gap in the literature regarding the decision making behind why the international community does not recognise the results of the illegitimate use of force.

The debate over why states grant recognition to some but not to other entities or situations has been carried on largely with reference to whether legal criteria, like those set out in the Montevideo Convention of 1933 including the effectiveness of the entity, are applied by states or instead whether recognition is given for political reasons. For example, Fabry (2010) analyses historical state recognition practice and justification, with particular attention to whether the de facto nature of the entity requesting recognition was relevant to state decisions. There is some awareness that nonrecognition might sometimes be intended to 'uphold' or 'preserve' norms or to prevent setting a precedent, but there are no coherent theoretical accounts either of how exactly that is supposed to work, nor are there detailed empirical investigations of whether this intention is in fact driving nonrecognition decisions.[17]

This book also provides an answer to the question of why symbolic sanctions, like nonrecognition, happen at all. The phenomenon of symbolic sanctions is important to International Relations (IR) theorists in several ways. First, as something that is often dismissed as useless, it is puzzling that situations like the nonrecognition of the TRNC or the Republic of South Ossetia exist. Nonrecognition is an enforcement mechanism of the norm against aggressive war, but it is primarily a diplomatic sanction, rather than an economic or coercive sanction. For Realist scholars, some of whom deny the importance of international institutions, symbolic sanctions largely consisting of moral condemnation are the epitome of Idealist futility. Economic sanctions have frequently been condemned as 'not working' (e.g. Pape 1997). Some have tried to explain them by their symbolic use (e.g. Baldwin 1985). However, the question of why states use symbolic sanctions against rule-breaking is not adequately answered in the IR literature. Many theories assert that sanctions must be costly in order to be effective. The use of the symbolic sanction of nonrecognition is puzzling because nonrecognition does not appear to be especially costly to the norm violator. Compared to economic sanctions, like boycotts or blockades, or coercive sanctions, such as military intervention, nonrecognition hardly does any harm to an aggressor. If a sanction is not costly to the norm violator, then it seems unlikely that it will affect the violator's cost–benefit calculation. Similarly, if a sanction is not costly to the sanctioner, then it cannot serve as a credible signal of intent or resolve. If this is true, then a reasonable actor would not use nonrecognition either to compel the violator to stop violating the norm or to signal the resolve of the sanctioner to punish future violations.

Symbolic sanctions like social shaming or expressions of disapproval are a fundamental part of the constructivist research tradition. Finnemore and Sikkink (1998) appeal to shaming both as a mechanism for promoting adherence to social norms and also as an indicator of the existence of norms. Socialisation theory (Johnston 2001; Checkel 2005) relies upon the mechanism of social shaming and other sanctions for promoting attitudinal change in new members to a group. However, these shaming arguments rarely problematise the *supply* of shaming. Both constructivist and rationalist literatures have not paid enough attention to explaining why states use symbolic sanctions.

METHODS

I choose to focus my study on some of the most prominent cases where recognition of the results of force was withheld. In contrast to some approaches, my goal is to delve deep into the decision-making process, using precise analytical tools to understand how and why particular outcomes came about. I try to discover how the actors involved in formulating and carrying out the policy of nonrecognition thought about, argued about and tried to convince others of the rightness of what they were doing. The rigorous analysis and interpretation of historical sources is the best tool we have for finding out the purposes, intentions and legitimation strategies of the people involved. In the following chapters, I provide an in-depth analysis of the decision making and legitimation involved in the reactions of third-party states to four cases of the cross-border use of military force: the Japanese incursion into Manchuria from 1931, the Italian conquest of Abyssinia (Ethiopia) in 1935, the Turkish invasion of Cyprus in 1974 and the Indian intervention in East Pakistan, later Bangladesh, in 1971. The first time that nonrecognition was collectively adopted was during the Manchurian Crisis. This involved substantial explicit policy debate and so this case is especially useful for evaluating those reasons for the policy treated as convincing. The Abyssinian Crisis, in which Italy conquered Ethiopia and this possession was recognised by numerous states, provides a revealing comparison to the Manchurian case. After World War II, nonrecognition became an accepted part of the rules of international behaviour and formalised in international law. The Cyprus and Bangladesh cases extend the findings of the rule maintenance model to a period in which the norm of nonaggression is more institutionalised.[18]

While deep case investigation is necessary to identify mechanisms and processes, an important question is how generalisable the results of those cases are. In order to test whether the model of rule maintenance helps to explain the broader universe of cases where nonrecognition is at stake, I survey twenty-one cases of nonrecognition debate. This survey also allows for elaboration on the sources of variation in nonrecognition that are suggested by the in-depth case studies.

PLAN OF THE BOOK

Chapter 1 lays out the theoretical arguments of the book. First, it surveys the pre-existing literature on sanctions and identifies this literature's theoretical blind spot concerning seemingly ineffective sanctions. Then it lays out the model of rule maintenance, elucidating the various concepts involved and how they fit together, as well as drawing out some of the observable implications of the model. A number of other motivations for engaging in sanctions are then outlined and contrasted with rule maintenance. The chapter ends with a consideration of the methods used to provide evidence that allows the adjudication between alternative explanations.

Chapter 2 investigates the first time that nonrecognition was used as a sanction against aggression. During the Manchurian Crisis, start-ing in 1931, first the US, in the person of US Secretary of State Henry Stimson, and the League of Nations collectively threatened and then imposed nonrecognition on the newly declared state of Manchukuo. From an analysis of decision making in the US, the UK and the League of Nations, I find that there was explicit discussion and consideration of nonrecognition, both as a policy to deal with the immediate situation, and in general as a rule for international relations. While several differ-ent reasons and justifications for the policy were considered and used, over the course of the crisis one reason became dominant: to maintain the rule among the states of the world that disputes should be resolved peacefully.

A mere two years after the League collectively agreed not to rec-ognise Manchukuo, Italy invaded and conquered Ethiopia (also called Abyssinia). Chapter 3 investigates why numerous states, including the UK, despite initially imposing widespread economic sanctions on Italy, decided to recognise Italian possession of another state. This negative case of nonrecognition, that is, the acceptance and legitimation of the fruits of premeditated aggression, thus provides a powerful answer to the question asked of nonrecognition, 'Why *not* do it?' The main finding is that, consistent with the rule maintenance model, resistance to aggression was being discarded in favour of appeasement. Thus, main-taining the rule of nonaggression made no sense to states who were not interested in perpetuating that rule.

Chapter 4 extends the results of the Manchurian case to the more recent case of the Turkish invasion of Cyprus in 1974 and the subse-quent nonrecognition of the Turkish-Cypriot state that emerged as a result of that invasion. Despite sympathy with the Turkish-Cypriots' claims to vulnerability as a minority on the island, the international community opposed their claims of a separate state because it was the result of Turkey's violation of the rules against aggression and using force for profit and territorial aggrandisement. Some policymakers in the US, especially US Secretary of State Henry Kissinger, were primarily concerned with maintaining good US–Turkey relations. However, in the UK and the UN many were concerned that recognition of the TRNC would pose a threat to the illegitimacy of using force to resolve international political disputes in one's favour. In general, the primary justification for the nonrecognition policy was that to do otherwise would be to 'condone' or 'legitimise' Turkey's use of force.

The Manchuria and Cyprus cases are instances where one state used premeditated military force against a neighbouring state, occupied a portion of the territory of that state and then supported the creation of a new state in that portion. This is also a good description of the case analysed in Chapter 5: the Indian invasion of East Pakistan in 1971. However, in this case the newly declared state of Bangladesh was recognised by most states in a few months and by the UN in 1974. This is thus another negative case of nonrecognition. Chapter 5 analyses the decision making involved in the American, British and UN reactions to the crisis and demonstrates that legitimising aggression was a central concern in the discourse surrounding policy options. Despite this concern, Bangladesh was recognised and admitted as a member of the UN. Why was this case different from the Manchuria and Cyprus cases? This chapter shows that the model of rule maintenance and the sources of variation that it identifies can be used to understand various aspects of the Bangladesh case. In particular, various features of Bangladesh's situation were seen as relevant, such as that its government was democratically elected before the Indian invasion and India's quick and very public commitment to withdrawing all troops from Bangladeshi territory. These were used to excuse India's use of force, or redefine it away from aggression, so that rule maintenance actions like nonrecognition were not necessary for the norm against aggression to continue.

Chapter 6 takes the insights from the in-depth case studies and applies them to the broader range of cases of 'nonrecognition debates' since World War I. The rule maintenance model explains the variation in nonrecognition over twenty-one cases where it was at stake. A survey of these cases provides more details and identifies more specific mechanisms by which cases exit the ideal-typical process leading to nonrecognition. In particular, one mechanism involving ambiguity over whether the use of force counted as aggression turns out to be the most common barrier to collective nonrecognition by the international community. Russia's annexation of the Crimean peninsula is singled out to show the relevance of the rule maintenance model to the most recent case of collective nonrecognition.

Finally, the Conclusion briefly summarises the main findings before extending the implications of those findings for various literatures. It also points to important areas of future research that are suggested and motivated by these conclusions.

NOTES

1. For example, a draft Security Council resolution (S/2014/189) supporting the territorial integrity of Ukraine, and reaffirming that no territorial acquisition resulting from the threat or use of force shall be recognised as legal, was only not adopted because of a Russian veto. A General Assembly resolution (68/262) along the same lines was passed on 27 March 2014 by 100 to 11 (58 abstentions).

2. For example, the European Union (EU) and the United States of America (US) publicly and repeatedly condemned both Russia's use of force and a referendum held in Crimea (BBC 2014).

3. 'Miliband warns Russia against starting a new Cold War', *Independent*, 27 August 2008, <http://www.independent.co.uk/news/world/europe/miliband-warns-russia-against-starting-a-new-cold-war-909861.html> (last accessed 23 January 2017).

4. 'Cheney backs membership in NATO for Georgia', *The New York Times*, 4 September 2008.

5. There has been an attempt to define aggression in international law, for example the United Nations General Assembly resolution 3314 (14 December 1974). However, people in practice apply the term aggression to some situations in order to express moral disapprobation or to influence others' perception of an action. What matters here is not whether various actions are or are not aggression, but whether the actors involved denounce those actions as a violation of the norm against using force aggressively and for private gain, rather than in support of collective or public goals, and treat them accordingly. For a general account of an anti-essentialist approach to social concepts see Jackson (2006).

6. An important question is what counts as the international community. Unanimity is not necessary, nor is a formal legal instrument like a UN Security Council resolution. This question is considered in more detail in the case studies and in Chapter 6.

7. The Covenant of the League of Nations, The Avalon Project, Yale Law School, <http://avalon.law.yale.edu/20th_century/leagcov.asp> (last accessed 23 January 2017).

8. Kellogg-Briand Pact 1928, The Avalon Project, Yale Law School, <http://avalon.law.yale.edu/20th_century/kbpact.asp> (last accessed 23 January 2017).

9. League of Nations Official Journal Special Supplement (LNOJ SS). Referenced with the supplement number, year and page number.

10. Charter of the United Nations, Preamble.

11. United Nations Treaty Collection, <https://treaties.un.org/Pages/ViewDetailsIII.aspx?src=TREATY&mtdsg_no=XXIII-1&chapter=23&Temp=mtdsg3&clang=_en> (last accessed 23 January 2017).

12. Declaration on Principles of International Law Concerning Friendly Relations and Co-operation Among States in Accordance with the Charter of the United Nations, UN General Assembly Resolution 2625 (XXV) 24 October 1970. From Principle 1: 'The territory of a State shall not be the object of acquisition by another State resulting from the threat or use of force. No territorial acquisition resulting from the threat or use of force shall be recognised as legal.'

13. UN General Assembly Resolution 3314 (XXIX) 14 December 1974. Article 5(3): 'No territorial acquisition or special advantage resulting from aggression is or shall be recognised as lawful.'
14. See for example, Fabry 2010; Caspersen and Stansfield 2011; Caspersen 2012; Ker-Lindsay 2012; Agne et al. 2013; Coggins 2016.
15. Crawford relates the suggestion that 'the "great debate" over the character of recognition has done nothing but confuse the issues, that it is mistaken to categorise recognition as either declaratory or constitutive in accordance with some general theory'. (2007: 26)
16. Speech acts have various elements: locutionary (the meaning of an utterance), illocutionary (the type of social act, e.g. promise, request, excuse, condemnation) and perlocutionary (the effect of the act, e.g. persuading, convincing, frightening).
17. See Peterson (1982), Pegg (1998: 196), Ker-Lindsay (2012: 13), Coggins (2016).
18. For more of the reasoning behind methods and case selection, see Chapter 1.

Chapter One

Rule maintenance: the logic of symbolic sanctions

This book asks why states engage in nonrecognition. This chapter presents the theoretical underpinnings of possible answers to this question. In the first section, addressing the question of the purpose of nonrecognition, I discuss different possible purposes to which sanctions could be put. In the second section, I lay out the methodology for the book and explain how the evidence will enable us to choose between the possible answers.

The logic of symbolic sanctions

The norm against aggression seems to be in some sense responsible for the use of nonrecognition. But how, exactly, are the two related? One plausible way would be that actors, believing so strongly in the moral wrongness of aggressive gain, unthinkingly reacted to each instance of aggression with condemnation and social sanctions (Elster 2007: 355–6). This conception relies upon a problematic mechanism: an unthinking reaction to a norm violation. While a common phenomenon in interpersonal relations in everyday life, this mechanism seems implausible when applied to the behaviour of states. This is especially the case when numerous states coordinate and sustain nonrecognition over long periods of time. Even those wholeheartedly convinced of the immorality or undesirability of aggression think strategically about how to enforce or perpetuate the norm against it. A better account of the use of nonrecognition would involve a process of strategically weighing various options when faced with a case of aggression. One of those options is nonrecognition. This still involves a normative position concerning aggression. Actors value a world without war and view the use of international violence for selfish gain as wrong. But their actions taken in pursuit of peace are not unreasoned. So, what might their reasoning be?

Why sanction?

The traditional attitude towards sanctions is that if sanctions are severe or costly enough, they will harm a state's economy, which will bring about pressure on the leaders of that state to change their policy. The goal is inducing policy change. The problem with this line of thought is that sanctions rarely work in this sense, and often seem obviously unlikely to do so (Pape 1997; Morgan and Schwebach 1997). Some work has tried to explain sanctions either as the result of mistakes and miscalculations (Hovi et al. 2005) or, more popularly, because leaders were trying to satisfy the demands of domestic constituents (Lindsay 1986). In a recent example, Whang, condemning the 'analytic failure to explain the recurrence of seemingly ineffective sanctions', appeals to the effects of sanctions on a president's domestic political popularity via 'cultivating an image of strength' (2011: 788). Even work arguing that the benefits of sanctions can be long term, and also that the free-rider problem is not crippling to coercive explanations of sanctions, relies on sanctions imposing costs or demonstrating a willingness to bear costs (Thompson 2009).

The puzzle of low-cost sanctions

The literature on sanctions largely ignores the strategic issues involved in low-cost sanctions, including diplomatic or symbolic sanctions. Often low-cost sanctions are dismissed as useless. For example, Tostensen and Bull lament 'only symbolic – and ultimately ineffective – acts' (2002: 378). Three features of low-cost sanctions make their repeated occurrence puzzling. First, they do not inflict enough costs on the target to justify using it as a coercive tool. Second, they are not costly enough to those imposing the sanctions to serve as a credible signal of resolve to punish future violators of a rule. Third, there are still negative potential consequences for the sanctioners, even if these are not relevant to the costly signalling of resolve (Maller 2010). Taken together, these imply that according to costly signalling logic, we should not expect to see states engaging in low-cost sanctions as the sanctioner has plenty to lose and little to gain.

Norm dynamics and sanctions

Many analyses of sanctions ignore the context of norms and social institutions in which they are applied. In many frameworks, there is no analytic difference between sanctions enacted as a response to a violation of a strongly held norm, and sanctions enacted purely on the whim of the policymaker in pursuit of some isolated benefit.

16

That said, some work has noted the relevance of the institutional or normative context. Nossal argues for conceptualising international sanctions as retribution, or 'the infliction of pain on an offender in return for an evil inflicted on the community' (1989: 314). Nossal tries to distinguish this from 'punishment for its own sake', but undercuts this attempt by claiming that 'there is nothing in the retributive punishment that is directed toward the future actions of either the offender or others'. What he is identifying is exactly the emotional or irrational use of sanctions for their own sake.

Relatedly, sanctions have sometimes been said to have an 'expressive' function. For example, Chesterman and Pouligny claim that 'sanctions may be designed primarily to express outrage but without a clear political goal' (2003: 505). Barber sees a secondary objective of sanctions being 'to express a sense of morality' or 'symboliz[e] a general stance' (1979: 380, 381). Sometimes this expressive function is explained by saying that inaction represents approval. Galtung argues that sometimes 'doing nothing is tantamount to complicity' and that a non-instrumental purpose for the imposition of sanctions is that it 'serves as a clear signal to everyone that what the receiving nation has done is disapproved of' (1967: 411). This intriguing idea has been referred to by others. For example, Lindsay claims that 'had Britain not placed sanctions on Rhodesia, most countries would have seen it as a sign of British approval of the Smith regime' (1986: 166). Similarly, Giumelli includes 'shap[ing] normality in what is allowed and what is forbidden in the international system' as an objective of sanctions (2011: 35). Baldwin points out that 'if the principal alternative to economic sanctions is appearing to condone communism, racism, terrorism, or genocide, the observation that they are a "notoriously poor tool of statecraft" may miss the point' (2000: 84). Nossal (1991) rightly focuses attention on the symbolic functions of sanctions, with particular regard to weak state sanctions on strong states. Inter alia, he argues that the role of Australian and Canadian sanctions on the USSR after its invasion of Afghanistan was to indicate that 'the sanctioner disapproved of this behavior, and thus was reaffirming a commitment to the norms of sovereignty and territorial integrity' (1991: 34–5). Similarly, Crawford and Klotz suggest that one reason for imposing sanctions is 'to establish international norms by punishing a state for breaking global standards and multilateral rules' (1999: 27).

However, despite appeals to the general idea of upholding, establishing or reaffirming norms, the current literature provides no detail, leaving it unclear how the mechanism is supposed to work. Also, the trend of much existing work is to treat the norm-violating state as the primary target of the sanctions, rather than the international audience.

Rule maintenance

I argue that nonrecognition of aggressive gain is driven by actors' desire to maintain the rule against international aggression. That is, declarations of nonrecognition were not coercive tools or hypocritical moves to placate domestic constituencies, nor were they unreasoned expressions of emotion. Instead they were aimed at rule maintenance. How does this work?

Symbolic sanctions can be used to maintain the legitimacy of a rule of behaviour. They do this by creating common knowledge that coordinates future collective action. Symbolic sanctions can create or reproduce common knowledge, or shared understandings, of what the rules of international society are. In order to understand how this works, first we have to define the strategic situation via attention to the social institutional context (see Figure 1.1).

This model of rule violation and maintenance indicates the conditions that have to obtain in order for a rule maintenance action to make strategic sense.

Imagine that a community of actors knows that there is a rule of conduct between them. When one of the actors breaks the rule, or is judged to have broken the rule, the other members of the community have a choice. They can 1) impose material sanctions on the violator and *enforce* the rule; 2) they can do nothing or accept the action and its results, potentially *abandoning* the rule; or 3) they can impose symbolic sanctions and thereby *maintain* the rule.

If the other actors in the community do not engage in material or highly costly sanctions against the rule violator, there is uncertainty as to whether the rule still exists, has changed or has been abandoned altogether. In order that the community of actors knows that the rule still exists, the rule is reaffirmed. That is, action is taken that is intended to communicate that, in future, actors will judge behaviour according to that rule and potentially take costly action to enforce the rule. There are two pathways underlying the reasoning behind rule maintenance. First, it can affect expectations about whether the community will be able to coordinate costly sanctions on rule violators in the future. Second, it can affect actors' beliefs about what is considered legitimate behaviour in the international system.

Symbolic sanctions, common knowledge and collective expectations

The expectation created or reproduced by rule maintenance sanctions is that even though costly sanctions were not used in the current instance, they may be used against future violations of the rule as the rule still

Rule

There is an agreed rule of behaviour

Action interpreted as violation

One actor performs an action and one or more actors denounce it as a rule violation, or question whether it is permitted under the rule

Absence/failure of material sanctions

Actors either do not deploy costly material sanctions or these sanctions do not induce compliance to the rule

Uncertainty about status of rule

As costly sanctions were either not deployed or were ineffective, actors are unsure whether the rule is still the rule or has changed or disappeared

Rule maintenance action

The rule is reaffirmed. Action is taken to communicate that in future the members of the community will judge behaviour according to the rule

Rule

There is an agreed rule of behaviour

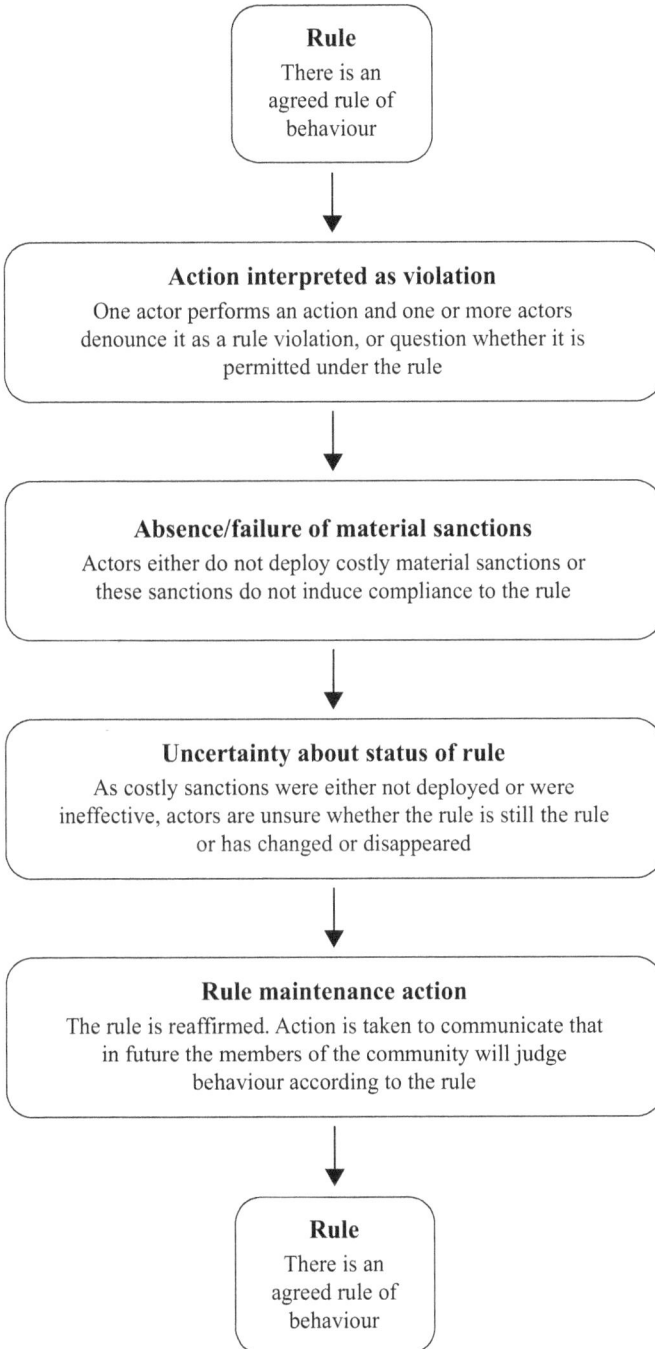

Figure 1.1 Rule maintenance

applies. This is different from a direct deterrence argument. Deterrence is premised on the idea that expectations of future action change because actors have demonstrated their ability or willingness to bear costs, thus enabling the differentiation between those actors willing to bear costs and those unwilling to do so. Rule maintenance actions have an effect on potential rule-breakers because rule maintenance means that actors have common knowledge of the community will to contribute to future sanctions on rule-breakers. Absent rule maintenance, potential rule-breakers can draw the inference that not only is the community currently unable to enforce the rule, but that they do not even value the rule itself.

It is clear in principle from analysis of signalling games that symbolic sanctions can reveal preferences to a limited degree.[1] The weak signal is not costly enough to demonstrate a willingness to bear the costs of enforcement. However, it is enough to differentiate between a type that does not value the rule (or the state of the world in which the rule is complied with) and a type that does values the rule, even if that latter type may not actually want to pay the costs of enforcing the rule.

In addition, if symbolic sanctions are collective, then even more information can be communicated. Norm enforcement sanctions present a (second order) collective action problem. That is, even if all actors would benefit from the norm being enforced, they would be better off if other actors paid the costs of enforcing the norm, that is, free riding on the efforts of others. So, a factor in a potential norm violator's calculations should be the extent to which actors will be able to coordinate on the imposition of sanctions. Symbolic sanctions can reveal the preferences of actors not just to potential norm violators, but to other members of the community. If actors agree to participate in collective symbolic sanctions, it suggests that they disapprove of the violation. Absent collective symbolic sanctions, even actors who would be willing to participate in future costly sanctions in concert with the community will be less likely to be able to coordinate collective action. So, it is thus more likely that certain actions will be sanctioned with the common knowledge that those actions are considered norm violations by the community.

Common knowledge can be defined formally in terms of the partitions of information sets (Geanakoplos 1992: 65) but can be understood informally; a proposition p is common knowledge if everyone knows it, everyone knows that everyone knows it, everyone knows that everyone knows that everyone knows it, and so on. Common knowledge is thus different from aggregated individual knowledge.

However, existing models of signalling are too limited to be able to account for common knowledge creation or recreation. In fact, it is impossible within game theoretic models for common knowledge to be created. Rubinstein (1989) shows that if there is a finite number of messages being sent between rational players, then they cannot be sure that the other one knows the information, even though intuitively they would believe it.[2] Instead, we have to use alternative theories. Clark and Marshall (1981) analyse this problem and posit relatively simple heuristics used to get to a state of common knowledge. One important heuristic is inference from the copresence of A, B and some state of affairs to common knowledge. If p happens when both A and B are present, and they know that the other is also present, they infer that p is common knowledge. This is called the mutual experience heuristic. Chwe (1998, 2001) analyses public rituals as examples of attempts to use mutual experience to create common knowledge aimed at helping or hindering coordination. In addition to other features of public rituals, like the content or the emotional resonance, the publicness of the rituals generates common knowledge. Because the ritual is performed in public, everyone present can see that everyone else present is also experiencing the ritual and can infer that the ritual and its content are common knowledge. Wendt points out that the concept of common knowledge is the same as the concept of intersubjectivity used by constructivists (1999: 160). Katzenstein et al. argue that common knowledge is a point of complementarity between rationalist and constructivist approaches to IR (1998: 680). In particular, given that what is common knowledge is highly influential, the processes by which common knowledge, or intersubjective understandings, of the rules of the game get created are 'highly contested' and often the object of strategic social construction (Finnemore and Sikkink 1998: 911).

The effect of common knowledge is to introduce an element of certainty into our interactions. If something is common knowledge, we can take it as given. If there is common knowledge of a rule, actors can treat the rule as existing objectively. They have to orient their behaviour around the rule even if they do not believe in the rightness of it individually. This conception is similar to Searle's idea of how the social world is created by speech acts (2010). One class of speech acts both represents the world and changes the world by declaring that a state of affairs exists. Searle calls these Status Function Declarations. These create objective facts about the world by virtue of people's collective acceptance or recognition of those facts.[3] The rules of a society are an example of this type of objective fact. To create, or recreate, them requires stating that they exist.

This rule maintenance argument is consistent with recent work on social norms and rules as coordinating devices. One example is Tyran and Feld who conducted public goods provision experiments and found that mild law, that is, law backed only by non-deterrent sanctions, significantly increases cooperation if endogenously imposed, that is, the participants jointly agree to the law. They argue that 'voting for mild law is interpreted as a signal for cooperation, and induces expectations of cooperation' (2006: 137).

Kier and Mercer (1996) address the setting of precedents in international relations. However, their focus is on demonstrative instances, that is, where performing action A in situation B may or may not generate a convention with the content that actions of type A are permissible or appropriate in situations of type B. They mention the reaffirmation of a prohibition convention via the further prohibition of actions, but they do not specifically theorise situations where there is intent to set a precedent, not by performing the action that they want to be expected, but by agreeing that a principle is the principle by which future behaviour will be judged.

Symbolic sanctions, legitimacy and norm reproduction

Another element of rule maintenance is that symbolic sanctions make certain acts illegitimate, or sustain their illegitimacy. Rule maintenance is a crucial part of the politics of legitimacy. Knowledge of the rules of international behaviour is important for states' expectations because when considering an action leaders of states cannot predict what others will do. There is a fundamental uncertainty faced in the real world over the capacities and intentions of others. However, actors can know what the principles involved are, what the terms of debate over the interpretation of the proposed action will be. Actors will then take these principles into account when deciding what actions to take. The key role of international law under this conception is that leaders of states have an idea of what types of actions will be investigated and in what terms they will be evaluated. As Reus Smit notes, 'international law can serve as a focal point for discursive struggles over legitimate political agency and action' (2004: 20). This makes knowledge of what rules are considered authoritative and accepted an important part of states' calculations over the likely consequences of their actions. Rule maintenance is an important part of the creation of international order because it reinforces the stability of the rules of international behaviour. Rule maintenance is one type of the public talk that Mitzen places at the centre of global governance. She argues that when states 'jointly and publicly commit to pursue a project together, publicity can exert a centripetal pull on individual actions capable of countering centrifugal tendencies and pulling individual acts toward the shared project' (2011: 54).

22

In order to understand what is being claimed here, it is important to distinguish between a) moral beliefs of individual people and b) norms. Rule maintenance does not necessarily involve any effect on what individual people think is morally wrong. However, it does affect what people believe to be the authoritative norms of society. Jaeger's (2008) analysis of 'world opinion' forcefully makes the claim that there is something beyond the aggregate of individual minds or opinions that actors refer to as something that exists. Steffek's (2003) account of the legitimation of international governance foregrounds two aspects of legitimation that are core parts of rule maintenance. The first is that, as international governance is dependent upon explaining and defending the actions and policy decisions of international actors in terms of shared justificatory reasons, moments of explicit consensus are crucial for defining the values, goals and procedures that make up the rules (or regimes) of international governance. Rule maintenance actions, like the symbolic sanction of nonrecognition, are examples of these moments of consensus. They provide, in Steffek's language, 'the consensual reference points for the regime's discursive justification and thus legitimacy' (2003: 264). The second aspect of Steffek's account of international legitimacy is the need for maintenance: 'international governance . . . requires permanent consensus-building' (2003: 265). International rules and norms are constantly open to renegotiation and previous agreement is no guarantee of present or future agreement. This means that rule maintenance actions are necessary for the continuation or reproduction of what makes up legitimate governance.

Symbolic sanctions thus can be effectual, and made comprehensible, if we see them as rituals of rule affirmation or attempts to create common knowledge of actors' common disapproval of certain classes of acts. This use of symbolic sanctions can be understood as consciously adopted norm reproduction. Actors declaring principles are aware that future interpretations of potential violations will involve consideration of previous incidents and action taken now will influence those future interpretations by providing a clear indication of appropriate action.

Variation in rule maintenance

The model of rule violation and maintenance can also be used to suggest some hypotheses about variation in rule maintenance actions (see Figure 1.2). At various stages of the model conditions can be such that there is no progress to the next stage.

First, a crucial assumption is that states value the rule, want it to be maintained and are able to coordinate on a rule maintenance action. If,

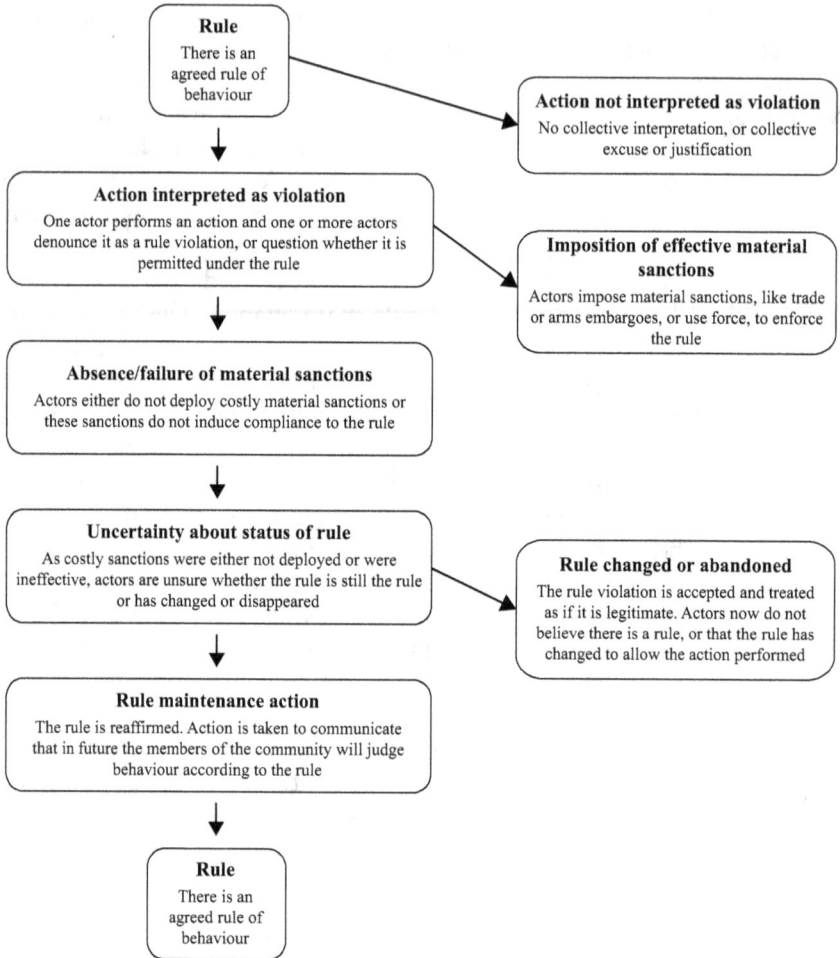

Figure 1.2 Pathways of variation in rule maintenance.

alternatively, states no longer value the rule, want to change the rule or are unable to coordinate on a symbolic sanction, then rule maintenance actions will not be performed.

Second, if material sanctions, like economic sanctions or the use of force, have been imposed and are successful, then there is no need for rule maintenance. For example, after 1991 there was no need to not recognise the results of Iraq's conquest of Kuwait because the violation had been overturned. This is not to say that the mere presence of material sanctions obviates the need for rule maintenance. An early rule maintenance action might facilitate the imposition of costly collective sanctions in response to the current violation, in which case the costly sanctions would come after rule maintenance, rather than before.

Finally, rule maintenance does not make sense if there is no rule violation. Whether some action is a violation of a rule is not given objectively. A violation is only a violation if actors treat it as such. Given the inevitable imprecision or vagueness of rules (or 'open texture' [Hart 1994: 123]) there is always the possibility that an argument can be made that any particular action is not a rule violation. Maybe the action is not of the right type to fall under the rule. Or maybe the action is of the right type, but there is some extenuating property or circumstance that means the action is a legitimate exception to the rule. See Chapter 6 for more extensive discussion of this issue.

Methodology

Process-tracing, mechanisms and explanation

The goal of this book is an exploration of the process by which non-recognition becomes accepted and the reasons actors had for doing so. The method of analysis is often called process tracing (George and Bennett 2005: 205–32). Recent work has distinguished three subtypes of process-tracing (Beach and Pedersen 2013). This book uses a combination of theory-building and theory-testing process-tracing, both theory-centric approaches. First, in the Manchurian Crisis case, I start with the empirical material and use an 'analysis of this material to detect a plausible hypothetical causal mechanism' (Beach and Pedersen 2013: 16). This causal mechanism is the rule maintenance model. Then, for the other positive case of nonrecognition, Turkish Cyprus, I apply theory-testing process-tracing to see whether this causal mechanism, rule maintenance, is present in the case and whether the mechanism functioned in the same way. Detailed case analysis is the only way to determine if the posited mechanism is operating and is vital for making convincing counterfactual claims. Empirical demands in the current study are high, as it is difficult to determine actors' purposes, ideas and their action in institutions without the use of multiple types of sources. Focused comparison of cases is also valuable, although the goal is not to test hypotheses about covariation. Comparison can demonstrate the limitations of the concepts or models used in explaining the cases they were developed for and motivate either the creation of new concepts or the modification of existing ones for the cases compared (Jackson 2010: 201).

A good description of the practicalities of this type of analysis is from the analytic narrative project.

> By reading documents, laboring through archives, interviewing and survey-ing the secondary literature, we seek to understand the actors' preferences, their perceptions, their evaluation of alternatives, the information they possess, the expectations they form, the strategies they adopt, and the con-straints that limit their actions. We then seek to piece together the story that accounts for the outcome of interest. (Bates et al. 1998: 11)

To this description I would add understanding the justifications for action that actors use to legitimate their choices.

Motives and evidence

Wendt identifies the major methodological challenge for institutional-ists when he critiques the rational design programme for being satis-fied when a design choice is consistent with a model. Consistency is a necessary but not sufficient part of determining which is the better explanation. To decide between explanations, 'we need to get inside the heads and discourse of decision-makers and see what is motivating their behavior' (2001: 1028). How can we know why people do what they do? It is impossible to introspect another's motives and intentions (O'Mahoney 2015). However, we can look at what actors said and did. In particular, the ways in which they justified their actions to others, both publicly and in private, can be the evidence for what they were trying to do. This is especially useful when a group of actors are trying to come to a decision on a joint action, like in a government or a group of governmental actors. Individuals are being honest about their reason-ing, or they are trying to be convincing to others, or they are trying to avoid censure for violating shared rhetorical standards. In all three of these situations, speech acts are potential evidence of the reasons that are thought convincing. As Schimmelfennig points out, 'whether or not political actors really mean what they say, they will choose their argu-ments strategically; and both opportunistic and truthful arguments have real consequences for their proponents and the outcome of the debate' (2001: 66).

Case selection

In order to come to a conclusion on why states engage in nonrecognition it is necessary to study instances of actors' decisions not to recognise

26

aggressive gain from war. The unit of analysis is the *nonrecognition debate*. A nonrecognition debate is a situation where there is some contestation over the decision by a state or an international organisation to recognise or not recognise gains made in war. There are three conditions that must obtain for a case to constitute a nonrecognition debate:

1. At least one state uses military force against another state, that is, across international borders.
2. There is some de facto 'spoils of war', that is, political change of some sort asserted by the militarily victorious state and contested by other international actors.
3. The cross-border use of force is not collectively authorised by an international organisation.

The first condition excludes many cases of civil war or of secession. Recognition of a government within a state is a different type of thing from recognition of a new state or of the transfer of territory from one state to another. The international law literature maintains a strict division between the two ideas (Crawford 2007). Civil war and secession raise their own interesting questions concerning when and why states choose to recognise (see e.g. Coggins 2016) but are different from situations where sovereign states break the international rule against profiting from war.

The interest in this study is in cases where recognition was in doubt. Hypothetically, almost any state action could be a candidate for recognition, but the concern here is in the results of the use of force. In particular, there must be some lingering contestation of the results of the use of force. The 'lingering' criterion excludes cases where the results of the use of force are relatively fleeting. For example, during the war in the Ogaden in 1977, Somali forces had conquered a large amount of territory in Ethiopia. However, within a few months, and before there had been any formal end to the fighting, Ethiopian forces reversed all those territorial gains. Thus, there was no subject for a nonrecognition debate. The 'contestation' criterion concerns a challenge on normative grounds, which excludes cases where the political issues are redistributed by mutual consent, such as in a peace treaty or other agreement. Alternatively, this criterion also excludes the numerous cases of conquest during World War II. By the time of Nazi Germany's invasion of Poland, there had ceased to be even a semblance of global norms. International order was in an extreme crisis and arguably did not exist; the period of World War II is the situation closest to pure anarchy since at least the Napoleonic era.

In the main body of this book I study four cases of nonrecognition debate: the Japanese conquest of Manchuria in 1931–3, the Italian conquest of Ethiopia (Abyssinia) in 1935–6, the Indian invasion of East Pakistan (later Bangladesh) in 1971 and the Turkish invasion of Cyprus in 1974. The Manchurian case is selected on the basis that the secondary literature identifies it as the first time nonrecognition was imposed on the results of the use of force. This means that policy discussion was more explicit and thus facilitates data collection. The Italian conquest of Ethiopia was selected as a comparison case to the Manchurian Crisis. The goal of comparison with negative cases in this study is to find out first whether the model of rule maintenance is useful in understanding the case at all and second why this case did not result in nonrecognition. That is, to identify sources of variation.

The next two cases are selected as a paired positive and negative case of nonrecognition. Arguably, the post-World War II era is qualitatively different in terms of the institutionalisation of the norm against the use of force for profit. The United Nations Charter makes clear the prohibition on acts of aggression. In addition, an important statement of the norms and rules of international society, the United Nations Declaration on Principles of International Law concerning Friendly Relations and Co-operation among States, was adopted by the UNGA in 1970.[4] In a world where there is a general consensus on the norms and rules of international relations, is rule maintenance still necessary? In order to address this issue, I selected two cases after 1970. Given the need for detailed information on the private communications of governmental actors, I selected cases where relevant documents have been largely declassified. The two cases that fit these criteria were the Indian invasion of East Pakistan (Bangladesh) in 1971, and the 1974 Turkish invasion of Cyprus resulting in the eventual assertion of a Turkish-Cypriot state in Northern Cyprus. Finally, I extend the analysis to the broader universe of cases of nonrecognition debate. I discuss the full list of cases and concepts used in Chapter 6.

Collective nonrecognition is largely that agreed upon within the forum of an international organisation – here either the League of Nations or the UN. The debates within and around the international organisation position will provide an indication of the spread of international motivations and those justifications that were persuasive across the member states, representing a kind of global consensus (bearing in mind that a formal resolution is not always necessary as evidence of such a consensus). However, much of the relevant processes also take place at the state level. A focus on a selected group of states will be manageable and constitute a plausibility probe. I select the UK and the US.

Table 1.1 Observable implications for explanations of symbolic sanctions

Reason for sanctioning	Costs	Oriented around	Intended audience	Other features
Rule maintenance	Not important	Rule or norm or principle	Community	Establish a precedent; define standard; protect a principle; provide basis for future action
Coercion	High cost very important	Behaviour of violator or future violators	Violator or future violators	Consideration of effect of costs on behaviour; publicly threaten costs
Graduated sanctions	Initially low, then high later	Behaviour of violator	Violator only	Avoid public condemnation initially
Vengeance	Not important	Personal sense of morality	None	No consideration of outcome; appeals to justice/rightness/fairness etc.; emotional
Domestic politics	Low cost is benefit	Domestic group	Domestic group	Existence of pressure group; consideration of electoral consequences
Generalised resolve	High cost very important	Perceptions of other states	Community	Link with other reputation, e.g. strength or reliability; use of current action as proof

Both are and have been powerful international actors and were central actors involved in all the conflicts concerned. Within these states, I focus on actors that are directly relevant to the recognition decision, primarily foreign policy decision makers.

Observable implications

In order to make a judgement over what the reasons for sanctions were in a particular case we must define the relevant empirical evidence that allows us to distinguish between alternative explanations in this particular case (see Table 1.1). How are we to know whether maintaining the rule against aggression actually was an important driver of action in decisions over whether to recognise various situations? What are the types of justifications that are consistent with wanting to create common knowledge of the rules? It is possible to identify evidence that indicates that rule maintenance was an important, or the main, reason for action. Rule maintenance as an action has several central properties. The first is that it is *concerned with rules*. Whether these are called rules, or principles, standards of behaviour, precedents, laws or something else, rule maintenance is specifically oriented towards a social rule. Rule maintenance actions then should be justified in the context of saving or promoting a rule rather than influencing behaviour in a specific instance. Another property is that it is *future-oriented*. The desired effect of rule maintenance is not immediate; instead it is a kind of deferred gratification. Moreover, it is not oriented primarily towards norm violators but towards the members of the community as a whole; it is not aimed at affecting specific actors but instead is aimed at creating common knowledge. Some of the observable implications of rule maintenance are that the reasons for action given are that the sanction will establish a principle, define a standard of behaviour or establish a precedent (unless setting a precedent involves the costly signalling of ability or resolve). Actors could be worried that not performing the rule maintenance action will legitimise or normalise the rule violations that have prompted the whole discussion. This reasoning should be coupled with the explicit denunciation of the sanction itself as efficacious in deterring violations. Actors might also emphasise that stating or proclaiming the principle, maintaining the legitimacy of the rule, will help to coordinate action, or provide a basis for action, in the future.

Alternative reasons to engage in sanctions

What are the alternative possible reasons to engage in sanctions? The most straightforward reasons for engaging in sanctions are either to compel compliance in the current case or to deter future instances (Schelling 1960). Deterrence or compellence in a specific instance involves the use of actions by a state S intended to inflict such costs on an actor, or rule violator, V, that V stops doing the action that S does not want performed. Another possible deterrence related view is called general deterrence. Here the intention is not to stop actor V from doing the current action of type A, but instead to prevent actors from doing actions of type A in the future. Again, the deterrent action must either itself inflict costs or indicate the intention to inflict costs later. If nonrecognition is intended to compel or deter, we should see policymakers explicitly asserting that the costs of nonrecognition are high, considering whether these costs will be sufficient to change the cost–benefit calculation of the target state(s), and publicly threatening the target or future aggressors with the costly consequences of noncompliance.

Another possibility is that a low-cost sanction is used as part of a policy of graduated sanctions. Ostrom notes that in the event of a rule violation, a low-cost sanction might be useful. 'A small penalty may be sufficient to remind the infractor of the importance of compliance' (1990: 97). A similar idea is behind the use of a police 'caution' to first-time offenders. The main function of the sanction is to let the violator know that they have been caught without causing resentment. The sanctioner may be in a similar situation in the future and would value some understanding of her own mistakes or weakness of will. However, in the event of continued non-compliance, 'one can expect the appropriator-monitor to escalate the imposed sanctions in an effort to halt future rule-breaking by such offenders' (1990: 98). Policymakers engaged in this activity should be taking pains in the initial stages of a crisis to avoid public condemnation of the norm violator. We should also see the adoption of more costly, public sanctions if the violator continues to break the norm.

Another view, which I term 'vengeance' for convenience, is that actors sanction norm-breakers through a strong form of logic of appropriateness. That is, the shaming or condemnation of norm-breakers is a fundamental part of human action that occurs in the absence of any calculation of its expected outcome. Durkheim approaches the urge to condemnation as a normal part of the human condition. Sanctioning or condemnation is an almost automatic response to norm-breaking: 'vengeance is . . . an automatic, purposeless reaction, an emotional and senseless impulse, and an unreasoned compulsion to destroy' even if it happens to defend society against a threat (1984: 45). 'What we are avenging [when society sanctions criminals] is the outrage to morality' (47). Others posit the operation of a 'fairness' norm. Falk et al.'s results from prisoners' dilemma experiments indicate that 'retaliation, i.e., the desire to harm those who committed unfair acts, seems to be the most important motive behind fairness-driven informal sanctions' (2005). If vengeance is the motivation for sanctioning, we should not expect to see sustained justification of the sanctions in cause and effect terms. Instead, we should see appeals to justice, moral rightness or other values as reasons for action. Vengeance is an emotional reaction, so we should see evidence of anger and indignation on the part of those making the decision to sanction.

As stated, another prominent alternative reason is that there is some domestic political benefit to being seen to engage in sanctioning. If domestic politics is the reason for engaging in nonrecognition, policymakers should be subject to pressure, publicly, privately or both, to adopt a nonrecognition policy or to take action against the aggressor state. This could include media campaigns, congressional or parliamentary debates and statements, or private meetings with non-governmental organisations, community leaders or businessmen. Policymakers might privately deplore the need to do anything but describe nonrecognition as a relatively cheap way to please a domestic interest group. Alternatively, they might display a concern with the electoral consequences of not taking punishment action. They might also appeal to the lack of commitment to take further action as a positive feature of nonrecognition.

Sanctions might also be motivated by the desire to signal generalised resolve (Schelling 1960; Mercer 1996). That is, if a state backs down on this issue, other states might view them as being easier to defeat in subsequent interactions. In order for this motivation to be analytically separate from the deterrence motivation, the information or resolve communicated must be oriented towards something other than the issue of aggression. If this is this case, decision makers should explicitly link the current situation with broader issues of global importance, or worry about the effect of their actions on others' views of their reliability or will to stand up to aggressors. They might also try to use their actions in the current crisis as proof of resolve when communicating with allies or opponents.

NOTES

1. Assume there are three types of state. One type (A) cares not for the rule. One type (B) values the rule and would be willing to use highly costly sanctions to enforce the rule under some circumstances. And the third type (C) values the rule and would be willing to send a weak signal that they are willing to enforce the rules, but not actually enforce the rules. There is a semi-separating equilibrium in which A always does nothing and both B and C send a weak signal. See Gibbons (1992: 215–7) and McCarty and Meirowitz (2009: 225).
2. This is the basic point of the 'coordinated attack problem' or 'two generals problem'. An informal version involves two generals who will only win the battle if they attack together sending messages to each other, for example by messenger on horseback, about when to attack. They are never sure if the last horse rider they sent got through until receipt of the other's reply confirming receipt. But they then have to confirm receipt of the message to the other, who does not know if the last confirmation of receipt got through. And so on.
3. Acceptance or recognition does not require approval. I can deplore the fact that tipping is customary while still recognising that it is customary.
4. UN General Assembly Resolution 2625, 24 October 1970.

CHAPTER TWO

The Manchurian Crisis

INTRODUCTION

The Manchurian Crisis was a major international diplomatic incident arising from Japan's use of force in Manchuria in Northern China over the period 1931–3. It was the setting for the first use of nonrecognition as a sanction against the illegitimate use of force. In the previous chapter, I outlined various types of reasoning underlying the imposition of sanctions. I focused on rule maintenance, the idea that symbolic sanctions create common knowledge of the rules by which states feel the international system should be governed. This chapter analyses the Manchurian Crisis in order to answer the question of why nonrecognition was adopted as a sanction against aggression in this case. Numerous commentaries identify the Manchurian Crisis as a seminal event in the development of the rule of nonrecognition and the laws of war. For example, Langer asserts that events during the crisis were 'epoch-making' (1947: 285). As it was the first instance of the nonrecognition of aggressive gain, the actors in the crisis had no prima facie expectation that nonrecognition was a viable policy option, let alone the default or expected reaction. This has two implications for the ensuing analysis. First, the reasoning behind the policy of nonrecognition is likely to be more explicit and more clearly laid out. When a policy is enacted for the first time, actors often need to spell out why it is worth doing, both for themselves and when persuading or legitimating the policy to others. This is a benefit if we are trying to understand the motivations behind a policy. However, the second implication is that the process by which the nonrecognition policy is decided upon is indirect, convoluted and messier than after it became a regular occurrence. There is a long, drawn-out process whereby people come to see a particular reason for a policy as persuasive and determinative. This means that there are changes over the course of the crisis, while various reasons are considered, offered and evaluated. That said, by the denouement of the crisis, the dominant reason why nonrecognition was enacted in the Manchurian Crisis was rule maintenance. The US and the League of Nations said that they refused to recognise the outcome of Japan's use of force because they wanted to maintain the illegitimacy of aggression.

I first outline some important events to provide an empirical framework. Then I discuss the theoretical findings from an analysis of the crisis. This is followed by a detailed investigation of the decision-making processes of the US, the UK and the League of Nations as they relate to the adoption of nonrecognition.

HISTORICAL OVERVIEW

The historian Arnold Toynbee called 1931 *annus terribilis*. The Great Depression was in full swing and the recent electoral success of the Nazi party in Germany was only one of the indicators that the relative peace after World War I might be fragile (Marks 2003: 122). Then, on 18 September 1931, the Japanese Kwantung army in Manchuria used an explosion on the railway at Mukden (Shenyang) as an excuse for the preconceived seizure of the arsenal there and of various other towns in the area. This became known as 'the Mukden Incident'. Almost immediately, the Nationalist Chinese government brought the issue to the attention of the Council of the League of Nations under Article 11 of the League Covenant, and appealed to the US under the terms of the Kellogg-Briand Pact. Reaction in the West was initially one of indifference. Many considered China 'unorganised' and Japan a civilised great power. The Japanese troops were stationed in Manchuria under a system of treaty rights similar to those enjoyed by many powers under instruments like the Boxer Protocol of 1901.[1] Credible information about the situation on the ground was scarce. A League Council resolution on 30 September 1931 merely noted 'the importance of the Japanese Government's statement that it has no territorial designs in Manchuria' (LNOJ 1931: 2307) and urged both sides to settle their differences peacefully.

However, the Japanese military, effectively autonomous from the civilian government, continued its operations. On 8 October they started aerial bombing of the city of Chinchow (Jinzhou). This generated a reaction. On 24 October the Council issued another resolution that called for the Japanese troops to be withdrawn into the railway zone allocated to Japan by treaty. Instead of doing so, the Japanese army continued its operations, which included seizure of revenues and replacement of administrative personnel. By 20 November, the Japanese had occupied Tsitsihar (Qiqihaer). The League responded on 10 December by appointing a five-man commission to investigate the facts on the ground, in particular who was responsible for the Mukden Incident and whether either side was acting in self-defence. This commission was chaired by the British Lord Lytton. Both the Chinese government of Chiang Kai-shek and the Japanese Wakatsuki Cabinet fell in December, loosening restraints on the Kwantung Army, which occupied Chinchow on 3 January 1932.

The occupation of Chinchow angered the US Secretary of State Henry L. Stimson. He responded on 7 January with a note sent by telegram to both the Chinese and Japanese governments, which included a statement that the US 'does not intend to recognise any situation, treaty or agreement which may be brought about by means contrary to the covenants and obligations of the pact of Paris of August 27 1928' (FRUS 1932 III: 8).[2] No other states issued similar notes. UK Foreign Secretary Sir John Simon notably refused Stimson's request to do so. However, at the end of January, Japan attacked Shanghai, where there were numerous legations and communities of citizens of Western states. Reports and newsreel footage of shelling and air bombardment were relayed back home by foreigners in the International Settlement. Whereas the dispute was approached officially as if the question of who was in the wrong was not settled, after the attack on Shanghai, Japan was increasingly treated as if it were the responsible party. This was clear in a League Council appeal of 16 February that was sent only to the Japanese. This appeal included an affirmation of the nonrecognition doctrine: 'no infringement of the territorial integrity and no change in the political independence of any Member of the League brought about in disregard of this article ought to be valid and effectual by Members of the League' (LNOJ 1932: 383–4).[3] Stimson sought to push further for the idea that nonrecognition was a good idea in a public letter to Senator Borah of the Committee on Foreign Relations on 23 February. The Assembly then passed a resolution on 11 March 1932 which said that it was 'incumbent upon the Members of the League of Nations not to recognise any situation, treaty or agreement which may be brought about contrary to the Covenant of the League of Nations or to the Pact of Paris' (LNOJ SS 101 1932: 8).[4]

Japan withdrew from Shanghai on 5 May in an agreement brokered by the Western powers and large-scale military action ceased. In the meantime, on 9 March the former Emperor of China Henry Pu-Yi declared an independent state of Manchukuo in Manchuria. Japan formally recognised Manchukuo on 15 September, defying the League and the US. The Lytton Commission's report was published in October and discussed by the League Assembly in December. While several of the larger powers were leaning towards accepting Manchukuo as a fait accompli, the Kwantung Army renewed military action with the seizure of Shanhaikuan in January 1933. This led in February to a League Assembly resolution adopting the first eight chapters of the Lytton Commission report, which, while not explicitly condemning Japan or recommending sanctions, did insist on the withdrawal of Japanese troops and Japanese recognition of Chinese sovereignty over Manchuria. Rather than agree to these terms, Japan formally withdrew from the League on 27 March 1933.

THEORETICAL DISCUSSION

Reasons for the adoption of nonrecognition

Any explanation of why nonrecognition was adopted in the Manchurian Crisis needs to account for the non-adoption of other measures. This is because there was such uncertainty at the time as to what should be done in the event of great power aggression that multiple options were prima facie possible and so the adoption of, say, economic sanctions, could have served as a pre-emptive substitute for nonrecognition. Nonrecognition was only considered as an option after other options had been discarded. An important aspect of the situation facing decision makers was then that other options seemed too problematic. Any states with potential military or economic leverage on Japan, including the US and the UK, excluded the use of force or sanctions because they were seen as too costly or unpopular. If Britain had not been so weak in the Far East relative to Japan, or if the US had not been in the grip of an economic crisis, it is possible that measures other than nonrecognition would have been implemented. This would have obviated the need to search for policy alternatives that produced the nonrecognition policy.

Explanations of why other sanctions were not adopted only go so far.[5] They do not help us to explain why states adopted nonrecognition rather than doing nothing. Answers to the general question of 'why sanction?' include coercing compliance in the current case, deterring future instances, out of a fit of irrational emotion and domestic politics (see Chapter 1 for an elaboration of these and other possibilities). None of these answers helps us to make sense of policymaking and the adoption of nonrecognition during the Manchurian Crisis. Henry Stimson justified his initial nonrecognition note, to others in the State Department, president Hoover, the domestic press and foreign diplomats, in terms of its effect on Japan. This effect was as a signal of US intention to take measures against Japan to stop its actions in Manchuria. However, this explanation of the sending of the Stimson note does not extend either to actors other than Stimson, nor to Stimson himself after the Japanese attack on Shanghai had seemingly demonstrated the inefficacy of the note.

Rule maintenance

The most prominent reason provided privately by several of the key actors in the US and the UK, as well as publicly in the League Assembly debates, was rule maintenance. This can be understood as consciously adopted rule or norm reproduction. In the Manchurian Crisis, there were at different times several different types of justifications given for the policy of not recognising the results of Japan's use of force in Manchuria. Across the US, UK and the League of Nations, the many actors involved in reacting to the Far Eastern Crisis expressed various thoughts, intuitions and reasoning. Some did occasionally entertain the idea that a threat of nonrecognition might work, especially against an 'Oriental nation like Japan' (President Herbert Hoover, quoted in Stimson Diary, 21 February 1932). Sometimes people expressed a wish to support China; sometimes they wanted to support Japan and thought that nonrecognition would not have any effect. Others thought that nonrecognition would look like action but without committing to do anything in the future. However, all of these motivations were temporary and isolated. Maybe they were subjectively plausible initially, but they proved unsustainable. In an interactive process, rule maintenance became the justification that was intersubjectively valid across the states in the League and the US. Other reasons did not command wide acceptance, either in private where consideration of personal benefit was more prominent or in public where consistency with principle was emphasised. These alternative motives became offered less and less as the crisis progressed. Instead, rule maintenance emerged as the dominant justification for the policy of nonrecognition. It was the only socially sustainable motive by the time of the adoption of the Lytton Report by the League Assembly in 1933.

In order to demonstrate how the decision making played out, I now investigate the adoption of a nonrecognition policy first by the US, then by the UK and finally by the League of Nations Council and Assembly. Using both private and public statements, I establish the reasons given for not adopting another type of sanction as well as those specifically for nonrecognition.

THE US AND NONRECOGNITION IN THE MANCHURIAN CRISIS

In 1931, President Hoover was fully engrossed in his task of responding to the economic problems his country was suffering. The seemingly unprecedented economic slump of the Great Depression took up almost all of his personal attention. Consequently, not only was Hoover adamant that foreign policy decisions should be subordinated to the demands of the domestic economy, but he left Henry L. Stimson, his Secretary of State since March 1929, with a considerable degree of decision-making autonomy during the period in which the nonrecognition policy was formulated and enacted. However, at numerous points Hoover's influence on the proceedings was significant. First, it was actually Hoover who was the first to conceive of the idea of nonrecognition as a distinct policy alternative. On 9 November 1931, he conceived of the idea of 'an announcement that if the treaty [between China and Japan] is made under military pressure we will not recognise it or avow it' (Stimson Diary 9 November 1931). It is clear that Hoover was not concerned with creating international law or legal precedents as it was not until over a month after Stimson sent his note that Hoover 'said that the more he thought of it, the more he was convinced that that would be one of the greatest steps forward in international relations that he knew of' (Stimson Diary 8 February 1932). While it was Stimson's name that became attached to the policy, Hoover tried to get Stimson to declare it instead the 'Hoover Doctrine' (Castle Diary 18 February 1932, quoted in Current 1954: 533). However, there were significant differences between Hoover's and Stimson's conception of what exactly the policy entailed. In an authoritative analysis of the formulation of the nonrecognition doctrine, Richard Current (1954) argues that Hoover's position was that the nonrecognition doctrine was a substitute for action, something that obviated the need for any stronger sanction. Stimson instead sought to use nonrecognition as a way of signalling to Japan the potential for future more potent action. At one point, Stimson had to talk Hoover out of making a public statement that the US would never use anything but moral sanctions (Stimson Diary 26 February 1932).

As this makes clear, Hoover did have opinions about foreign policy during the Manchurian Crisis. Most importantly, he set strict limits on Stimson's freedom of action. Despite Stimson's occasional consideration of robust measures, particularly economic sanctions, Hoover was insistent that war must be avoided. Speaking to his Cabinet during November 1931, he said 'We will not go along on war or any of the sanctions, either economic or military, for those are the roads to war' (Steiner 2005: 727). Stimson's reactions to Japanese military action throughout the crisis were emotional and after the Japanese attack on Tsitsihar, Stimson again favoured economic sanctions but Hoover was adamant that sanctions would lead to war and so they were to be avoided. In December 1931, three of four State Department experts recommended economic sanctions to Stimson (Current 1954: 520) but Hoover's fear of domestic political repercussions meant that this option was not seriously considered.

The decision makers

There were four primary formulators of Far Eastern policy at this time (Smith 1948: 11). Apart from Hoover, there were Stimson, Secretary of State, Stanley K. Hornbeck, the Chief of the Far Eastern Affairs Division at the State Department, and William R. Castle, Jr., who was Under Secretary of State. Hornbeck and Castle, considered pro-Chinese and pro-Japanese respectively, provided policy guidance to Stimson, who was ultimately responsible for making the decision, although Castle was less involved.

Hornbeck and 'no immediate effect'

In the face of Hoover's and hence Stimson's avoidance of economic sanctions, Stanley Hornbeck considered alternative policy options. His position on nonrecognition was a particularly nuanced one. Unlike any other major commentator, Hornbeck drew a distinction between a legal condemnation and a moral one. On the 21 November 1931, he wrote of a declaration of nonrecognition:

> In terms of action, this view, if adopted, would mean that, if and when the time comes for the American and other Governments most concerned to give notice that they will not recognise any treaty or treaties which may be concluded between Japan and China under the compulsion of Japan's military occupation of Manchuria, the attempt should be made, in such evidence and points of law without attempting to pass or to suggest a moral judgement. (Doenecke 1981: 87–8)

This commentary reveals that Hornbeck viewed the role of nonrecognition to be to tell Japan that its actions were disapproved of, but that an excessive amount of moral condemnation might prevent future reassimilation into traditional diplomatic practices (Burns and Bennett 1974: 105). This position is implicitly underwritten by a lack of faith in the effectiveness of nonrecognition to achieve a change in Japanese behaviour. Hornbeck makes this explicit in a memo of 5 December 1931 (Doenecke 1981: 91–3) where he considers the possible courses of action for the Powers. Apart from an economic boycott,

> The Powers could join in a public denunciation of Japan as a law breaker. This would be painful to Japan, but it would not be likely to cause her to desist from what she is doing or to undo what she has done.

This public legal denunciation is differentiated from nonrecognition; however, nonrecognition would also in all probability have no immediate effect in relation to the objective at this moment under consideration, namely that of restraining Japan and causing her to accept the terms of the [League of Nations] Resolution the fate of which now hangs in the balance.

Instead, the 'possible effect' of nonrecognition 'would lie in the future'.

This posited future effect of nonrecognition was further elaborated on 15 December (Doenecke 1981: 84–5). Nonrecognition might 'amount to more *morally* than anything . . . done so far'. Hornbeck's statements at this point emphasise the flexibility of notice not to recognise certain treaties.

It would involve no question of use of force or of sanctions of any sort. It would conflict with no action or position taken hitherto and would establish no limitations as to action which may be taken hereafter. As a notice, it could later, if and when circumstances might warrant, be canceled or revoked.

The next claim, often quoted in the secondary literature, seems oddly inconsistent with the rest of Hornbeck's writings. Nonrecognition would, 'show the powers "mean business". It would give the Pact of Paris "teeth". It would answer the charge that the League and the various governments are impotent.'

Out of context, this claim seems to place Hornbeck firmly on the side of nonrecognition and to justify it in terms of its direct causal impact on the situation at hand. However, Hornbeck puts 'mean business' and 'teeth' in quotation marks, suggesting that he is responding to criticism and that nonrecognition might deflate that criticism. More plausible indicators of Hornbeck's attitude are the arguments made in this memorandum and others that nonrecognition would be relatively useless.

When it came time to actually make the declaration of intent not to recognise Japan's gains in the Stimson note of 7 January 1932, Hornbeck was not in favour of it. Stimson reports that 'Hornbeck fought rather tenaciously against a definite statement' (Stimson Diary 6 January 1932). Hornbeck later said that he tried 'to convince Stimson that nonrecognition would not work because the world was full of rascals' (quoted in Ferrell 1957: 156 fn20). Current reports that Hornbeck was responsible for changing the wording of the note from 'will not recognise' to 'does not intend to recognise' (1954: 524). It seems plausible that Hornbeck thought this wording would be more flexible if the US had to back down or change position subsequently.

Stimson and his note

At the time of issuing the notification Stimson viewed it as sending a sig- nal to Japan, a bluff that the US was considering further action concern- ing Manchuria. However, once the signal was sent, once public opinion both in the US and internationally seized upon it as a precedent for international law, and particularly after it appeared to have had little deterrent effect, Stimson began to justify his adoption of nonrecogni- tion in terms of setting a precedent, that is, the creation of international law. This dual reasoning is encapsulated by Stimson in his second auto- biographical book covering the crisis: 'At the best this policy [nonrec- ognition] might in fact deter the Japanese. At the worst it would lay a firm foundation of principle upon which the Western nations and China could stand in a later reckoning' (Stimson and Bundy 1947: 258).

On 7 November, only a couple of weeks after the incident at Mukden, Stimson spoke to Hoover concerning Manchuria; specifically, what they would do if the Japanese military got 'control of the situation' (Stim- son Diary 7 November 1931).[6] Hoover apparently ruled out economic pressure or an embargo as it would 'lead to war' but raised the idea of withdrawing the US ambassador. However, he also wanted to 'give out a statement at the same time putting war out of the question, an announce- ment that we would not under any event go to war'. Stimson disagreed with this policy because 'it would remove from Japan any fear of any further economic blockade'. This account reveals the distinction between Hoover's and Stimson's approach to US action towards Japan. Stimson is clearly advocating the signalling of policy intentions to Japan, using graduated sanctions as a tactic to warn Japan that the continuation of current behaviour will lead to increased costs.

Hoover changed his mind over the weekend and Stimson reports that on 9 November the president had now decided to 'give an announcement that if the treaty is made under military pressure we will not recognise it or avow it' (Stimson Diary 9 November 1931). This is the genesis in the administration of the idea that nonrecognition might be used. Stimson then writes that Hornbeck said 'this remedy didn't amount to anything because we had tried it in 1915'. Stimson disagreed with this diagnosis. First, 'if the disavowal is made by all of the countries, it ought to have a very potent effect'. Second, former Secretary of State William Jennings Bryan's note in 1915 'was one of the potent forces then by which in 1921 and 1922 the Japanese twenty-one demands were finally rectified as far as Shantung was concerned'. At this early stage of the crisis it seems that Stimson held that diplomatic sanctions, like a note of nonrecognition, would be effective in a policy of using threats and bluffs to deter Japan.

By late December Stimson was concerned that Japanese action constituted aggression. He noted in his diary a meeting about Chinchow with the Japanese Ambassador Debuchi in which he said his information was 'that there had been no preparation on the Chinese side at all and nothing to provoke an attack. So that an attack if it came against the regular forces, would necessarily be in the nature of an aggression' (Stimson Diary 23 December 1931). After Christmas and New Year, Stimson received news that the Japanese had finally occupied Chinchow. Stimson said 'this brings the Manchurian matter up to a final climax' and that he considered it a 'final slap in the face' (Stimson Diary 2 January 1932). Ferrell interprets this reaction as that 'Stimson was furious' (1957: 152). Hornbeck attempted to rationally evaluate the situation, claiming that this action was no different from previous actions, calling Chinchow 'the last dish in a set of dishes' that were being broken by the Japanese. Stimson greeted this with anger, leaving Hornbeck to worry if he were going to be fired (interview with Hornbeck quoted in Ferrell 1957: 153). It was in this frame of mind that Stimson set out to compose the Stimson note.

The next day Stimson composed his first draft of the note, showed it to his advisors and 'went over all the precedents' with them (Stimson Diary 3 January 1932). After agreeing the language with Hornbeck and others, Stimson showed the note to Hoover, who 'approved it'. Stimson recounts that he discussed with Hoover 'the dangers which we would have if the Japanese called our position, so to speak, and tried to annex Manchuria', but that the president was 'willing to take that risk' (Stimson Diary 4 January 1932). Stimson at this point seems to be viewing the sending of the note to be the sending of a warning, a signal of resolve to engage in future action. He describes the language of the note as 'rather clear and strong' and that 'the advantages of that upon the Japanese will probably outweigh the embarrassment of any position which we may be put in in [sic] after years by it' (Stimson Diary 4 January 1932). This is evidence that Stimson's reasoning at this time involved an attempt to deter Japan from pursuing further military action and to deter Japan from attempting to profit from their military success. His motivation does not appear to be the setting of a precedent, given his unconcern with the future position of the US. At least, his characterisation of the potential effects for the US being embarrassed does not constitute evidence that at this point he was conceiving of his notice of nonrecognition as creating a new standard in international law. There is no mention of Chinchow or any specific reference to Japan's actions in Manchuria in the note. Referencing this fact, Doenecke concludes that 'assistance to China for its own sake was not the issue' behind the note (1984: 48).

Stimson and the Shanghai incident

After sending the note of nonrecognition on 7 January 1932, Stimson's attitudes towards nonrecognition were in flux. He offered a post hoc justification of the note on 9 January. He credits his action with causing the Chinese to decide against breaking off relations with Japan and thus giving 'Japan just the opportunity she wants to have a free hand in acting as if there was war' (Stimson Diary 9 January 1932). Also on the 9th, Stimson spoke to Senator William E. Borah, chairman of the Committee on Foreign Relations of the United States Senate. Borah approved of the note and had made a public statement of that approval. In the discussion, Borah 'agreed with me [Stimson] that one of the main things to consider was the preservation of our interest in and the effect upon China' (Stimson Diary 9 January 1932).

After the Japanese attack on Shanghai starting on 28 January, endangering numerous Western citizens and considerable Western investment, Stimson was shocked. He framed his reactions following the Shanghai attack in moralistic terms:

> The attack on Shanghai has made very much the same repercussions that the German invasion of Belgium made in 1914. It has shocked the whole world. It has seemed to be a perfectly indefensible act of aggression against an undefending populace. They have bombed an unoffending civilian city without any occasion whatever except their own policy, and now the question is what we shall do as outsiders looking on. I recall how outraged we were when President Wilson did nothing to show the shame that we felt in regard to Belgium, and I am very anxious that Mr Hoover should not be put in the same position here. (Stimson Diary 8 February 1932)

The extension of Japanese military action into Shanghai seems to have changed Stimson's thinking. While working towards a restatement of the US intent not to recognise treaties made under the current circumstances, Stimson explained his motivations: 'What I am trying to do is to get a chance to sum up the situation officially to answer the Japanese Government's propaganda and to put the situation morally in its right place' (Stimson Diary 8 February 1932).

Considerations of deterrence of the Japanese, of any 'potent effect' of statements of nonrecognition, are already gone from Stimson's justifications. On 18 February Stimson reported that:

> The whole situation is beginning to shake me up and get me back to a little bit nearer my old view that we haven't yet reached the stage where we can dispense with police force; and the only police force I have got to depend upon today is the American Navy. (Stimson Diary 18 February 1932)

However, this swing back towards a more Realist belief in the efficacy of force alone did not turn him away from his intent to make a further statement of nonrecognition. Stimson commented that 'the prospect of the cessation of hostilities in Shanghai', the nominal goal of the recent flurry of diplomatic action, made him 'unhappy because if they cease they will cease without America having said her word on the morality of this great situation' (Stimson Diary 18 February 1932). Stimson was so convinced at this point that action short of sending battleships or the use of 'real guns' was destined to be ineffective that he privately condemned in his diary the League Council declaration of 16 February which 'adopts my doctrine rather feebly of not recognizing future situations which are produced by a breach of treaty' (Stimson Diary 19 February 1932).

Hoover was much more enthusiastic about nonrecognition, a state of mind attributed by Stimson to the upswing in domestic economic policy. The president took the position that 'the main trouble before the Assembly is that they have not yet adjudged Japan to be in the wrong. We cannot discuss punishment until there has been a judgement' (Stimson Diary 21 February 1932). If a judgement were made then the US would go along with punishment in terms of 'a universal declaration of non-recognition of any treaties, etc., and even the withdrawal of envoys'. Stimson reports that Hoover is not yet disenchanted with such a policy's deterrent effect, saying, 'The President thinks that this would have enormous and controlling effect upon an Oriental nation like Japan' (Stimson Diary 21 February 1932).

Despite the differences between his reasoning and Hoover's, Stimson pursued their mutual goal of a joint statement of nonrecognition through the League. This resulted in what was to be known as the Borah letter, publicly sent by Stimson to Senator Borah. Discussing this letter, Stimson calls it both 'a statement as to the policy of the "Open Door"' and a means to pursuing the president's programme of getting the League Assembly to make a declaration of nonrecognition.

Stimson's letter to Senator Borah

Stimson does not explain in his diary his view of the effect of the letter to Senator Borah, who was thought to be already in agreement with Stimson on the issue. Castle recounts the aims of the letter to Senator Borah as being:

> setting forth the ideas of this Government as to the Open Door, etc. in a fashion which would get public sentiment behind us in this country and at the same time show the League how far we were willing to go. (Castle Diary 21 February 1932, quoted in Current 1954: 529)

The text of the letter is interesting in terms of the justifications used for the policy of nonrecognition (FRUS 1943 I: 83–7).

The letter opens with an extended review of the Open Door policy of the US and the subsequent Nine Power Treaty which formalised some of the principles behind that policy.[7] Under the justification that a free, self-governing China would best serve the interests 'of all nations which have intercourse with her', that Treaty was 'a covenant of self-denial among the signatory powers in deliberate renunciation of any policy of aggression which might tend to interfere with [China's] development'. This self-denial was reinforced and extended, Stimson claimed, by the Pact of Paris or Kellogg-Briand Pact. He says the situation in China does not indicate that these two treaties should be modified; instead the covenants therein should be observed. Then he references his note of 7 January and describes what will happen 'if a similar position [of nonrecognition is] taken by the other governments of the world'.

> a caveat will be placed upon such action which, we believe, will effectively bar the legality hereafter of any title of right sought to be obtained by pressure of treaty violation, and which, as has been shown by history in the past, will eventually lead to the restoration to China of rights and titles of which she may have been deprived. (FRUS 1943 I: 87)

There are two reasons for pursuing nonrecognition stated here. The first is to create a standard or precedent in international law. This is not exactly the same as the one Stimson had been expressing in his diary. Making clear the US view of the morality of the situation could be done without reforming a fundamental principle of international relations (*pacta sunt servanda*). The restoration of Chinese rights is a separate goal and one that is not prevalent in the writings of the policymakers. The only partial exceptions are the occasional statement of empathy for the Chinese, but this is usually in reference to the violence at Chinchow and Shanghai. Also, the entire discussion up to this point was directed towards a peaceful renegotiation of Chinese rights, which, in the current circumstances, would almost certainly lead to their replacement with further Japanese rights and titles. Desire to provide support to the victim of aggression does not seem to be a driving reason behind the adoption of the nonrecognition policy.

US public opinion and nonrecognition

Public opinion in the US during the Manchurian Crisis period was not measured by polls and there was a distinctly regional character to the printed press. Two studies covering a wide range of newspaper, periodical and governmental writings, Tupper and McReynolds in 1937 and Doenecke in 1984, come to reasonably similar conclusions about the distribution of opinion during the crisis. In the first period, September 1931–January 1932, reactions in the press were 'wildly divergent' and 'there was no general condemnation of Japan's reaction to the September 18th incident' (Tupper and McReynolds 1937: 296). Even the bombing of Chinchow, which exercised Stimson, did not shift this overall division. Plenty of observers supported Japan's action. Elihu Root told Stimson that the US should 'recognise [Japan's] real claims to Manchuria' (Stimson Diary 14 November 1931). The former editor of the *Christian Science Monitor*, W. G. Abbot said:

> Far from blaming Japan for the trouble in Manchuria, the world would marvel at the patience and endurance of Japan if the truth were known about the situation. The Chinese attempt to repudiate solemn treaty obligations involved in the building of railroads, and their aggression upon Japanese citizens justified strong remedial if not punitive action.[8]

Though reaction was mostly positive, there was negative feedback on the Stimson note. Some predicted the collapse of Japan's society as a result of the condemnation. Some saw nonrecognition as a precursor to other pressures, both political and economic. Peace and religious organisations mostly saw the note as reinforcing the Kellogg Pact. Many spoke of the efficacy of the note, for example: 'Secretary Stimson has done all that can be done to stigmatise and check Japan's aggression against the integrity of China' (*Washington Evening Star* 8 January 1932, in Tupper and McReynolds 1937: 315). Congress and business were silent on the issue. The negative feedback focused on the lack of efficacy of the note. An article in the *New Republic*, criticising a statement by James McDonald of the Foreign Policy Association that the note 'put teeth' into the Pact of Paris, said that 'American policy was just about as effective as saying to a man who has just burned a neighbour's house, "I refuse to take cognizance of the conflagration, and shall continue to send letters to the old address"' (quoted in Doenecke 1984: 52).

After the attack on Shanghai opinion swung overwhelmingly against the Japanese (Hamilton 1953: 107). Even then public opinion in the form of letters to the President, up to 100 a day in February 1932, was heavily directed against armed entanglement. Press and congressional opinion was similarly cautious and wary of using force. Peace and religious groups advocated only 'wholly pacific methods' and several groups specifically included nonrecognition as such a method (Doenecke

1984: 55). However, the attack reflected for some the ineffectiveness of Stimson's nonrecognition policy. Edwin James (1932) wrote that:

> Whether or not one wishes to agree with the criticism that Colonel Stimson has used too much note paper during the recent developments, it is plain that the diplomatic communications we have sent abroad since September last, in which we brought our moral pressure to bear in an effort to restrain the advancing Japanese, have scored a signal failure.

Contrary to Stimson and others, James also saw trouble for 'the plans for ensuring world peace, based upon the efficacy of moral force, upon the strength of an aroused public opinion' which had suffered 'a serious setback'. In fact, apart from the *San Francisco Chronicle*, which ignored the deployment of naval forces and regarded Japan's withdrawal from Shanghai as 'a triumph of the moral force of world opinion led by the United States', nonrecognition was not credited with any effect beyond vague references to allowing for future action (Tupper and McReynolds 1937: 338).

The role of public opinion in the formulation of the US nonrecognition policy was not straightforward. It is clear from Hoover's forbidding of action that might lead to war that he was concerned about the public reaction to action that would be economically costly or that might interfere with his plans for the recovery of the domestic economy. This attitude coupled with Britain and other European powers' lack of support for economic sanctions goes a long way to explaining the non-adoption of a stronger sanction, as secondary analyses claim (Thorne 1972; Ostrower 1979; Marks 2003; Steiner 2005). But this constraining effect of public opinion on foreign policy does not account for the use of nonrecognition. None of the justifications for the policy made by Stimson and other policymakers, either public or private, refers to the need to placate a domestic constituency. Doenecke claims that there was no link between administration policy and public opinion. Stimson, Hoover and Hornbeck, when they were not being 'patronizing' to peace groups, ' refused to be pressured by businessmen, intimidated by leaders of peace societies, or swayed by editorials' (1981: 15). At one point, Stimson spoke to Roy Howard and the chief editorial writer of *The New York Times* in order to convince them that action other than diplomatic sanctions was 'folly' (Current 1954: 520). Ferrell doubts that 'Stimson before promulgating his Doctrine made any calculation of the American psyche' (1957: 168). It seems then that domestic political considerations, while making the use of force or economic sanctions prohibitively costly, were largely irrelevant in the formulation and enactment of nonrecognition by the US.

Conclusion of US section

During the active phase of the Manchurian Crisis, in which two of the most widely cited documents in the history of nonrecognition were made public, few people in the US thought that a declaration of intent not to recognise treaties or situations resulting from aggression would change the behaviour of the aggressor. Secretary of State Stimson, caught up in anger at what he saw as Japan's aggressive use of force, justified sending his note in terms we can understand as deterrence, an attempt to signal to the Japanese that further more costly actions would be forthcoming if they continued to use force. However, a few weeks afterwards, when this attempt at deterrence had apparently failed, Stimson changed his justification of the policy. Now he was trying to make a statement on 'the morality' of the situation and 'bar the legality' of aggressive gain. Public opinion formers in the press accepted this justification, and even Hornbeck, seemingly convinced that nonrecognition was not only useless but potentially constraining, accepted the role of a statement of nonrecognition as having an effect on future morality.

THE UK AND NONRECOGNITION

The position of the British Empire during the Manchurian Crisis was both very similar and very different from that of the US. Both countries were experiencing alarming economic problems and both were militarily weak in the Far East compared to Japan. The economic problems took up most of the attention of Prime Minister Ramsey MacDonald and meant that, like Stimson in the US, the Foreign Secretary Sir John Simon 'was free to chart his own course' (Steiner 2005: 725). One difference between the UK and the US concerns the general attitudes towards, or culture of, diplomacy (see for example, Pratt 1971: 226–9 and Thorne 1970: 1638); high level British foreign policymakers were more Realist and oriented towards the long term, and also characterised by pessimism about the strategic weakness of an empire in decline rather than the energetic optimism of one on the rise. When considering the strategic position of the UK, it is important to remember that the Manchurian Crisis was only a minor issue in British domestic politics. Other questions, such as the economy, a shocking naval mutiny at Invergordon, leaving the Gold Standard, war debts and reparations and the troubles in India, were all seen as more important than a minor spat in the Far East far from any British interests (Dutton 1992: 126). Also, the UK was a member of the League of Nations and as such had the option of taking action as part of that collective body rather than separately. This does not make an analysis of British policy during the crisis superfluous. Even though action was often taken through the League, the position and influence of the UK makes British attitudes towards nonrecognition important. In addition, despite opinion being against it, Foreign Secretary John Simon was influential in passing the 11 March League Assembly resolution.

British attitudes towards Japan

In general, there was considerable sympathy in British political circles for Japan. Even on 23 November 1931, after much Japanese military action, Simon wrote that there was 'a widespread feeling, which I believe to be justified, that although Japan has undoubtedly acted contrary to the principles of the Covenant by taking the law into her own hands, she has a real grievance against China'. Simon initially rejected the claim that this was a case of aggression, saying 'This is not a case in which the armed forces of one country have crossed the frontiers of another in circumstances where they had no previous right to be on the other's soil' (DBFP 2, VIII, no. 769).[9] Even after the attacks on Chinchow and on Shanghai, Simon still had a respect for the Japanese that was lacking in regard to the Chinese. On 17 February he said to the Cabinet, 'From the point of view of the security of the [Shanghai] Settlement it appeared better that the Japanese should succeed than the Chinese' (Thorne 1970: 1631). Japan was seen to have a strong case against China by most of the interested British public in 1931 (Bassett 1952: 31–2). For example, the *Daily Telegraph* wrote on 23 October, that 'The right of a government to protect its interests against barbarism and anarchy is a well-recognised one' (Dutton 1992: 125). Even after the establishment of Manchukuo, there was a considerable section of British public opinion in favour of the Japanese position. Member of Parliament (MP) Mr Loyat-Fraser asked Simon in the House of Commons on 14 March, regarding potential recognition of the newly declared Republic of Manchuria, 'Does not the right hon. Gentleman think that it is very desirable to encourage this beginning of order against chaos and anarchy in China?' (HC Deb 14 March 1932 vol 263: cc10–11).[10]

Even apart from any accord between the two powers on imperialist policy, British policymakers held Japanese goodwill to be important for the maintenance of British interests in China and the Far East more generally. A memorandum by Victor Wellesley, Deputy Under-Secretary for Foreign Affairs, on 22 December 1931 noted that: 'A major postulate of [British policy in the Far East] and of the safeguarding of [British] interests is the maintenance of really cordial relations with Japan, for in the absence of such relations our Far Eastern policy would necessarily fail . . .' (DBFP 2, IX, no. 21)

Hecht encapsulates this policy: 'Fearful of Japanese military strength, much greater than their own in the Pacific, the British practiced a form of appeasement in the Far East, hoping that Japan would continue to honor British rights and privileges in the conquered provinces' (1969: 178). This attitude had direct consequences both for the British reaction to the Manchurian Crisis generally and the nonrecognition policy in particular. It meant that one of the most important considerations for Simon when considering options was not to antagonise Tokyo. As Wellesley put it: '[Solution of the] Manchurian imbroglio . . . is a secondary function for His Majesty's Government's interest in the territorial status of Manchuria is infinitely less than their interest in maintaining cordial relations with Japan' (DBFP 2, IX, no. 21).

Economic sanctions

As a policy option during the crisis, economic sanctions were never genuinely considered by those responsible for making British foreign policy. The view was generally held that sanctions against Japan 'were likely to lead to an armed clash with that country' (Thorne 1970: 1619–20). In a Cabinet meeting on 11 November, shortly after Simon became foreign secretary, he said that economic sanctions were out of the question and that instead 'we ought to cooperate in any course that will preserve the moral authority of the League and a futile reference to Article XVI [concerning sanctions] would surely have the opposite effect' (Dutton 1992: 128).

The British response to Stimson's note

Stimson had reacted to the Japanese attack on Chinchow with indignation. The British viewed the situation as now being under control, as there were now no more Chinese troops in Manchuria for the Japanese to fight. Prior to the attack, Simon had considered privately warning Japan, but Under Secretary of State Wellesley and Foreign Office China Expert John Pratt both advised against it. Pratt said that

> The chief danger is that if the Chinese believe that the powers are stepping in to protect them against Japan they may elect to refuse to evacuate Chinchow whereas if they realise that they are face to face with Japan an arrangement will probably be reached under which the Chinese troops will quietly march away to Jehol before December 31. (Quoted in Hecht 1969: 182)

Pratt's concern here is that a public warning to Japan would encourage the Chinese to resist. This was viewed as counter to British interests in stability. At the same time, Wellesley expressed to Simon the claim that all of British diplomacy and investment in the Far East was built on a basis of Japanese cooperation: 'No other nation stands to lose as much as we do from a hostile Japan which is in a position to do us untold mischief' (in Hecht 1969: 183).

Stimson, under advice from Castle, notified the other members of the Nine Power Treaty a day before issuing his note that he would do so, asking them to do the same thing (Stimson Diary 6 January 1932). After the US notified the UK of the note, requesting similar British action, there were meetings of Far Eastern experts who 'unanimously advised rejecting the American invitation' (Hecht 1969: 181–5). One expert, MacKillop, characterised such a declaration as 'gratuitous discourtesy' and emphasised only the danger to Anglo-Japanese relations. Wellesley agreed, saying that a statement of nonrecognition 'would be premature and might cause considerably and unnecessary irritation'. Whitamore predicted that the note would cause the Japanese to become irritated with the US. Head of the Far Eastern Department Charles Orde, however, thought that Japan could be denied the fruits of her aggression (DBFP 2, IX, no. 67). Also, Lindley (ambassador to Japan) wrote in a telegram on 11 January 1932 that the 'American note has made an impression here and we believe Japanese will now follow conciliatory policy in Manchuria towards foreign interests in Manchuria' (DBFP 2, IX, no. 67). This view was sporadic at best and overwhelmed by dismissals of nonrecognition notes as useless. Anthony Eden, speaking for the Foreign Office in the House of Commons, said when questioned about the possibility of Britain joining Stimson in a declaration, 'I do not think that a further note on this subject would, even if it were addressed to both parties . . . serve any useful purpose' (Willoughby 1935: 207). In retrospect, John Pratt writes:

> Rightly or wrongly we attached little importance to this *demarche*. Nonrecognition was a peculiarly American technique, the fruit of American isolationism, and it was wholly out of harmony with the British tradition in international affairs. On the previous occasion in 1915 the nonrecognition notes had had no effect at all, and the repetition of the gesture in 1932 seemed to be in the nature of a formality. (Pratt 1971: 226)

Instead of a nonrecognition note to Japan, Simon sent Stimson a response on 11 January, saying he 'understands the action taken by the United State Government in addressing to the Chinese and Japanese Governments their note of January 7th' and that it 'corresponds with [UK] feelings'. However, the Japanese delegate to the League said 'that Japan had no territorial ambitions in Manchuria and was the champion in Manchuria of the principle of equal opportunity and the open door for the economic activities of all nations'. There is no mention of aggression, or the Pact of Paris, nor does Simon threaten nonrecognition, merely that he will discuss recent Japanese action in Parliament (FRUS 1932 III: 22–3). This was a compromise measure. As foreign secretary, Simon needed to find a way to reconcile two desires. The first was to cooperate with the US and the second was to not insult Japan. Hecht claims 'the primary reason for Simon's rejection of Stimson's invitation' was that he 'simply believed that at that particular juncture he could not afford for political, strategic, and economic reasons to offend Japan' (1969: 190). In line with this, on 8 January, the day after Stimson sent the note, the Japanese Ambassador Matsudaira met with Simon, who told the ambassador that the British were trying to find a way to 'deal with the American request that we associate with them in their recent Note in a way which we should regard as most consistent with our friendly relations with Japan' (DBFP 2, IX, no. 61). If Stimson had intended his note as a bluff, a signal of resolve to try and deter further Japanese action, Simon was going out of his way to assure the Japanese that the British were uninterested in Japanese action as long as it could be reconciled with British interests in the 'open door' policy. This policy seemed to bring results. By 20 January, Matsudaira had replied to Simon, noting that 'the fact that His Majesty's Government in the United Kingdom had not followed the example of the United States Government in addressing a formal note to Japan' meant that the Japanese government viewed the British as having a 'friendly attitude' (DBFP 2, IX, no. 98).

Simon and nonrecognition

There is a problem with concluding that the British diplomats did not want to join Stimson in declaring a policy of nonrecognition because Japanese goodwill was so valuable. Not only was Britain party to the League Council declaration in February and the Assembly resolution in March which took a position of nonrecognition, John Simon was an important influence on those actions. Some secondary analyses, for example Hecht (1969), attribute Simon's perceived change of attitude towards nonrecognition resulting in the League Assembly resolution of 11 March as being due to the increased importance to Simon of Anglo-American cooperation. Dutton also claims that Simon's active participation in the drafting of the League Council declaration of 16 February

1932 was a result of his desire 'to avoid upsetting American sensibilities' (1992: 133).

These conclusions are inadequately supported. Simon was well aware that Stimson was not especially pleased with British insistence on going through the League, and the Borah letter was only drafted after Stimson realised that he would not get Simon's cooperation. Simon does say to Macdonald that 'We have to remember . . . that Japan is the strongest power in the Far East . . . But we cannot afford to upset the United States of America over this, and I do not mean to do so' (Simon in letter to Macdonald 29 January 1932, DBFP 2, IX, no. 153). However, there was no actual change in policy. A separate note was not sent out. As Simon had been planning since November (see below) action was taken through the League. Ostrower sees the appearance of Anglo-American cooperation as a side benefit of the Assembly resolution rather than a driving motivation (1979: 131).

So, why did the UK participate in the League actions in February and March? As we have seen, there was scepticism about the effect of a nonrecognition declaration on Japan's behaviour. This did not change. Instead, the goal of the action was framed in terms of the League, the Covenant and the principle of the peaceful settlement of disputes.

Upholding the authority of the League

John Simon wrote in a letter to Macdonald on 17 November 1931 that the League could not solve the situation through force or moral persuasion, 'but it would be much better I think for the League to face that fact' and that even though 'this is not satisfactory . . . if all efforts at adjournment fail it is better than pretending (what nobody believes) that the League is really in a position to control the situation' (Dutton 1992: 129). In a memorandum presented to the Cabinet on 23 November (DBFP 2, VIII, no. 769), Simon laid out the case for the League 'in some manner reaffirming the . . . fundamental principle that a State may not, without prior recourse to the recognised means of peaceful settlement, take the law into its own hands'. A decision on this issue 'will necessarily have a most material influence upon [the League's] future as an effective international instrument for restraining military action and securing peaceful settlements'. Ignoring the fact that the League was in this case powerless to enforce this principle (as Simon was predicting even at this early stage) would be unwise. Instead a declaration by the President of the League of the principle would be an honest confession of weakness on the part of the Council, but that would be better than a cynical abandonment of the fundamental principle, upon which it has been attempting to build during these last 12 years an organization for the preservation of peace. (DBFP 2, VIII, no. 769)

Abandonment of that principle would risk 'that the League in refusing to reaffirm its true function, will lose so much respect as may yet be accorded to it in the face of its failure to enforce its demands upon the parties' (DBFP 2, VIII, no. 769). That is, even if a declaration of principle did not enforce compliance, even if it did nothing in terms of affecting Japan's behaviour, it would still be worthwhile because it would in some way promote the continuation of the principles of the League.

This position regarding the League was supported on 30 January by several major members of the foreign policymaking establishment. For example, the following statement was explicitly agreed to by Wellesley, Vansittart, Simon and Anthony Eden.

> The question at issue is surely a far more important one than that of Japan's and China's grievances against one another and the disturbance of our interests in the Far East. It is the question of whether the League of Nations is a reality or a sham, whether respect for the Covenant can or can not be maintained. It is surely essential, especially on the eve of the Disarmament Conference, that the League should not abdicate its authority [and] not be denied the chance of dealing with the greatest issue that has arisen in the history of the League, an issue which will probably decide whether the League is worth preserving or not. (DBFP 2, IX, no. 176)

Simon was consistent throughout the crisis concerning the issues that were at stake. In public, when justifying himself at all, he shifted emphasis towards the issue of the moral authority of the League. In the House of Commons on 22 February, Simon responded to a question about British policy towards China, Japan, Manchuria and Shanghai with a speech in which he explicitly addressed the 'lamentable fact' that despite all of the treaties of peace fighting was going on between two members of the League. He said 'the full influence of Britain' would be directed towards supporting 'the moral authority of the League of Nations'. Defending this policy he said 'it is only by affirming with boldness and sincerity the principles of the League that we shall find the best means of restoring peace'. In further justification, he hoped that

> if we show ourselves devoted to the purposes of the League, the time may soon come, notwithstanding the wreckage of our hopes, when the moral

authority of the League will be seen to exercise its influence on the side of peace. (HC Deb 22 February 1932 vol 262: cc173–84)

Here Simon is appealing to future occasions where the principle of non-aggression might be able to be enforced. Declaring the principle of non-aggression, that is declaring the illegitimacy or illegality of gains made by aggression at this point in time, would mean that that would be the standard used in the future to judge behaviour.

Conclusion of UK section

Fears of war and acute awareness of strategic weakness in the Far East were used in private by Simon and the Foreign Office as reasons to avoid the use of force or economic sanctions against Japan. Compared to Stimson's writings, there is a palpable absence of moral outrage at Japan's actions in China. There was never a sense that a statement of nonrecognition would be effectual in deterring Japan, and decision makers had little sympathy for China. The UK did not, in the face of repeated American requests, issue a unilateral note threatening Japan with nonrecognition of its gains. Instead, Simon participated in League action, both in the Council and the Assembly, justifying this action in terms of maintaining both the authority of the League and the principle that aggression was illegitimate.

THE LEAGUE OF NATIONS AND NONRECOGNITION

The Council and prevarication

The discussions in the League Council beginning in late January and continuing until 19 February are notable in their lack of explicit attention to the question of nonrecognition. Paul-Boncour, president of the Council, read out a declaration that referenced the Stimson Note of 8 January but did not explicitly target Japan, apart from noting that Japan's statement that she 'harbours no territorial designs in Manchuria and she will uphold the principles of the open door and equal opportunity, as well as all existing treaties relating to that territory' was 'hopeful' (LNOJ 1932: 336). However, during the sessions, the mood turned against the Japanese position. The substantive outcome of these Council meetings was an appeal on 16 February that, contrary to previous form, was addressed only to the Japanese government. This appeal constitutes a statement of intent not to recognise. It is clear that the principles being appealed to include non-use of force as well as territorial integrity and political independence, because reference is made to the Pact of Paris as well as the League Covenant.

> The twelve members of the Council . . . recall once again the solemn undertaking of the Pact of Paris that the solution of international disputes shall never be sought by other than peaceful means . . . and the terms of Article 10 of the Covenant, by which all the Members of the League have undertaken to respect and preserve the territorial integrity and existing political independence of all other Members. It is their friendly right to direct attention to this provision, particularly as it appears to them to follow that *no infringement of the territorial integrity and no change in the political independence of any Member of the League brought about in disregard of this article ought to be recognised as valid and effectual by the Members of the League of Nations*. (LNOJ 1932: 383-4, emphasis added)

Stimson later dismissed this Council Appeal as not a 'positive declaration by the entire body of nations' (Stimson 1936: 177). Walter Lippman of the *New York Herald Tribune* reacted to the Council note by admitting that the 'declarations may conceivably amount to nothing' but went on to be optimistic about the potential of this announcement of principle to be 'one of the great moments in the evolution of international law' (Lippman and Nevins 1932: 202).

The Assembly and the affirmation of principles

By the time the League Assembly convened in a special session on 3 March 1932, the violence in Manchuria was five months old and the attack on Shanghai had been going on for over a month. Not only the Stimson note but numerous attempts at persuasion, reconciliation and negotiation, as well as threats of force in the form of naval manoeuvers and movement of troops, had been employed by the great powers. The atmosphere at the special session was not an especially optimistic one. The mood had turned against the Japanese; several statements in the general discussion reference the opinion that 'aggression' had taken place, that self-defence was not a legitimate excuse in the present case and that Japan was thus at fault. There is a complete absence of explicit condemnation of the Chinese position, except from the Japanese delegation.

The dominant sentiment during the general discussion was that the Assembly should pass a resolution that constituted

> a clear affirmation of the principle that, after the establishment of the League as a great international organization based on law and the adoption of the

Pact of Paris, no new right can be created by force. No agreement secured by force can be registered by the Secretariat under Article 18 of the Covenant. That is a *sine qua non* for the validity of any agreement concluded between Members of the League. (Munch (Denmark) LNOJ SS 101 1932: 51)

The most striking feature of the discussion was that the efficacy of a declaration of principles was not defined with reference to the immediate short-term payoff in terms of changing Japan's behaviour. Even though almost all of the delegates advocated an affirmation of the principles of the League, which included nonrecognition of situations in violation of Article 10 of the Covenant, very few statements were made that explicitly or implicitly rested upon the idea that a statement of nonrecognition was going to cause a cessation of hostilities. Several delegates explicitly acknowledged the futility of nonrecognition. The Chinese representative, W. W. Yen, in a speech preceding the general discussion, declared that nonrecognition was useless:

[The League] has joined the United States in declaring that any situation de facto brought about by means contrary to the Covenant, the Pact of Paris and the Nine Power Treaty cannot gain legal recognition. None of these measures has had the slightest effect. (LNOJ SS 101 1932: 30)

The distinction between short-term effectiveness in terms of solving the current controversy and some form of future-oriented norm-building or rule-making was made explicit by several representatives. For example, the Irish delegate said: 'It is clear that the duty of the Assembly is not only to settle the dispute between two Members of the League, but also and above all to uphold the sanctity of the Covenant' (Lester (Ireland) LNOJ SS 101 1932: 70).

Specific compellence or deterrence is thus not consistently or even frequently cited as a reason to engage in nonrecognition of the outcome of this conflict. Instead, justification for the action revolves around the ideas of 'duty', 'moral value', 'precedent', and the continuation of the League and the current international order.

The future of the League

There was a consensus that the actions taken in this special session, the first time that the Assembly had considered a claim under Article 15 of the Covenant (the one that asks the League 'to effect a settlement of the dispute' under consideration), were consequential for the future of the League. One strand of thought concerned the existence, vitality and authority of the League. Braadlund (Norway) said, 'The Assembly should constantly bear in mind that principles are involved the violation of which might produce incalculable effects on the future of the League. The very authority of the League is at stake' (LNOJ SS 101 1932: 47).

Many made a causal linkage between a failure in the current circumstance and the failure or collapse of the League. Often the League and the peace treaties were mixed in with the current international order. Zulueta of Spain put the matter bluntly, 'In brief, the question for the League is, To be or not to be?' (LNOJ SS 101 1932: 53). A statement of principles was presented as a way to maintain the League and the interlocking system of post-war treaties legally guaranteeing states' protection against aggression.

Proclaiming principles

Another predominant theme was that the present actions would create a precedent and this precedent would be influential in affecting the future course of the international order. Statements by several delegates took note of the historical importance, in terms of precedent, of their potential actions. John Simon's speech is especially important as, fortunately for this analysis, it explicitly addresses the question of the rationale behind the proposed action of a declaration of the principles of the League:

> What should such a declaration accomplish? It would reassert, in terms which would, I trust, receive the adherence of every State here represented, the conditions under which every Member of the League is pledged to conduct relations with every other Member. It would direct the attention of the world once more – the fresh and specific attention of the world – to the proper means of solving disputes. It would be a proclamation not only of the interest but of the duty of us all to stand by the League in this hour of its severest trial. I agree with what was said from this tribune a short time ago by a previous speaker. *It would be far better for the League to proclaim its principles, even though it failed to get them observed, than to forsake those principles by meaningless compromise.* Lastly, this declaration that I suggest would be a recognition that the ultimate progress of the world cannot be secured by any other means which the League has been formed to organise and supply – the means of peace and justice. (John Simon (UK) LNOJ SS 101 1932: 63, emphasis added)

Simon here not only does not justify the action in terms of affecting Japan's behaviour, but actively implies that the action will not fulfil this function. Instead, the reasons revolve around the idea of rhetorically upholding a principle as a definition of what counts as 'pledged . . . conduct', 'proper means', or the 'the means of peace and justice'. Simon explicitly asserts that enforcing adherence to the principles in the current case is not the primary aim of the proclamation. This position was reaffirmed by the German representative.

Titulesco's encapsulation

The speech by the Roumanian representative makes an explicit causal argument that encapsulates several of the strands of the debate. Several points are worth quoting (LNOJ SS 101 1932: 60). He argues that even if 'the League is over-ambitious' it would be better to fail in Manchuria because conditions are exceptional, 'than it should fail because it had changed its law to suit special cases and circumstances'. The reason for this position is that consistency is valuable:

> In the former case, it would be the League's action that had failed in a particular circumstance and not the League itself, for it would have remained faithful to its doctrine as conceived and known by the majority of its members. In the second case, that in which there would be multifarious doctrines to suit the exigencies of the moment, it would be the League itself that would founder.

Titulesco's reasoning, his justification for the action of a proclamation of principles, relies on the idea that having an explicit, clear set of principles and rules is valuable and that affirmations or declarations of those principles are consequential in making them common knowledge and increasing the belief that they will be used as standards to judge behaviour in the future. He contrasts consistency of principles with ad hoc accumulations of hybrid precedents. In an explicit appeal to future contingencies, Titulesco points to the role of declarations of principles in affecting beliefs about what the community standards of behaviour are:

> To reject [an appeal to affirm principles] would be to eviscerate our faith in the League and to rob the countries that are not parties to this conflict of their most precious possession – the legitimate hope that, in case of war or threat of war, the contractual guarantees they enjoy will be converted into tangible realities.

The Assembly's resolution

The Assembly resolution was unanimously adopted on 11 March, with Japan abstaining. It noted three principles: 1) a scrupulous respect for treaties, 2) to respect and preserve as against external aggression the territorial integrity and existing political independence of Members of the League, and 3) the obligation to submit any dispute to procedures for peaceful settlement. The resolution stated that the Assembly:

> Proclaims the binding nature of the principles and provisions referred to above and declares that it is incumbent upon the Members of the League of Nations not to recognise any situation, treaty or agreement which may be brought about by means contrary to the Covenant of the League of Nations or to the Pact of Paris. (LNOJ SS 101 1932: 87)

Willoughby claims that the Assembly declarations, including that of nonrecognition, were important 'since they firmly established the principles by which the Assembly declared it would be bound in its future handling of the controversy' (1935: 307). In a *New York Times* article the day the Assembly adopted the resolution, Clarence Streit (1932) sees the resolution having 'far-reaching constitutional developments for the League'. Despite the temperate language, the resolution makes it 'as binding as the Assembly legally can on League members not to recognise anything done in violation of treaties'. Another implication is that nonrecognition does not only apply to this Sino-Japanese affair, but as a 'general doctrine everywhere'.

Conclusion of League of Nations section

The declaration of principles, which included a clear statement of nonrecognition, was mostly not justified in terms of its efficacy in the current situation. The predominant reason given for engaging in this proclamation of principles was that it would define the agreed standard of behaviour between states. The League of Nations would cease to exist as an authoritative dispute resolution body if it did not make a statement on the bearing of the case at hand. These two reasons were intertwined but analytically separable. Presumably the League could maintain its authoritative status if it exhausted the procedures for dispute resolution written down in the League Covenant. The way in which a declaration of principles promotes the League's relevance is that it is not a lack of action. A complete lack of action would mean the League had nothing to offer to an international dispute. However, this is not a reason for any specific action. A reason that is specific to the proclamation of principles is that the common standards of behaviour among states have been brought into question by the current dispute and the common assertion of 'the conditions under which every Member of the League is pledged to conduct relations with every other Member', as John Simon put it (LNOJ SS 101 1932: 63), would make it clear what those standards are. In the future, states can expect that their behaviour will be judged by these standards and orient their behaviour around them.

THE LYTTON COMMISSION AND ITS REPORT

The Stimson note, the League Council notes and the Assembly resolution of 11 March 1932 were all threats of nonrecognition. The adoption of the League Assembly report on the Lytton Commission 24 February 1933 was not a threat of nonrecognition but an act of collective nonrecognition of Manchukuo.

Waiting for Lytton

In the period after the Assembly resolution of 11 March and before the League discussion of the Lytton Commission report, Japan withdrew its troops from Shanghai starting 5 May under an agreement brokered primarily by the British. With this threat to Western interests removed, attention to the Manchurian situation waned considerably. In the US there was some consideration of the merits of Stimson's policy. Lawrence Lowell, the president of Harvard, wrote an article in *Foreign Affairs* magazine criticising the nonrecognition policy (Lowell 1932). Once a nation, believing itself in the right, conducts military operations, mere public opinion has little effect, he wrote. Worse, if Stimson's policy means that 'any signatory of the Pact has a right at any future time to refuse to recognise the provisions of a treaty' then it would be 'highly likely to produce an extremely dangerous situation'. For example, suppose

> that China should feel compelled to cede, not the sovereignty, but the control and administration of all Southern Manchuria, and that our merchants, supported by our government, should pay no attention to Japanese officials and customs duties, how long would peace last? Yet if we do not do this we are recognizing a condition brought about by means which Mr Stimson's note implies would, in the event supposed, be contrary to the covenants and obligations of the Pact of Paris. (Lowell 1932: 367)

Lowell draws out the distinction between nonrecognition and the adoption of other sanctions, like the use of force. The former without the latter, or 'the Pact of Paris, with an interpretation whereby the signatories are under no obligation to prevent war, yet are at liberty to disregard its results, might well create more causes of strife than it would allay' (368). The stability of treaties and of relations between states was at stake. The international evil of indefinite claims is 'a festering sore for any nation to probe thereafter, or . . . an excuse for action that would otherwise be without justification'. Lowell made the case that if the US would not go to war to obtain a fair settlement, then 'it must ultimately recognise the situation that develops' for the sake of international order. Lowell's high profile article represented a prominent strand of the reaction to the nonrecognition policy.

Stimson responded directly to this criticism in a speech to the Council on Foreign Relations in August 1932 that was also printed in *Foreign Affairs* (Stimson 1932). This speech was a justification of the nonrecognition policy. The Briand-Kellogg Pact had made war illegal; therefore war could not be the source of rights. Many legal precedents were obsolete and so new ones must be set. The force of public opinion could 'be made one of the most potent sanctions in the world'. The Stimson note and the League Assembly resolution were motivated by 'a new viewpoint towards war'. The note was an expression of 'moral judgement', a 'refusal to recognise the fruits of aggression'. This by itself 'might be of comparatively little moment to an aggressor' but 'Moral disapproval, when it becomes the disapproval of the whole world, takes on a significance hitherto unknown in international law.' That nonrecognition is aspirational is clear. Stimson explicitly represents nonrecognition as crucial for sustaining the hoped for new international order:

> The determination to abolish war which emerged from that calamity [WWI] must not be relaxed. These aspirations of the world are expressed in this great [Kellogg-Briand] Treaty. It is only by continued vigilance that it can be built into an effective living reality. (1932: ix)

The Lowell–Stimson debate is interesting in that it does not turn on a disagreement about the practical efficacy of nonrecognition for coercion or deterrence; both are similarly pessimistic. Instead, the disagreement is about the implications for international order. Lowell's picture of the future is of aggressors running around unchecked and grievances multiplying. Stimson's is of a stable, policed, aggression-free society of nations. This division of opinion dominated subsequent discussion of the viability of nonrecognition. Throughout debates in various League forums the axis of disagreement was the value of short-term order and stability against the prospect of a longer-term transformation in the practices of international relations.

Lytton Report published; the Council transmits it to the Assembly

The Lytton Report was published 2 October 1932. Much can be and has been said about the aims, the process of drafting, the failures and the achievements of the Lytton Report, which had multiple parts and was noted for running to hundreds of pages, but for present purposes the most important feature was that its recommendations specifically mentioned nonrecognition of Manchukuo. In the section on 'Principles and Conditions of Settlement' (Chapter IX) the report admits that the issues are 'exceedingly complicated'. Part of this complexity is that

> This is not a case in which one country has declared war on another country without previously exhausting the opportunities for conciliation provided in the Covenant of the League of Nations. Neither is it a simple case of the violation of the frontier of one country by the armed forces of a neighbouring country, because in Manchuria there are many features without an exact parallel in other parts of the world. (Willoughby 1935: 400)

That said, the report continues and states that

> It is a fact that without a declaration of war a large area of what was indisputably Chinese territory has been forcibly seized and occupied by the armed forces of Japan, and has in consequence of this operation been separated from and declared independent of the rest of China. (Willoughby 1935: 400)

These two conclusions appear to differ in emphasis. The first seems pro-Japanese, the second pro-Chinese. The Commission clearly went to lengths to avoid an outright condemnation of Japan as a formal aggressor, but does not avoid stating the facts as they saw them. Given that there is no formal aggressor, economic sanctions are not recommended, but given the use of force, the current situation cannot be approved of. Not only was a return to the status quo ante unacceptable, but

> The maintenance and recognition of the present regime in Manchuria would be equally unsatisfactory. Such a solution does not appear to us compatible with the fundamental principle of existing international obligations, nor with the good understanding between the two countries [China and Japan] . . . (LNOJ SS 111 1933: 34)

The Lytton Report thus advocated nonrecognition of Manchukuo. There were three bodies that were to consider the Report: the Council of the League, the Committee of Nineteen appointed by the League Assembly (which was to draft a resolution that was then considered by the Assembly) and the Assembly itself. The Council session in November

1932 was inconclusive. After lengthy statements by Japan and China, there was no discussion by other members of the Council. Instead, consideration of the report was transmitted to the Assembly.

US and UK attitudes going into the Assembly debate

The dominant British attitude to nonrecognition was that it would be better not to do it because censure of Japan would hurt relations and might mean Japan's leaving the League, but that the UK would have to go along with the League consensus. Simon laid out his position:

> For ourselves, the controlling considerations must be (1) be faithful to the League and act with the main body if possible (2) do not take the lead in an attitude which, while necessarily futile, will antagonise Japan seriously (3) be fair to both China and Japan (4) work to keep Japan in the League. (Thorne 1972: 294)

Prior to the Assembly debate, Simon wrote a Cabinet memo in which he explicitly considered a potential reaffirmation of the 11 March nonrecognition statement and called it 'an abstract declaration'. The fear was that 'the attempt will now be made from some quarters to apply it specifically to the findings of the Lytton Report' (DBFP 2, XI, no. 53). He was concerned that pledging 'all eternity never to recognise the new State if it becomes definitely established' would be a mistake, even considering 'its illigitimate [sic] origin'. If nonrecognition were a League policy, however, 'It is impossible to abandon loyalty to the League and its principles merely because Japan would prefer this: we must explain to Japan that the course we take is *pro* League and not *anti* Japan.'

This position was pervasive in the British foreign policy establishment. Pratt, a foreign office China expert heavily involved in policymaking during the crisis, saw the issue of recognition as a problem.

> Difficulties however will begin to arise if, as seems probable, a demand is pressed that something should be said with regard to recognition. Quite clearly we should resist any wording which implied that the members of the League must never recognise Manchukuo to the end of time. We should also use our influence to prevent any statement about recognition being so worded as to imply a censure on Japan. We can argue that so long as our aim is conciliation that aim can only be frustrated by censuring one of the parties. (DBFP 2, XI, no. 85)

At this point the British appear willing to accept the fait accompli of Manchukuo and avoid upsetting Japan. Pratt said that they should not 'pronounce academic judgements on the question of recognition' but instead be practical and find a government for Manchukuo 'which can be recognised without injury to the fundamental principles of the League of Nations' (DBFP 2, XI, no. 85).

Discussion moved to the Assembly

The issue of censure of Japan in general and nonrecognition in particular was the primary axis of discussion in the League Assembly 6–9 December 1932. The representatives of the major powers were unenthusiastic about proposed action against Japan. A group of smaller states (Switzerland, Spain, Ireland and Czechoslovakia) drafted a resolution in which Japan was condemned and nonrecognition reiterated. The major powers equivocated, emphasising complexities, realities and, in the case of Simon, the Lytton Report's criticisms of China. The Assembly referred the report to a Committee of Nineteen that would draft its own report on the report that would be considered in February 1933. The rhetorical positions taken in the Assembly debate are revealing because they demonstrate a clear divide in positions between the major and minor powers.

The smaller powers and righteousness

On 5 December 1932, the day before the debate opened, there was a secret meeting of ten smaller powers to coordinate strategy during the debate. Dr Benes of Czechoslovakia chaired the meeting and recommended the adoption of the first eight chapters of the Lytton Report, a vote of censure on Japan and 'a vote of eternal non-recognition of Manchukuo' (DBFP 2, XI, no. 88). This programme was presented in the Assembly through strident speeches that revolved around two concepts: the survival of the League itself, and the survival of the principles of the League Covenant. In his Assembly speech Benes fixated on the fact that whatever solution was presented 'will constitute a precedent of the first importance' (LNOJ 111 1933: 35). The concern was that inaction would mean a 'temptation to copy the example of operations that have proved successful'. The 'injustices' of the current crisis 'must . . . be put right'.

In no case could they be recognised by Members of the League, as has already been proclaimed, in connection with the present conflict, by the Assembly resolution of March 11, 1932, which reads: 'The Assembly declares that it is incumbent upon the Members of the League of Nations not to recognise

any situation, treaty or agreement which may be brought about by means
contrary to the Covenant of the League of Nations.' (LNOJ 111 1933: 37)

Benes realised the limitations of the programme he and his fellow
minor power representatives were putting forward. He did not evoke
immediate practical results as support of censure and nonrecognition.
Instead, the main aim is that 'there must be no doubt as to the view,
the convictions and the real decision of the Assembly'. The principles
of the League must be proclaimed, thus known and thus defended.

> For one thing must be made absolutely clear to all – namely, that we must
> do our whole duty in safeguarding our principles, and that the League of
> Nations, a body essentially based on the principle of conciliation, may
> compromise on this or that practical solution, but can never and must
> never compromise on matters of principle. Any compromise on matters
> of principle, and especially such important principles as are involved in
> the present case, would mean the bankruptcy and the end of the League.
> (LNOJ 111 1933: 38)

Adopting a resolution that included censure of Japan and nonrecognition of Manchukuo would be a 'great historic act . . . an act of international morality which cannot but bear fruit'.

Benes was not alone. The Swedish, Dutch, Irish, Swiss, Greek and
Norwegian representatives all made explicit statements supporting his
position. Lange of Norway said, 'The all-important thing is to safeguard
the primary object of the League – namely, the maintenance of the principles of peace and right and the application of those principles in all
cases arising for the League' (LNOJ 111 1933: 39).

Connolly, the Irish representative, declared:

> it [the League] will only achieve its purpose if it is prepared to stand defini-
> tively with courage and determination behind the Covenant and its own deci-
> sions. If it falters or hesitates, fearing lest by its action it may offend, then as
> an organization, built up by moral support of what is right, it will not survive
> and, in my opinion, will not deserve to survive. (LNOJ 111 1933: 33)

It was the responsibility of the Assembly 'to uphold at all costs the
terms under which the Covenant must be applied by the Members of the
League' by declaring 'their intention of refusing to recognise the "State"
of "Manchukuo"' (34).

Paul Hymans, President of the Assembly, was determined that they
must 'restore the authority and proclaim the principles of the League'.
This was necessary because:

the League would find its Covenant pine and perish of mortal disease if, by default, we were to allow the public to become convinced that Article 10 permits of Chinese Manchuria becoming Japanese Manchukuo, that Article 12 allows of military invasion becoming permanent, and that the principles of the Covenant must be waived in exceptional cases, when, in fact, all cases are and always will be exceptional cases. (LNOJ 111 1933: 42)

The major powers and pragmatism

In contrast to the smaller powers' idealistic determination to proclaim the principles of the Covenant, the major powers strove to present a case against censuring Japan and favoured further attempts at conciliation. Perhaps the most noteworthy, and certainly the most vilified in the British press and academic literature, was John Simon's speech. He read out the section of the Lytton Report that stated Japan had not declared war without exhausting opportunities for conciliation, nor had it violated the frontiers of China with its armed forces (because it had rights to station troops in China under the Boxer Protocol and subsequent agreements). He pointed out that, in the face of the one-sided attitude of previous speakers, the report condemned both China and Japan. He also emphasised Japan's frequent assertions that it desired to be a good member of the League of Nations. He did also make comments similar in substance to those of the smaller powers. However, he qualified these sentiments with frequent exhortations to practicality, which meant accommodation of Japanese control of Manchuria. Simon said he believed 'that, while we all firmly hold by the principles and the ideals of the League, we sincerely wish to act in this matter as practical men. We must concern ourselves with the realities.' He quoted the report as saying 'Criticism alone will not accomplish this [settlement]; there must also be practical efforts at conciliation' (LNOJ 111 1933: 51).

Baron Aloisi of Italy took a similar line and was the most outspoken opponent of 'mere abstract and rigid statements'. He continued the theme of denying that responsibility for the crisis was definitively established and that a practical solution meant accommodation to the current situation.

the dispute . . . has put the Covenant to a severe test . . . but that does not justify our proceeding to conclusions not based on a sense of realities or the responsibility of Government representatives. The latter are called upon, not to establish academic principles, but to discover a solution based on realities. (LNOJ 111 1933: 53)

League action must be 'to facilitate this *rapprochement* between China and Japan rather than concern ourselves with more or less theoretical considerations regarding our own responsibility'. The German representative concurred, stating that 'the League must not, in its efforts to find a solution of the conflict, merely approach the question on the basis of more or less abstract principles' (LNOJ 111 1933: 54). Cahan of Canada explicitly advocated against setting a precedent of nonrecognition, saying that they should not 'establish a precedent which in the future may be deemed to exceed the terms of this article as already construed by competent authority' (LNOJ 111 1933: 59). That is, the League should adopt no new methods.

Assembly report, Japanese military action and nonrecognition

The outcome of the Assembly debate was a resolution passed on 9 December to refer the Lytton Report to a special Committee of Nineteen to 'draw up proposals' for the consideration of the Assembly. While this report was being negotiated and written, the Japanese military, having been relatively unengaged for the past few months, embarked upon several more offensive campaigns throughout early 1933, including the occupation of Shanhaikuan in January. This continued military action and Japan's absolute refusal to compromise on the recognition of Manchukuo were the background to the Committee of Nineteen's report.

There were several attempts at reaching a formula which would be acceptable to all sides (Steiner 2005: 742). Secretary-General of the League Eric Drummond tried approaching a Japanese League official, Sugimura Yotaro, but this was judged a breach of the neutrality of his office and rejected. Matsuoka Yosuke, Head of the Japanese delegation to the League of Nations, tried to avoid the confrontation that would result from a stalemate, but was unsuccessful. The Committee of Nineteen, initially interested in exploring a conciliation outcome, was presented by the Japanese government with several proposals and counter-proposals, none of which involved any withdrawal from the position that recognition of Manchukuo by Japan and the League was essential to any settlement. Eventually the special committee abandoned its attempts at conciliation and recommended adopting the first eight chapters of the Lytton Report and, among other things, that the Pact of Paris and the 11 March 1932 Assembly Resolution should be observed. A final statement of the report (Willoughby 1935: 481) was that the status quo was unacceptable as was the maintenance and recognition of the existing regime in Manchuria, such maintenance and recognition being incompatible with the fundamental principles of existing international obligations and with the good understanding between the two countries on which peace in the Far East depends.

Instead, the Members of the League should adopt this report, which meant that:

the Members of the League intend to abstain, particularly as regards the existing regime in Manchuria, from any act which might prejudice or delay the carrying out of the recommendations of the said report. They will continue not to recognise this regime either *de jure* or *de facto*.

Despite the positions taken by the major powers in the Assembly debates in December, the Lytton Report was thus adopted and explicitly included a declaration of the intent not to recognise Manchukuo. The only reasons given in favour of this course of action at this point were protecting the League and its principles. The maintenance of the rule against aggression was the primary justification for adopting the policy of nonrecognition.

Deterrence and the cost of nonrecognition

The intuition that sanctions are undertaken for direct deterrence purposes is strong. In arguing against a deterrent intent in the nonrecognition of Manchukuo, I have suggested that nonrecognition is not costly enough to be a plausible candidate either for a deterrent, or for a costly signal of intent. This issue of costliness requires some attention. The issue is not whether we as scholars can conceive of some possible way that cost might arise from a policy, but the extent to which decision makers thought that the policy would be costly. The foregoing empirical analysis shows that the main attitude towards nonrecognition was that it would not be costly enough to serve as a deterrent for Japan, nor to indicate an individual state's capacities to punish aggression. Further support for this position is provided by a consideration of the actual costs imposed.

There was some cost to Manchukuo of the nonrecognition policy. An advisory committee was set up by the League Assembly on 24 February 1933, which appointed a subcommittee to consider measures to be taken in relation to the collective nonrecognition of Manchukuo (Willoughby 1935: 520–8). The subcommittee recommended that Manchukuo be denied access to all international conventions and international organisations, even those formally open to administrative and private associations. These included the Universal Postal Union (UPU). In the event that Manchukuo tried to join the UPU, the Manchukuo postal service would be suspended, Manchukuo stamps would be considered invalid, and all post should be routed through China. Manchukuo currency was not to be allowed on international exchange markets. Passports issued by a Manchukuo government could not be given visas. Consuls stationed in Manchuria could be replaced but should be advised that they were to do nothing to indicate recognition of Manchukuo. As Manchukuo could not accede to the 1925 Geneva Opium Convention, opium could not be exported into the territory. All of these recommendations were agreed to by the Members of the League. However, these restrictions were not especially onerous to anyone. The *North China Herald* reported on 2 January 1935 that the postal restrictions had been dealt with by the creation of a new franking stamp and an injunction on writing 'Manchukuo' in the address (Willoughby 1935: 528). Also, instead of visas individuals living under the Manchukuo government could be given alternative identity documents.

An issue that might have been costly to all parties was barriers to trade. Japanese policymakers offered application of the Open Door policy, that is, preferential tariffs, to states recognising Manchukuo. However, when international companies investigated the possibility of tapping into the Manchurian market, they found that the Manchukuo government was engaged in protectionist measures, making the foregone trade opportunities under nonrecognition relatively less attractive (Nish 2002: 92).

Conclusion

The primary reason why nonrecognition was both threatened and enacted in the Manchurian Crisis was to maintain the illegitimacy of aggression. There is a crucial methodological issue in interpreting the evidence presented in this chapter for this claim. Much of the evidence in favour of the rule maintenance explanation of the nonrecognition of Manchukuo (and indeed for any explanation) is statements made, verbally and in written form, both public and private. How can we infer what people were thinking from the statements they made? The inherent limitations of historical evidence mean that we have no way of getting irrefutable proof of what was in the heads of the people at the time. Instead we must work with what is available. If we allow for the possibility of using evidence, then we can say that there are more and less convincing inferences. For individual actors, we can try to use statements to rule out certain reasons why they acted and support others.

We can infer from statements to private motives, or what people were actually thinking.

Using the available evidence in the Manchurian Crisis, including diaries and original intragovernmental documents, the evidence on Stimson's and Simon's thinking provides reasonably clear support in favour of rule maintenance as the motivation for not recognising Manchukuo. Stimson's threat of nonrecognition seems to have been motivated by a combination of anger, a desire to punish and the idea that Japan would be deterred from continuing their attacks in Northern China. He expressed indignation that the Japanese army took Chinchow after he had told them not to and Japanese diplomats had assured him that this would not happen. He seems to have been trying to punish them. This seems partly emotional, but Stimson also expressed a desire to show the Japanese that their actions were unacceptable to him, that they carried a cost, and that they might carry a greater cost in the future.

However, after the emotion had faded, Stimson realised the futility of deterrence with a weak policy instrument. Yet he maintained his faith in nonrecognition and tried to convince others to join him. The reason for doing so was, as he said both privately and publicly, to set a precedent, to maintain the principle that aggression was unacceptable, that society disapproved of the use of force to settle disputes or extract concessions.

In stark contrast, John Simon remained emotionally detached from the situation throughout. His private communications to others in the government weighed his options calmly and strategically. Simon was very concerned not to upset the Japanese if could avoid it. And yet Simon still advocated for some action that would reaffirm the principles of the League. Nonrecognition of Manchukuo was a means to this end. Pragmatic calculations meant that Simon did not seriously consider stronger sanctions against Japan. But it was a pragmatic choice to not recognise Manchukuo. Simon valued the principle of nonaggression and wanted to take action that would show that it was still a rule of conduct among states.

However, the state of mind of two individuals, centrally important though they were, does not constitute an explanation of the adoption of nonrecognition by the entire international community (absent Japan). What does it mean to say that something was the primary reason for a collective decision? We have the public statements of the decision makers and we have some more private accounts of what they said about what they were trying to do and why they were trying to do it. The evidence from the Manchurian Crisis supports several claims, some more convincingly than others. From analysing debates in the League Council and Assembly sessions, as well as secret or classified diplomatic documents, we can see that one reason appealed to when trying to convince others that nonrecognition was a good idea was rule maintenance. Further, even though there were occasionally other reasons alluded to, rule maintenance was used as a reason far more consistently throughout the deliberations on nonrecognition of Manchukuo than any other reason. Also, rule maintenance was used by almost all international actors as their official position. This includes the US, the UK, small nations like Czechoslovakia and large nations like France. No other reason was as widespread. So, rule maintenance was the dominant publicly given reason. This makes it the most convincing candidate for being a 'socially sustainable justification'. That is, states were willing to accept from each other rule maintenance as a justification for performing the action of nonrecognition.

Apart from Secretary Stimson's short-lived initial hope that a threat of nonrecognition might deter Japan, none of the major decision makers in the US, the UK or in the League of Nations thought that nonrecognition would act as a compellent, a deterrent or was engulfed in the passion of vengeance. Neither were they aiming to support China or placate a domestic coalition. Instead, the adoption of the Lytton Report and the continued nonrecognition of Manchukuo was justified in terms of creating common knowledge of the 'conditions under which every Member of the League [was] pledged to conduct relations with every other Member' (John Simon (UK) LNOJ SS 101 1932: 63).

NOTES

1. Inter alia the Japanese had the right to station a Legation guard at Peking (Beijing), a garrison at Tientsin (Tianjin) and a railway guard along a section of line from Peking to the sea. The Chinese were forbidden to station or march troops within twenty Chinese *li* of Peking, or within two miles of the Peking-Tientsin railway (Thorne 1972: 329).
2. Foreign Relations of the United States (FRUS). Referenced with the year and volume number, followed by the document number.
3. League of Nations Official Journal (LNOJ). Referenced with the year and page number.
4. League of Nations Official Journal Special Supplement (LNOJ SS). Referenced with the supplement number, year and page number.
5. The rest of this section is a brief summary of the findings from the evidence analysed in detail in the main section of this chapter.
6. Stimson's Diaries are unusually regular and comprehensive. He started writing the day he took public office and stopped writing them when he stepped down. He dictated them to a secretary at the end of the day or the next day. As such, they are an invaluable resource as to his contemporaneous thoughts and attitudes. However, he did intend for them to be published as a public record, so some caution in interpretation is advisable.

7. The original nine powers were the US, Belgium, the British Empire, China, France, Italy, Japan, the Netherlands and Portugal.
8. 'W.J. Abbot upholds Japan in Manchuria: Member of Christian Science Monitor Board Says Tokyo Had Many Provocations', *The New York Times*, 20 November 1931.
9. Documents on British Foreign Policy (DBFP). Referenced with the series, volume and document number.
10. House of Commons Debates (HC Deb). Referenced with date, volume and column number.

CHAPTER THREE

The Abyssinian Crisis

INTRODUCTION

In this chapter, I analyse the crisis surrounding Italy's 1935 invasion and subsequent annexation of Ethiopia, or Abyssinia as it was sometimes referred to at the time. As in the other cases in this book, one state used premeditated military force against the army of another state. The victorious invader then occupied a portion of the territory of the other state and supported a change in the government authority over that territory. Whereas in the other cases the outcome was a new state, like Manchukuo, Bangladesh or the TRNC, in the Ethiopia case, the outcome was Italy's direct possession of Ethiopia. The King of Italy styled himself 'Emperor of Ethiopia'. In the Manchurian case, there was widespread uncertainty or disagreement over whether Japan's actions were aggression. The Japanese military had had relatively limited aims, in that only a portion of Chinese territory was occupied and outright annexation was foregone in favour of establishing a new state, at least nominally under the control of ethnic Chinese. By contrast, the Italian conquest of Ethiopia was obviously premeditated and was aimed at the formal annexation of the entire country.

The Italo-Ethiopian crisis is thus especially interesting because the use of force was unambiguously treated as a norm violation and yet within the space of a few years a large proportion of the international community was treating the spoils of that use of force as legitimate. In addition, because the collective security system embodied in the League of Nations Covenant collapsed, this case also shows that the threat of dissolution is not a phantom fate for an institutional rule. It provides a powerful answer to the common question asked of nonrecognition, 'Why *not* do it?'

The primary goal of the study of this case is thus to find out why nonrecognition did not happen. Why did states, such as the UK, that condemned Italian aggression and imposed economic sanctions on Italy, then turn around and recognise Italian sovereignty over Ethiopia? These findings help to build the model of rule maintenance. As the main purpose of this study is theory-building rather than theory-testing, the case comparisons are not used to falsify pre-formed hypotheses, but to aid in the construction of the model and suggest potential sources of variation.

I first outline some important events to provide an empirical framework. Then I discuss the theoretical findings from an analysis of the crisis. This is followed by a detailed investigation of the decision-making processes in the UK, the US and the League of Nations as they relate to the adoption of recognition and nonrecognition.

HISTORICAL OVERVIEW

In 1934 there was a border incident between Ethiopia and Italian-held Somaliland, in which Ethiopian troops protesting the Italian construction of a fort at Wal-Wal, inside the Ethiopian border, clashed with the Italian garrison. Both Emperor Haile Selassie of Ethiopia and Italian Prime Minister Benito Mussolini claimed aggression by the other. During 1935 (from December 1934 to October 1935) there was extended discussion over whether the Wal-Wal incident constituted aggression, with Ethiopia bringing suit against Italy in the League in January 1935. The League response was inconclusive and an arbitration committee did not put the blame for the incident on either party. However, more incidents led to an Italian military build-up and in March 1935 Ethiopia again appealed to the League, invoking Article 15 of the Covenant concerning a 'dispute likely to lead to a rupture' and the referral of the dispute to the Council. Talks between Italy and Ethiopia concerning arbitration did not produce agreement and the League bureaucratic processes took place slowly. During 1935 there was a series of talks between France, the UK and Italy concerning security cooperation, particularly aimed at Hitler's Germany. In April the three powers met at Stresa and produced an agreement that they would jointly resist any attempts by Germany to change the terms of the Versailles peace treaty. However, an agreement between the UK and Germany in June increasing the size of the navy that Germany would be allowed to have was just one of the ways in which what was known as the Stresa Front was honoured more in the breach than the observance.

By September, it was clear to everyone that Italy was planning to invade Ethiopia. There were moves to forestall Italian military action through negotiated Ethiopian concessions, but Mussolini desired the public relations effect of a military victory. Italy invaded Ethiopia on 3 October 1935. The US imposed an arms embargo on both belligerents starting on 5 October. The League Council found that Italy had resorted to force in violation of the League Covenant on 7 October (and the Assembly on 11 October). The League imposed economic sanctions on Italy, with fifty states participating. In December, UK Foreign Secretary Samuel Hoare and French Minister of Foreign Affairs Pierre Laval agreed to a peace plan that included substantial concessions by Ethiopia to Italy. Despite both UK and French governmental agreement, when the plan was leaked, public outcry was so negative that both disavowed the plan. Italian military progress led to the occupation of Addis Ababa, the Ethiopian capital city, in May 1936. On 9 May, Italy proclaimed the annexation of Ethiopia into the Italian Empire. The League deferred consideration of the sanctions regime for a month, but the will to sustain them was gone, along with the surge of optimism about the new system of collective security that had accompanied their imposition the previous year. In June, the US lifted the arms embargo. In July, the League voted to end sanctions, although there was no formal statement on a change of status of Ethiopia and Ethiopia was still considered a member of the League. Italy pursued recognition of its conquest of Ethiopia, and some states like Austria, Germany and Japan recognised the conquest in 1936.

The UK and France continued to pursue Italian help against Hitler. In 1938 the UK and Italy concluded the Anglo-Italian agreement, which was signed in April and then formally ratified in November. Part of the agreement was British recognition of the Italian conquest of Ethiopia. France followed soon after. Another part of the agreement was that the UK would appeal to the League to reverse its position on the status of Ethiopia. In May 1938, the League Council mostly agreed that the members of the League were no longer bound by the previous resolution, from March 1932 in the midst of the Manchurian Crisis, stating that it was 'incumbent upon the Members of the League of Nations not to recognise any situation, treaty or agreement which may be brought about contrary to the Covenant of the League of Nations or to the Pact of Paris' (LNOJ SS 101 1932: 8).[1] UK Foreign Secretary Lord Halifax was successful in getting agreement that 'the question of the recognition of Italy's position in Ethiopia is one for each Member of the League to decide by itself in the light of its own situation and its own obligation' (LNOJ 1938: 335).[2] By the end of 1938, forty-seven states had given recognition to the Italian empire.

Theoretical discussion

The extensive historiography on the Ethiopian crisis and the run up to World War II presents its own challenges.[3] This is especially true as regards the issue of 'appeasement' of which the Ethiopian case is a major part. However, while the issue of recognition and nonrecognition of the Italian Empire in Ethiopia has been written about many times, there is no existing consideration of the Ethiopian case in the larger context of nonrecognition as a symbolic sanction. That said, interestingly, there is a quasi-consensus in the most recent historical literature on the broad lines of why some major powers recognised the Italian conquest. Three themes that recur are the strategic position of Britain and France in relation to the rise of German military power and aggressiveness; the desirability of Italy as an ally or neutral in negotiations, or even a war, with Germany; and the decline of belief or confidence in 'collective security' as an organising principle for international relations and a consequent boost in the popularity of a search for a 'general settlement' in Europe, that is, 'appeasement'. The latter point in particular is important for the model of rule maintenance. The claim in the historical literature is that the recognition of Italian sovereignty over Ethiopia was not an isolated affair, but instead was part of a much broader institutional shift away from the existing, albeit incipient, rules, principles and practices that constituted interwar peacemaking. For example, according to Baer,

> When it became clear, in the course of the Ethiopian affair, that the status quo in Europe would not be effectively defended, future possibilities for a collective security system or even for an arrangement other than appeasement to accommodate peaceful change, disappeared. (1972: 178)

Sbacchi also attributes the *de jure* recognition of the Italian Empire to 'an admission of the failure of the League of Nations and of collective security' (1997: 209). Because the UK and France were unable or unwilling to apply the 'principles of general security', this meant that 'the vision of the League disappeared' to be replaced with appeasement (1997: 213). Given the ubiquity of the concept of collective security in today's global governance, 'it is easy to forget how new and revolutionary the concept proved in the 1920s and 1930s' (Strang 2013: 4). It is also true that even though the League and its principles existed and most states were members, not everyone was committed to collective security as a way to manage global conflict, making the Ethiopian Crisis, 'a collision of views between governments' (Strang 2013: 4).

The dynamics of the crisis map onto the different stages of the rule maintenance model (see Figure 1.2). First, there is a clear sense among the members of the League that there is a new rule against aggression or the use of force for profit. The Manchurian Crisis is only a year or so old and is fresh in the memories of the participants, many of whom are still in leadership positions. Second, Italy's invasion of Ethiopia is very obviously interpreted as a violation of that rule. Unlike Hitler, Mussolini did not try to legitimate his territorial and martial aspirations under a cloak of reparations and ethnic solidarity. The League of Nations formally declared Italy an aggressor state (in the League Council on October 7 1935 [LNOJ 1935: 1225] and in the Assembly on October 11 [LNOJ SS 138 1935: 114]). Third, widespread economic sanctions were imposed, although shipments of oil to Italy were not included. However, the threat and imposition of these sanctions by a large group of states did not prevent Italy from winning its war and occupying significant parts of Ethiopia, nor from claiming conquest. Fourth, partly as a result of the failure of material sanctions, there was a sense of uncertainty about the status of the rule. In particular, the procedures and principles of the 'new diplomacy' and the collective security apparatus are challenged by a different approach to managing international relations: appeasement. This line of thought, held by a significant section of the decision-making elite, was that trying to ignore changes in the balance of power would lead to more war than peacefully accommodating them. The situation was thus ripe for the abandonment of the rule against aggression rather than an attempt to maintain the rule by continuing to not recognise Ethiopia as an Italian possession.

Analysis of the Ethiopian Crisis case, then, suggests an interesting source of variation in the adoption of nonrecognition and hence of rule maintenance. If the international community no longer values the rule being violated, then there is no need to try to maintain it. This finding suggests some conditions under which potential rule maintenance actions might be more likely to be rejected. When rules or institutions are relatively new and less regularised and internalised, states might be more willing to jettison the rule or to try a different one. This implies that rule maintenance is less likely at the beginning of the life cycle of an institution than later on. Also, if there is a prominent or salient contender to the existing rule, one that the community could consider switching to, this also makes it less likely that states would choose to adopt rule maintenance actions. Finally, if the rule seems broken or unworkable for some reason, as collective security seemed after the failure of economic sanctions against Italy, then changing the rule would seem more desirable, and so maintaining the rule would be less likely.

These implications of the rule maintenance model appear fruitful directions for future research.

One notable exception to the majority of states abandoning nonrecognition was the US. When justifying their decision, President Franklin Roosevelt and Secretary of State Cordell Hull were explicit and consistent. Nonrecognition of the Italian conquest of Ethiopia was essential 'to reestablish and maintain principles of international law and morality' (FRUS 1938 I: 121).[4] Even so, the Roosevelt administration did flirt with the idea of changing policy from nonrecognition to recognition, at least in communication with the UK. However, this proposed shift was stated to be only possible in the context of a 'major world appeasement' (FRUS 1938 I: 148). This provides further support for the claim that the abandonment of the rule makes rule maintenance actions less likely.

In order to demonstrate how the decision making played out, I now investigate the shift in policy from initial condemnation and sanctions to the abandonment of a nonrecognition policy by the UK. I then analyse the foreign policy decision making in the US including the reasons and justifications for applying and adhering to nonrecognition. Finally, I lay out the actions and reasoning of the League of Nations. Using both private and public sources, I establish the reasons given for initially adopting the sanctions regime as well as those later used against nonrecognition.

INTRODUCTION TO UK SECTION

As one of the most famous episodes in international relations, British policy towards Italian and German uses of threats and violence in the 1930s has been extensively studied. The purpose of this section is not to evaluate the prudence or wisdom of the policies followed.[5] Instead, it investigates the historical evidence of the reasoning behind the UK's turn from active participation in the nonrecognition of Italy's conquest of Ethiopia to highly visible formal recognition. The Anglo-Italian agreement signed in 1938 constituted *de jure* recognition (using the language of the time) of Italian sovereignty over Ethiopia. Britain also sought and succeeded in changing the policy of the League of Nations towards nonrecognition by moving for acknowledgment of the position that nonrecognition of the results of aggression were no longer a duty of members of the League, as it had been stated in March 1932 in the midst of the Manchurian Crisis. Instead, 'the question of the recognition of Italy's position in Ethiopia is one for each Member of the League to decide for itself' (LNOJ 1938: 335). If we are to understand why nonrecognition is sometimes applied and sometimes it is not, a study of UK decision making in this period is a useful resource. In contrast to some other sections of this book, which ask the question 'why nonrecognition?', this section asks, 'why *not* nonrecognition?'

So, why did the British government change from nonrecognition to recognition? While there were numerous concerns with maintaining the League and upholding the principles of collective security during the Abyssinian crisis, the breakdown in nonrecognition of the Italian conquest was precipitated by a knotty strategic dilemma. Hitler's rise to power and subsequent German actions, rearmament and territorial readjustment and acquisition, in particular in the Rhineland, had prompted many decision makers to devise some means of dealing with the rise of German power and assertiveness. The problem was especially acute given Britain's ongoing decline in economic and military (particularly naval) power (see e.g. Kennedy 1976). Numerous policy options and varieties of approaches to this problem were considered, including the idea of reducing potential German power by preventing Italy from aligning with Hitler. The evidence presented herein indicates that recognition of Italian sovereignty over Ethiopia was offered to Mussolini as a carrot intended to draw him closer to the UK, or at least to induce him to be neutral in a future war with Germany. If this is true, how does this affect our understanding of what drives the adoption of nonrecognition? Why is this not just an idiosyncratic, unsystematic strategic decision, independent of any considerations of rule maintenance? The answer is that we can use this variation to improve our model of the conditions under which rule maintenance actions will be taken. In particular, the context in which the recognition decision was taken exemplifies a more general situation in which nonrecognition no longer seems worthwhile to those choosing what to do. From the creation of the League onwards, there was an incipient move towards an international conflict-management system based not on the use of force and rights of conquest but of arbitration, negotiated readjustment of political advantage, and peaceful change. However, the crucial question of how to deal with a significant change in the balance of power produced a split in these conceptions of a new global governance. Parker explains Britain's policy choices, as they were considered, in the 1930s in the face of Hitler's actions and rhetoric as four-fold (1993: 24). Two were to either do nothing or retreat into heavily armed isolation. The third was 'to seek strength for resistance to aggression from world-wide co-operation or from limited sets of collaborators'. This conception involved using the League and refusing to acquiesce and legitimate concessions made to states that had become more powerful and were demanding an improvement in their situation. Nonrecognition was a central part of this conception of international conflict management. Finally, the fourth option was 'the search for concession to Hitler to induce him, or enable him, to renounce armed force as a means for change'. This conception involved giving the rising states what they wanted (and likely could get through the use of force anyway) in the hope that this would prevent the horror of war. This latter conception became known as 'appeasement'.

In the UK in particular, the need to buy time for rearmament coupled with a sense of the inevitability of war with Germany, combined to induce Prime Minister Neville Chamberlain, Permanent Private Secretary of the Foreign Office Robert Vansittart and Foreign Secretary (from 1938) Lord Halifax to make concessions to Hitler. Scholarly opinion is that these concessions were intended to forestall an attack by Hitler so that British military power could catch up and overtake that of Germany, and perhaps, ideally, reach a broad settlement under which Germany would no longer feel the need to go to war at all (Ripsman and Levy 2008). Neville Chamberlain was the most famous but not the only proponent of a line of thought in which 'general appeasement' was seen as a replacement for the status quo-oriented collective security in which changes in the balance of power were resisted and ignored. Despite the opprobrium with which appeasement is regarded today, up until 1938 'the majority of the British public' regarded appeasement as a good policy because it reasonably rectified German grievances produced by French intransigence (Parker 1993: 10). While Hitler was almost uniformly seen as the primary concern, Mussolini's Italy was seen by many as a crucial element in the European balance of power. Policy towards Germany had implications for policy towards Italy and vice versa.

During the Ethiopia Crisis in the lead up to the outbreak of war, British policy was split between two tendencies (see e.g. Post 1993: 86–7). One, epitomised by the famously anti-German Vansittart, advocated preserving the League Covenant, the Stresa Front and other agreements with Italy[6] by appeasing Italy through peaceful concessions in Ethiopia, including substantial territorial changes. In April 1935, the UK, France and Italy met at the lake front resort of Stresa to discuss security policy in Europe. They agreed to resist any further German attempt to change the Treaty of Versailles. While it may be counterintuitive today, the Stresa Front was genuinely viewed as a potential military force that could deter or defeat Nazi Germany. Relations with Italy were thus both extremely important and intimately entangled with views of the future role of conflict management in Europe and beyond. Vansittart deemed the Ethiopian crisis as less important than Italian participation in the Stresa Front. Given the view in the British Cabinet that Mussolini might accept a pacific settlement of the dispute if he got enough prestige and concessions out of it, Vansittart concluded that the dictator would have to be 'bought off'. Otherwise Britain would 'put Italy for keeps into the arms of Germany, and thereby probably have contributed to the eventual undoing of Europe and of ourselves' (quoted in Roi 1997: 94).

The other line of policy, led by first League of Nations Affairs Minister and later Foreign Secretary Anthony Eden, pursued collective security as a means to peace in Europe by demonstrating the effectiveness of the League in punishing an aggressor. Confusingly, the administration of Prime Minister Stanley Baldwin did not choose between these two tendencies. The UK both participated in moral condemnation of and economic sanctions against Italy along with the League and also engaged in negotiations with France and Italy over a deal that would transfer territory and rights from Ethiopia to Italy. UK Foreign Secretary Samuel Hoare described his reasoning in a conversation with French Foreign Minister Pierre Laval on 10 September 1935:

> A double line of approach was essential. On the one hand, a most patient and cautious negotiation that would keep [Italy] on the Allied side; on the other, the creation of a united front in Geneva as a necessary deterrent against German aggression. (Templewood 1954: 168)

This dual policy led to the scandal over the Hoare–Laval pact.

NEGOTIATIONS FOR A PEACEFUL SETTLEMENT AND HOARE–LAVAL

An important part of the model of rule maintenance is the claim that the recognition of Ethiopia as Italian was part of a wider replacement of the existing rules with a new conception of global governance rather than an isolated strategic decision to which norm dynamics were irrelevant. An important piece of evidence for this claim is the negotiations between Italy, Britain and France over the future of Abyssinia, both before and even during the Italian invasion. The search for a peaceful settlement was intended to bolster the Stresa Front against Germany by keeping Italy as an ally of the UK and France instead of Germany. Perhaps most telling was what became known as the Hoare–Laval pact. This pact, nominally between Samuel Hoare and Pierre Laval although it was in fact approved by the Cabinets of both governments, was an agreement reached during the war, in December 1935. The agreement was to a peace proposal that involved various adjustments of sovereign territory by both Italy and Ethiopia as well as a large area in which Italy would receive an economic monopoly (Parker 1974: 313). When the pact was revealed the members of the League, as well as the US, was stunned.

While denounced at the time (and since) as the height of hypocrisy, the continued negotiations between Britain, France and Italy over the cession of territory and economic and political control of Abyssinia made very specific strategic sense. There was a widespread acknowledgment that if Italy went to war with Ethiopia, conquered it (as was expected, although Italy's military victories came quicker than predicted), the League and the international community would be forced to choose between approval and condemnation, between recognition and nonrecognition. Though not stated in these terms, the choice was between rule maintenance and rule abandonment, or at least rule modification. Those who valued the League and the rule of peaceful dispute settlement, as well as those who saw the domestic political value of appealing to League principles, wanted to avoid having to make that choice. However, if Italy could get the same or similar material outcome through negotiation rather than the use of force, the choice would not have to be made, as there would be no conquest, no aggressive gain to be recognised or not.

One good example of this line of though was John Simon, UK foreign secretary in the beginning of the crisis until being replaced by Hoare in June 1935. As in the Manchurian Crisis, Simon's reaction to the prospect of an attack aimed at annexation was not righteous indignation but a pragmatic assessment of the effect on what he saw as British interests. By May 1935, Simon had determined that there was an 'exceedingly difficult decision' between supporting League principles against Italy and supporting Italy against Abyssinia. The first option would 'break the close association at present existing between France, Italy, and the United Kingdom', demonstrate the impotence of the League (as Simon thought this option was bound to fail) and perhaps lead to Italy leaving the League. The second option would leave the UK 'open to grave public criticism' and prove that the League was unable to 'afford justice to a small country' (DBFP 2 XIV: 253).[7] Simon's solution was to accommodate 'legitimate Italian aspirations' by joining with the French to effectively establish an Italian protectorate over Abyssinia (DBFP 2 XIV: 250).

Conversely, Anthony Eden, who became foreign secretary after Hoare's resignation in December, seemed more sincere in his attachment to the League principles at stake than most. For example, on the day that Italy invaded Ethiopia, Laval proposed to Eden an agreement involving granting Italy a League mandate over 'those portions of Abyssinia inhabited by other than the Amharic races' as well as significant Italian control over the rest of Abyssinia. Eden communicated the proposal to Foreign Secretary Hoare, but advised rejecting it. His reason was 'when we had just received reports of Italian aggression upon Abyssinia it was scarcely possible to put forward proposals which went further than those previously offered. We should then be rewarding the aggressor' (DBFP 2 XV: 7).

The reaction to the publication of the leaked Hoare–Laval plans and then their official communication to the League was widespread and dramatic. At Geneva, delegates to the League expressed shock and distress. Whereas Hoare and others tried to argue that the limitation of bloodshed and the salvation of at least some autonomy and power for the Emperor were perfectly in line with the spirit of the Covenant, the dominant sentiment amongst the other League members was that the proposals rewarded, or as Haile Selassie phrased it, 'put a premium on', aggression (Baer 1976: 135).

The proposals represented to many the abandonment of the institution of collective security and instead a return to a system in which powerful states could gain rights and advantage through aggression. Baer's analysis of the period immediately following the revelation of the Hoare–Laval proposals was that 'the Covenant, *and what the Covenant stood for*, was betrayed' and that the world was asking, 'was this a change of policy, from opposing aggression to appeasement?' (1976: 132, emphasis in the original). Similarly, Walters claims that at this time the authority of the Covenant and the potential for collective security had lost 'all the ground thus gained, and much more' (1986: 672). The leader of the Opposition, Clement Attlee, expressed this sentiment in the House of Commons on 19 December 1935, when he said,

> That the terms put forward by His Majesty's Government as a basis for an Italo-Abyssinian settlement reward the declared aggressor at the expense of the victim, destroy collective security, and conflict with the expressed will of the Country and with the Covenant of the League of Nations, to the support of which the honour of this country is pledged; this House, therefore, demands that these terms be immediately repudiated. (HC Deb 19 December 1935 vol 342: c2017)[8]

Lord Halifax later described the Hoare–Laval proposals as

> not so frightfully different from those put forward by the Committee of Five [A League Committee tasked with facilitating negotiations]. But the latter were of respectable parentage: and the Paris ones were too much like the off-the-stage arrangements of nineteenth-century diplomacy. (Quoted in Feiling 1970: 275)

Hoare and Laval bore the brunt of the criticism over these plans, but they were not acting in isolation. Both the British and French governments were aware of and approved of the negotiations. Other governments were also interested in pursuing the same line of policy. The Chilean delegate to the League of Nations approached Eric Drummond, UK ambassador to Italy and ex-secretary general of the League of Nations, about the proposed agreement with Italy (which had become public knowledge at this point) and offered on behalf of the three Latin American countries on the Council to provide political cover for the Hoare–Laval pact. His idea was that the League could delegate authority to France and Britain to negotiate a settlement between Italy and Abyssinia. This would mean both that 'a solution might be found which would be more favorable to Italy than the previous recommendation of the Committee of Five' and that 'the Council would not be required to approve it'. Drummond commented that the Chilean delegate's motivation was to avoid being 'required to accept a solution by which the aggressor State would receive territorial aggrandisement' (DBFP 2 XV: 104). Here, again, we see actors trying to avoid having to make a choice between rule maintenance and rule abandonment.

A SENSE OF UNCERTAINTY AND THE SEARCH FOR A NEW INTERNATIONAL ORDER

The UK fully participated in the economic sanctions against Italy. However, there were concerns over the effectiveness of sanctions throughout the crisis. For example, Drummond wrote to Hoare a couple of days after the invasion to comment on the possibility of economic sanctions. He was emotionally engaged, describing Mussolini's policy as 'immoral and hateful'. Even so, he was pessimistic about the ability of economic sanctions to stop Italy, and said that 'only military measures will prove effective'. However, he also said that economic sanctions would be essential 'from the point of view of the maintenance of the League of Nations and of collective security' (DBFP 2 XV: 65). Hoare hoped that collective declarations of support for economic sanctions would be sufficient for rule maintenance. He argued that if all League members explicitly stated that they 'accepted both their share of the application and their part in any consequences' of economic sanctions, then 'on the basis of such virility alone could the League survive and prosper' (DBFP 2 XV: 76). The logic here is that a collective affirmation of commitment to the principles of the League would demonstrate the continued valuation of those principles.

After Italian military successes and the failure of economic sanctions to coerce Italy, British policymaking circles entered a period of uncertainty over the continuation of the present order, of the present set of rules set up to manage conflict resolution and maintain the peace and security of Europe and the rest of the world. This sense of uncertainty was initially precipitated or at least exacerbated by the revisionism of Germany and Italy. An early challenge was Germany's withdrawal from the League of Nations shortly after Hitler became chancellor. After Hitler remilitarised the Rhineland in March 1936, he proposed an entirely new 'system of peaceful security for Europe' to replace the Locarno Treaty (DBFP 2 XVI: 48). After being subject to economic sanctions and condemnation by the League, Italy proposed reform of the League and later withdrew and refused to consider re-entry without the abandonment of Article 16, the foundation of the system of collective security. But it was the failure of economic sanctions in the Italo-Ethiopian War that marked a turning point in attitudes towards collective security. Reform was on everyone's minds, whether they were in favour of strengthening the League or in favour of abandoning it and instead relying upon military arms build-up and alliances. In the following discussion, I focus on a few key individuals that represent alternative reactions.

In a clear-minded memo written in March 1936 (DBFP 2 XVI: 48), Eden stated awareness that Hitler would 'repudiate any treaty even if freely negotiated' if it is 'inconvenient' and 'Germany is sufficiently strong and the circumstances are otherwise favourable'. However, he also acknowledged 'Germany's material strength and power of mischief in Europe'. These two factors together prompted Eden to advocate a renegotiation of the current order in Europe, including a 'new Locarno', a new settlement in Eastern Europe, and the unconditional return of Germany to the League. Eden rejected an alternative, offered by France, of a formal condemnation by the League Council of Germany's remilitarisation of the Rhineland and possible economic and financial sanctions on Germany. These French proposals were aimed at proclaiming faith in the existing order, in existing institutions, but Eden viewed this as a mistake. Instead, Britain should 'induce or cajole France to accept' (DBFP 2 XVI: 48) renegotiations with Germany. More specifically, in an 11 June 1936 memo on maintaining sanctions on Italy, in which Eden recommended raising those sanctions, he wrote a paragraph on the 'Reconsideration of the structure of the League in the light of recent experience' (DBFP 2 XVI: 360). He advocated that 'immediate steps should be taken by Members of the League to study individually how the Covenant can best be applied henceforth in the light of recent experience'. Further, in another more wide-ranging memo, he rejected the idea that a Mediterranean Pact would 'in itself restore the general authority of the League' because 'More far-reaching measures affecting the essential character of the League as a whole will probably be found to be necessary to achieve this purpose' (DBFP 2 XVI: 361). Here we can see that the outcome of the Abyssinian crisis has so challenged Eden's view of the extent of collective support of the League that fundamental reform is necessary to re-establish that support.

In a debate in the Commons on the British reaction to the remilitarisation of the Rhineland, Eden spoke of his objective being 'the appeasement of Europe as a whole' and, obliquely, of avoiding British involvement in a French attack on Germany. This meant that the UK was not abiding by its commitments under the Locarno agreement to guarantee Germany's western borders. There was 'an overwhelming consensus of opinion' (according to Winston Churchill) that Eden's policy was a good one in that it effectively pursued peace. Neville Chamberlain proposed that the MPs 'must have been struck, and perhaps a little surprised, at the general consensus of opinion in this House upon the main lines of the proposals'. This shows that the intuitions towards appeasement were not limited to a small set of individuals. It also shows that this sentiment could co-exist with at least nominal support of the League (HC Deb 26 March 1936 vol 310: cc1435–1549). Post agrees, saying that the Rhineland crisis prompted a debate over how to buy time for British rearmament and that 'the weight of argument began to shift towards appeasement' (1993: 19).

A prominent advocate of the League and of nonrecognition as a means to deal with aggression, Philip Noel-Baker, an MP, academic and a former League of Nations bureaucrat, is a useful example of the passionate advocates of collective security. He may not have been in favour of appeasement, but he was very clear that there were different conceptions of global governance fighting for dominance. When commenting on the Hoare–Laval Pact, he opined that the League was defunct and that international diplomacy had taken a 'long step back toward the pre-war Concert of the Great Powers, and to the politics of the balance of power, alliances, and an arms race' (quoted in Johnson 2013: 65). Noel-Baker persisted in his pursuit of nonrecognition as a means of preserving the rule against aggression and the system of collective security in the House of Commons throughout the pre-war years. On 15 December 1936, he asked Eden whether the official position of the government was still that of

the declaration made by the Committee of Twelve of the League Council on 16th February 1932, to the effect that no infringement of the territorial integrity and no change in the political independence of any Member of the League brought about in disregard of the Covenant ought to be recognised as valid and effectual by the Members of the League, and whether the principle thus expressed will guide their action with regard to Abyssinia. (HC Deb 16 December 1936 vol 318: c2432)

Then, during the debate on the Anglo-Italian agreement in 1938, he claimed that the effect of renouncing nonrecognition would in fact mean the abandonment of the rule against aggression,

The League Assembly resolution of March 11, 1932, was perfectly precise, and it simply declared what was the existing law of the Covenant . . . If we recognise Italian sovereignty over Abyssinia today, whatever other Governments may have done, we are in fact setting aside the Covenant and we are doing it without any approval of any organ of the League. (HC Deb 2 November 1938 vol 340: c313)

THE ANGLO-ITALIAN AGREEMENT OF 1938

At a meeting in August 1937 to consider issues related to conversations with the Italians over a possible Anglo-Italian agreement, the first item on the agenda was 'the question of recognition of Italian sovereignty over Abyssinia' (DBFP 2 XIX: 90).[9] After being informed by Drummond that recognition was a '*sine qua non*' as the Italians valued it so highly, the participants worked out ways of framing the move of abandoning the previous position both of the League and that laid out in statements made by Baldwin and Eden. The inconsistency of continuing not to recognise Manchukuo while recognising Ethiopia as an Italian possession was noted and some arguments were floated as to how to distinguish the two situations. Apart from suggesting that recognition would be in the interests of the 'natives' as it would induce in them despair of ever regaining their independence and hence prevent their repression by the Italian occupiers, the main line of discussion was oriented around the replacement of the failed idea of collective security. 'Collective action against aggression has been attempted and, for whatever reason, has, anyhow for the time being, failed in its effect.' This failure had led to uncertainty surrounding the existing rules. As the minutes note, 'It is, indeed, a matter affecting the working of the Covenant, and the Assembly in appointing its committee on the application of the principles of the Covenant has recognised that this is a subject for enquiry.'

While the previous position was rejected, it was not to be replaced wholesale. The minutes record that 'There can be no rescission of previous resolutions', as well as that 'It is not suggested that the League as such should recognise that Italy has acquired a rightful title to the possession of Abyssinia' because 'to do so would be to condone a breach of the Covenant'. The aim of the British government still was international peace and cooperation. However, the 'maintenance of this principle' of nonrecognition was now felt to be less likely to bring it about. This was because nonrecognition would 'cause Italy to believe that [the UK] and other members of the League are actuated in this matter by motives of ill-will [and potentially revengeful]'. If this situation continued, it would be 'fraught with danger to European peace'.

Several phrases indicate the sense that a previous rule or principle was being rejected, avoided or amended. For example, it was claimed that 'politics is not an abstract science, and the League should not be the slave of abstract principles'. In the context of the nonrecognition of the League position on Manchukuo, it was worried that, unlike the UK, some South American countries would 'be unwilling to go back upon it in the case of Abyssinia'.

The most important decision maker behind the Anglo-Italian agreement was, of course, UK Prime Minister Neville Chamberlain. Chamberlain is famous for later acts of appeasement, but he worked out some of the reasoning behind his famous policy in the planning and negotiations for the agreement between Britain and Italy signed in April 1938. At a Cabinet meeting on 8 September 1937, Chamberlain indicated that he saw 'the lessening of the tension between this country and Italy as a very valuable contribution towards the pacification and appeasement of Europe' which would 'weaken the Rome–Berlin axis' (Self 2006: 274). Further crucial insight into the directions of Chamberlain's thinking in the run-up to the Anglo-Italian agreement comes from his diary entries written in February 1938 (Chamberlain Diary 19/27 February). His primary concern was to 'improve relations with the 2 storm centres Berlin and Rome' because he feared 'having ultimately to face 2 enemies at once'. His approaches to Germany coming to nothing, Chamberlain decided to approach Mussolini, who Chamberlain characterised to the Cabinet as 'resembl[ing] a hysterical woman' in that he 'deeply resented' being 'thwarted' over Abyssinia. Mussolini agreed to participate in conversations aimed at an agreement with Britain. In discussion with Eden and the Foreign Office over strategy in these conversations, Chamberlain rejected two ideas (Chamberlain Diary 19/27 February). First, he disagreed with Eden's view that trading *de jure* recognition for 'material advantage' was distasteful, because the UK would 'be giving away our best card for nothing and moreover we should draw down on ourselves a condemnation more scathing than that aroused by the Hoare Laval proposals'. Second, he also rejected the framing of the Foreign Office proposal to trade *de jure* recognition for 'sundry concessions' from Italy. Instead, Chamberlain wanted to 'approach the matter from the angle of obtaining general appeasement'. When Roosevelt warned Chamberlain against 'shocking public opinion by giving *de jure* to Italy', the prime minister mollified the president by making it clear that 'it is only on the hypothesis that the result of conversations with Italy would be a material advance towards world appeasement in one of the world's danger spots that we contemplate that recognition should be accorded' (DBFP 2 XIX: 458). Chamberlain's fears are laid out clearly and succinctly in his diary. Not giving Italy recognition would mean that

> the dictatorships would be driven closer together, the last shreds of Austrian independence would be lost, the Balkan countries would feel compelled to turn towards their powerful neighbours, Czechoslovakia would be swallowed, France would either have to submit to German domination or fight in which case we should almost certainly be drawn in. (Chamberlain Diary 19/27 February)

Nonrecognition was thus a small price to pay. Chamberlain by this time seems to have accepted that collective security was dead or dying and so maintaining the rule against territorial acquisition by force was not a feasible solution to the problems Britain, and Europe, faced.

Chamberlain's view was not unanimously held in his Cabinet. In particular, Anthony Eden disagreed with the way that appeasement was being pursued. This disagreement led to Eden's resignation and became very public. The Eden–Chamberlin quarrel, while wrapped up in personality and interpersonal issues, was over the way in which appeasement was to be pursued rather than being between two fundamentally different strategies. Eden's view, driven partly perhaps by intuitive distrust of Mussolini, was that British actions should be conditional on some Italian concessions. Successful cooperation on smaller, less consequential actions would lead first to trust-building and then to reciprocal exchanges of specific items of more importance. By contrast, Chamberlin's strategy was to trade British concessions for assurances and goodwill in the hope that Italy would change its long-term alignment away from Germany. Part of Eden's objection to the plans for the Anglo-Italian agreement was over the extent to which Mussolini could be expected to change his alignment away from Germany. The hope expressed by the prime minister was that 'the announcement of official negotiations would produce an immediate *détente* in Europe', but Eden disagreed. Instead, he felt that the world would know 'that the conversations would have to include *de jure* recognition and it would be regarded as another surrender to the Dictators' (DBFP 2 XIX: Appendix II).

The response to the Anglo-Italian agreement was mixed, but there was little variation in one important theme. The agreement meant that the UK, and consequently the other members of the League, had abandoned the rule against aggression and collective security as a means to enforce that rule. For example, in the House of Commons, opposition leader Clement Attlee laid out a response to the Agreement that was oriented around the complaint that 'it really means the destruction in the end of the League of Nations. It means the definite recognition of aggression' (HC Deb 21 May 1938 vol 332: c70). Others followed the theme. One MP said that the

> Agreement, moreover, deals another heavy blow at the League of Nations, the rule of law and the collective organisation of peace. It takes us back to where the prime minister belongs, pre-1914, with all the doubts and uncertainties of that time.

Lloyd George, referring to the League, said that 'It is no use any longer as a means of protecting weak countries against an aggressor; in supporting international right by collective action. That has gone.' Despite this opposition, both Houses of Parliament approved the agreement in April and it was eventually ratified in November 1938. Thus the UK recognised the Italian conquest of Ethiopia.

DOMESTIC POLITICS

Domestic political considerations were considerable and consequential in the negotiations over the Abyssinian Crisis. Part of the motivation behind Britain leading the charge in the League economic sanctions regime against Italy was to capitalise on domestic public opinion. There is evidence that the general election called by Baldwin in November 1935 was called early in part to benefit from the administration's popularity resulting from participation in League economic sanctions against Italy (Baer 1976: 49–50). Also, the withdrawal from the Hoare–Laval proposals and the breakdown of a negotiated settlement of the crisis that granted large concessions to Mussolini was entirely due to the domestic political backlash against the proposals and the perceived immoral betrayal of the spirit of the League, collective security and nonaggression (Waley 1975: 49). Steiner, however, notes that this 'dropping of the Hoare–Laval pact was one of the very few inter-war examples of the government in London giving way to public pressure, at least as it was filtered through parliament' (2011: 126). In particular, no domestic constituency had much, if any, impact on the Anglo-Italian agreement and the decision to recognise. British decision makers were more concerned with selling their policy to the public rather than responding to them. In Cabinet discussion of recognition as part of an Anglo-Italian agreement (DBFP 2, XIX: 630), there was much concern that domestic and international public opinion saw recognition as being exchanged for concrete concessions by Italy as regards the Spanish Civil War. Mussolini had sent Italian 'volunteers' to Spain to fight for Franco against the communists and the Anglo-Italian agreement was to involve the withdrawal of some or all of these volunteers and the cessation of other forms of Italian intervention in Spain. This was aimed at diverting public opinion away from the critique that recognition had been given away for nothing. In the end, despite the agreement, Mussolini took no steps towards bringing his 'volunteers' home from Spain (Steiner 2011: 570).

CONCLUSION TO THE UK SECTION

The overwhelming view in the UK was that recognition of the Italian conquest of Ethiopia meant the abandonment of, or at the very least a change in, the existing institutions of global governance. Even those who were in favour of nonrecognition, and hence trying to maintain the system of collective security, understood that recognition represented such a change. Chamberlain, the main force behind the Anglo-Italian agreement, realised that recognition was not consistent with the existing institutional rules, but viewed those rules as inadequate for the task at hand. He wanted to change the way that these conflicts were handled.

INTRODUCTION TO US SECTION

The US role in the Ethiopian Crisis and the nonrecognition of the Italian conquest followed a very different path from that of the European powers. Isolationist domestic politics had a strong influence on the foreign policy of President Franklin Delano Roosevelt (FDR), even to the extent of passing the Neutrality Acts, legislation designed to tie the president's hands in his ability to intervene in the crisis. Thus, unlike the members of the League, the US did not participate in the wide-ranging economic sanctions on Italy, although it did impose an embargo (on 'arms, ammunition and the implements of war' [US Department of State 1943]) on both belligerents. However, again unlike the UK and France, the US did not ever accord recognition to the Italian conquest of Ethiopia and so continued with nonrecognition until Haile Selassie was reinstalled as emperor during World War II. Study of the US reasoning thus provides an interesting contrast to that of the UK, France and others in the

League. This section first contextualises the attitude of the Roosevelt administration towards nonrecognition through an investigation of the effect of neutrality on US policy and actions. Then, the section addresses the question of Roosevelt's attitude towards appeasement, and its relevance to nonrecognition. Finally, the section presents evidence of the reasoning behind nonrecognition put forward by Roosevelt and members of his administration.

THE US AND NEUTRALITY IN THE ETHIOPIAN CRISIS

US President Franklin Roosevelt and Secretary of State Cordell Hull had broadly internationalist tendencies and were personally sympathetic towards Ethiopia. However, a split in domestic attitudes towards US foreign policy politics was highly influential during the crisis. Strong domestic isolationist sentiment was against any action whatsoever. This manifested itself in various ways. One example was that the Roosevelt administration refrained from even designating either country involved in the crisis as an aggressor (Harris 1964: 121). There were also two pieces of legislation that were aimed at preventing the president from becoming involved in the crisis. The first was the Joint Resolution on Neutrality in August 1935. The approval by Congress and the president of a neutrality resolution without the discretionary embargo came as a relief to Italy. In the event of war, this meant that the US could not single out Italy for more than moral condemnation, since the embargo on arms, ammunition and implements of war applied to Ethiopia as well. Prevented from formally discriminating between the two states, Hull and Roosevelt made an appeal for a 'moral embargo' (Baer 1976: 72). In effect, private businessmen were asked not to send various war materials to Italy. This moral embargo did not prevent trade with Italy, although Hull thought that it meant the rise in exports without the embargo would have been 'many times greater' than with it (Hull 1948: 461). The second piece of legislation was the emendation of the Neutrality Act in February 1936. The debate over the neutrality legislation became one over the issue of executive discretion. The isolationists favoured a neutrality policy that was both automatically applied and mandatory (Harris 1964: 122). The administration wanted discretion over what, when and who to embargo. The isolationists argued that it was 'not the business of the administration to designate aggressors in distant wars, to restrain trade accordingly, and so get America embroiled in foreigners' problems' (Baer 1976: 201). In the end the second neutrality act removed all discretion from the president and was to be applied to all belligerents regardless of other considerations. On 20 June 1936,

Roosevelt revoked the neutrality proclamations of 5 October 1935 and 29 February 1936. This meant a resumption of normal trade with Italy and was seen at the time as contributing to the League's lifting of sanctions a few weeks later.

During the initial phase of the war, Roosevelt and Hull did try to do various things that restricted trade with Italy, including the temporary threat to impound an oil tanker that had a contract to ship oil to Italy. They also sought to mislead private actors and without technically breaking the law make them believe that they were not allowed to trade with Italy. In response to inquiries, Hull would repeat Roosevelt's statement that attempts to trade with Italy would be undertaken at the 'own risk' of the parties (Harris 1964: 91). However, they did not have the legal power to embargo raw materials or discriminate between aggressor and victim.

Italian–American organisations strongly opposed the economic sanctions and their extension to oil during the war. A substantial Italian language press approved of the neutrality resolution of 1935 and argued against the administration discouraging private American citizens from trading with Italy. A large amount of form-letters from Italian-Americans to the White House and the State Department opposing administration policy were motivated in part by a letter-writing campaign sponsored by *Il Progresso Italo-Americano* in November 1935. Harris attributes the emendation of the 1936 neutrality legislation to exclude presidential discretion to ban exports if they would prolong or expand war, which could be applied to Italy, to the 'diffuse but mounting opposition' by this Italian-American pressure group (1964: 125).

These constraints and pressures on the Roosevelt's decision making were all in the wrong direction for a domestic politics explanation of nonrecognition. The general push was for less intervention. In a detailed study of the issue, DeSilvio argues that Roosevelt was mistaken about the extent of isolationism but, nevertheless, refrained from more active intervention due to his fear of a predominantly isolationist public (2008: 6). The mechanism where Roosevelt felt compelled to choose nonrecognition as a sop to domestic pressure for morally satisfying action is not a good characterisation of the situation.

ROOSEVELT AND APPEASEMENT

A much-studied issue in the historical literature is FDR's approach to a European war in the late 1930s. Among questions like whether the president sought full-scale intervention into the war, or whether he misled the American public on the extent of his assistance to Britain and the allies before US entry, there is a debate on the extent to which FDR was an appeaser. This debate is important for the current study because if FDR was pursuing appeasement in Europe, and yet did not recognise the Italian Empire, this casts doubt on the claim that the pursuit of appeasement in Europe led the UK, France and other countries to over- turn their previous stance of nonrecognition. A major proponent of the Roosevelt-as-appeaser thesis, Offner (1977) sees appeasement in a vari- ety of actions and policies. These include support for German rearma- ment, approval of the Anglo-German naval agreement, a lack of action in the Ethiopian crisis and approval of the Munich agreement. However, this is insufficient evidence to determine Roosevelt's attitudes towards both the role of nonrecognition and also the nature of the world order going forward.

Roosevelt did not draw the same dire lessons from the failure of sanc- tions to compel Italy as many others did. Far from having a profound change of mind about collective security after the crisis, he came up with the idea of quarantining aggressors, which he outlined in a speech on 5 October 1937 (the 'Quarantine speech'; Braddick 1962: 71). This was followed up with a proposal, initially Sumner Welles' idea, for a confer- ence of the US and neutral nations to agree the rules of international relations, including how to keep the peace. The great powers would be informed of the results, which, once followed, would produce world peace. This conference was intended to support Chamberlain's policy of appeasement (Wallace 1962: 5). As Welles put it in a memo to Roosevelt on 10 January 1938, 'it will lend support and impetus to the effort of Great Britain, supported by France, to reach the bases for a practical understanding with Germany both on colonies and upon security, as well as on European adjustments' (FRUS 1938 I: 116).

Chamberlain responded to Roosevelt's proposal for a conference a week later, effectively making the point that his own negotiations with Italy and Germany would be stymied by such a conference. In particular, Chamberlain wrote that

> if the President's suggestions are put forward at the present time Germany and Italy may feel constrained to take advantage of them both to delay consideration of specific points which must be settled if appeasement is to be achieved, and to put forward demands over and above what they would put forward to us if we were in direct negotiations with them. (FRUS 1938 I: 120)

Chamberlain explicitly mentioned the UK's willingness 'to recognise de jure Italian conquest of Abyssinia' (FRUS 1938 I: 119).

When reacting to the crisis and break in foreign policy represented by Chamberlain and Eden's disagreement over Anglo-Italian negotiations and Eden's resignation on 20 February 1938, Hull further made the point that he hoped the appeasement policy would succeed. However he defined success in terms of 'general world appeasement' and said that the goal of the policy was 'the reestablishment of those principles of international conduct to which [the US] is so firmly committed and without which it did not believe any permanent peace could be found' (FRUS 1938 I: 138).

In light of the rule maintenance model, it is perhaps no surprise that the foremost advocate of appeasement in Roosevelt's circle, Sumner Welles, both favoured recognising Mussolini's conquest of Ethiopia and appeasing Germany, although he was not pro-Nazi (Offner 1977: 385). Welles was sent to Europe by Roosevelt in 1940 on a mission to pursue the possibility of a peace agreement. During talks in Rome from 26 to 28 February, Welles said to Mussolini that Roosevelt desired to meet with him and saw no objection to recognising Italy's conquest of Ethiopia within a general settlement. Welles also was involved in talks in Berlin with the German leadership, including saying that the US desired a just peace and discussed German retention of Austria, Danzig, the Sudetenland and a protectorate over Bohemia-Moravia as part of a general settlement (Offner 1977: 386–7). However, Welles' mission was the last gasp of a policy that sought to appease Germany and Italy as part of a plan to avoid a European war. On Welles' return, Roosevelt made a statement that he had realised there was 'scant immediate prospect for the establishment of any just, stable and lasting peace in Europe'.[10] Later, in July, Roosevelt said to Congress that 'We must always be wary of those who with sounding brass and tinkling cymbal preach the "ism" of appeasement.'[11]

Arguing against Offner, Cole denies that Roosevelt was ever an appeaser. Cole sees the president as hoping Chamberlain's policies might bring peace, but without any conviction behind them (Cole 1990). Perhaps the best relevant summary is Farnham's analysis of Roosevelt's decision making up to and during the Munich crisis. Farnham argues that 'Far from supporting appeasement, Roosevelt disapproved of it and sought throughout the [Munich] crisis to strengthen the will of the democracies' (1997: 91). Farnham emphasises Roosevelt's adaptation to circumstances and the fact that the president simply did not have a clear idea of the best way to deal with Hitler until the Munich Crisis made clear the nature of the situation.

So, despite collaborating with Chamberlain and being initially hopeful about the prospects of success of the Munich agreement, Roosevelt was not a convinced proponent of an appeasement policy designed to change the way that international relations was regulated. Roosevelt was committed to the existing international order as much as was practical, but when he did explore appeasement he was also willing to consider jettisoning the nonrecognition policy as part of the replacement of that order with something else.

Nonrecognition of the Italian conquest

Roosevelt's foreign policy from the Ethiopian Crisis to the outbreak of war in Europe was thus not rigidly ideological, but did have a guiding theme: the maintenance of international order. Similarly, Cordell Hull's actions were aimed at 'encouraging the development of those institutions and practices which he believed ultimately to be necessary for the maintenance of order in the international community' (Braddick 1962: 64). Nonrecognition was an important part of this approach. Given the separation of what they called de facto recognition, meaning conducting relatively normal economic and diplomatic relations, and *de jure* recognition, meaning moral approval and formal legal recognition, it is unsurprising that few saw nonrecognition as a form of coercion. Instead, the only stated reasoning in favour of nonrecognition was in terms that can be interpreted as rule maintenance.

Responding to Chamberlain's demurral over the proposed peace conference in early 1938 (see above), Roosevelt expressed particular concern over Chamberlain's willingness to 'recognise the *de jure* Italian conquest of Abyssinia'. He reminded Chamberlain of 'the harmful effect which this step would have, especially at this time, upon the course of Japan in the Far East and upon the nature of the peace terms which Japan may demand of China'. He followed up by saying that 'respect for treaty obligations [is] of vital importance in international relations'. Here Roosevelt is viewing the issue as one of global rules and norms and not simply current crisis. Roosevelt then said that 'A surrender by [the UK] of the principle of non-recognition at this time would have a serious effect upon public opinion in [the US]' because public opinion wanted 'to reestablish and maintain principles of international law and morality' (FRUS 1938 I: 121). This is an interesting statement because while it quite explicitly refers to rule maintenance as the reason to continue with nonrecognition, Roosevelt also implies that the problem is US public opinion. However, far from being under explicit domestic pressure to take action, Roosevelt was the one pushing against public opinion. For example, the reaction to Roosevelt's Quarantine speech (see above) in October 1937 was significant. Hull described the situation:

> As I saw it, this had the effect of setting back for at least six months our constant educational campaign intended to create and strengthen public opinion toward international cooperation . . . Six of the major pacifist organizations issued a declaration that the President 'points the American people down the road that led to the World War'. (Hull 1948: 545)

In attributing the rule maintenance view to public opinion, Roosevelt may very well have been trying to avoid personally disagreeing with Chamberlain while also removing the possibility of Roosevelt changing his mind. The president went on to say that while the conquest of Ethiopia may 'at some appropriate time . . . have to be regarded as an accomplished fact', recognition should only be considered 'as an integral part of measures for world appeasement' (FRUS 1938 I: 121).

The attitude of the Roosevelt administration towards the nonrecognition of the Italian conquest was summed up by Secretary of State Cordell Hull in a reply to the British ambassador to the US, Sir Ronald Lindsay in January 1938 during the negotiations that led towards the Anglo-Italian agreement (FRUS 1938 I: 133–4). Hull discussed his concern with what he saw as the Japanese plan 'to abolish and for an indefinite time destroy the operation of the spirit and principles relating to the sanctity of international treaties and international law and, in fact, relating to all the laws of war and humanity as well'. He then noted that 'the principle of non-recognition has been very carefully kept alive by this and certain other governments during recent years' but that

> if any important country like Great Britain suddenly should abandon that principle, to the extent of recognizing the Italian conquest of Ethiopia, for example, such would be capitalised by desperado nations and heralded as a virtual ratification of the opposing policy of outright treaty violation, and treaty wrecking, and the seizure of properties by force of arms.

Hull went on to say that the US

> fully realises the difficulties which the policy of nonrecognition presents as a policy of indefinite operation, but we here have assumed that the policy is of universal importance as a factor and agency in the restoration and stabilization of international law and order.

This justification is referencing the two elements of *concern with rules* and *future-orientation* that are characteristic of rule maintenance. Hull did not see nonrecognition as having a coercive effect on Mussolini's decision making. Hull also addressed the circumstances under which the US would be willing to consider 'how the permanency of this policy might be interrupted or modified': only 'by some general arrangement or understanding entered into by all or most of the nations of the world proceeding in a peaceful and orderly manner'.

This was the line taken by the Roosevelt administration in internal communication and with allies. For example, when the French ambassador to Washington called on Welles after the president's statement on the Anglo-Italian accord, he asked Welles about recognition of the Ethiopian conquest. Welles stated that the US position had been consistent for two and a half years, that is, that the US

> had been outstanding in its support of the principle of nonrecognition of the acquisition of territory through force and the consideration of any deviation from that stand could only be undertaken if in the independent judgement of this Government it believed it desirable to do so as an integral part of a major world appeasement. (FRUS 1938 I: 148)

The practice of nonrecognition

What actually constituted the US's *de jure* nonrecognition? There was an absence of any act aimed at declaring a state of recognition, like the Anglo-Italian agreement. However, there were also other actions taken by the US that were part of the practice of nonrecognition. The Italian approach to seeking recognition of their conquest was subtle. The first part of the plan was to submit to other governments a formal notification of the annexation of the Empire of Ethiopia to the Italian crown without requiring a response. As William Phillips, US Under Secretary of State, put it, 'This would mean an official awareness of the change of territory on the part of foreign governments without, however, any overt act on their part to indicate acceptance and approval' (Phillips 1952: 178). Subsequently, Italy tried to acquire recognition through the accreditation of representatives. Ambassadors from Italy had credentials from 'the King of Italy and Emperor of Ethiopia' and ambassadors to Italy were requested to have that phrasing in their documents. However, when both the US ambassador to Rome and the Italian ambassador to Washington were replaced in June 1936, the US government refused both of these formulations and would only accept the new representative Fulvio Suvich if Italy accepted Phillips without the new phrasing and explicitly agreed that acceptance of Suvich would not signify American recognition of the act of annexation. Breckenridge Long, the US ambassador in Rome during the crisis, requested that Roosevelt accredit Phillips to the Emperor of Ethiopia on the basis that the US would lose advantageous trade agreements that Italy would sign with recognisers (Sbacchi 1997: 218). But Roosevelt refused.

Further, in June 1936, the US terminated the Italian–American Treaty of Commerce and Navigation of 1871. This was partly to do with its potential conflict with neutrality legislation, partly because it advantaged Italy in trade relations, but also as an oblique condemnation of Italian actions in Ethiopia (Harris 1964: 144). The implication became less oblique when the US explicitly refused to include a recognition of the King of Italy as Emperor of Ethiopia in a new, replacement treaty. During negotiations over a new treaty, Hull told Ambassador Phillips to change the proposed wording of the preamble of the treaty because 'we are unwilling that the words "Emperor of Ethiopia" or the word "Ethiopia" appear in the treaty, namely, in any instrument signed on behalf of the United States' (FRUS 1937 II: 480). Phillips then reported that this nonrecognition issue became a crucial sticking point in negotiations. In response to Hull's objections to the preamble wording, Italian Foreign Minister Count Galeazzo Ciano spoke with Mussolini who rejected both of Hull's alternative suggestions for preambles not including 'Emperor of Ethiopia' and said 'therefore the treaty could not be signed'. Ciano further commented that 'to sign without the full title would raise a political issue' (FRUS 1937 II: 492). Instead, the two nations would continue with the existing provisional arrangement. It is possible that other considerations were also behind this breakdown in negotiations, but the nominal reason was nonrecognition.

CONCLUSION TO THE US SECTION

The main people responsible for the decision to not recognise the Italian conquest of Ethiopia were clear and explicit in their stated reasoning for the policy. Roosevelt justified continuing the policy as that it was essential 'to reestablish and maintain principles of international law and morality' (FRUS 1938 I: 121). Hull emphasised that 'the [nonrecognition] policy is of universal importance as a factor and agency in the restoration and stabilization of international law and order' (FRUS 1938 I: 133–4). The rule maintenance model thus provides an explanation for their actions during and after the crisis. Also, valuably, these two actors' reasoning included an assessment of the recognition actions taken by other states and thus an evaluation of the conditions under which they thought they might change their nonrecognition policy. Only as part of a 'major world appeasement' (FRUS 1938 I: 148) would recognition make sense for the members of the Roosevelt administration. That is, only if the existing, though obviously under threat and failing, international order were to be changed and replaced with a different set of rules for conflict management. The US case thus offers some insight into the sources of variation of nonrecognition, similar to that gained from the study of the UK above.

Introduction to League section

In this section, I discuss the role and reasoning of the League of Nations and of states other than the US and the UK. I focus on a series of episodes that capture the shift of attitudes throughout the crisis away from the system of collective security and specifically of nonrecognition as a way of maintaining that system. Generally, the widespread participation in the economic sanctions regime against Italy on the basis of resistance to aggression was followed by an abandonment of collective security both in principle and practice after what was seen as the failure of sanctions to prevent or reverse war. Nonrecognition was largely also abandoned primarily on the basis of its being unnecessary when there was no intention to preserve a system that was aimed at resisting aggression.

Support for the League, sanctions and collective security

In Geneva, the mood in the period leading up to the Italian invasion of Ethiopia was against aggression and hence against Italy. Despite the mutual accusations of aggression during the Wal-Wal incident in December 1934, it was Ethiopia who appealed to the League (Baer 1967: 97). In March 1935, Ethiopia invoked Article 15 (notice of a 'dispute likely to lead to a rupture') and Article 10 (preservation against external aggression) of the Covenant (LNOJ 1935: 572). It was 'generally assumed' that Italy intended to pursue a war against Ethiopia (Steiner 2011: 106).

On 11 September 1935, Samuel Hoare gave a speech to the League of Nations Assembly that not only encapsulated a stand of support for the League and the system of collective security against aggression but seems to have created a burst of enthusiasm for it. The statement that was so popular was Hoare's claim that 'In conformity with its precise and explicit obligations, the League stands, and my country stands with it, for the collective maintenance of the Covenant in its entirety and particularly for steady and collective resistance to all acts of unprovoked aggression' (LNOJ SS 138 1938: 43). Hoare was surprised by the 'universal acclamation' the speech received (Templewood 1954: 169–70). Following Hoare's speech, the atmosphere at Geneva became one of optimism and resolve to protect the Covenant through collective security (Baer 1967: 335). Many countries spoke of their allegiance to the

League and the Covenant, although a few, like Australia and Canada, rejected the idea of punitive sanctions against a violator.

This spirit continued through the invasion of Ethiopia by the Italian armed forces on 3 October. Two days later, Anthony Eden said that 'At this moment international politics are passing through a phase of evolution when far the greater part of the nations of the world are striving to substitute the rule of law for the rule of force in international dealings' (quoted in Baer 1976: 131). A League Committee was appointed to consider and report on whether either side was in violation of Article 12 of the Covenant, which stated that parties to a dispute had to wait three months before a resort to war after arbitration. On 7 October, the report of the Committee was presented to the Council and the last sentence of the report was: 'After an examination of the facts stated above, the Committee has come to the conclusion that the Italian Government has resorted to war in disregard of its covenants under Article 12 of the Covenant of the League of Nations' (LNOJ 1935: 1605–27). The report was accepted unanimously by the Council (excluding Italy), with the President of the Council stating that this meant 'the establishment of the existence of a state of war' (LNOJ 1935: 1225). In the Assembly, Italy was also declared in violation of Article 12 in a resolution that was adopted in a vote by fifty to four, with Italy against and Austria, Hungary and Albania abstaining (LNOJ SS 138 1938: 114). During discussion, General Nemours of Haiti was forthright, saying that, 'The situation is clear: one State, a Member of the League of Nations, has invaded the territory of another State which is a fellow-Member of the League' (LNOJ SS 138 1938: 107). He also explicitly referred to Italy as an 'aggressor, who has deliberately taken the responsibility for his act'. However, most states expressed friendship with Italy while deploring the state of war and the breach of the Covenant this represented. Despite the qualifications, these acts in the League Council and Assembly constitute an interpretation of the Italian use of force in Ethiopia as a rule violation and also designated Italy a rule violator.

The members of the League then engaged in economic sanctions against Italy. These sanctions did not include all materials relevant to the conduct of war, with oil notoriously being exempted, but they were genuinely collective with fifty states participating (Baer 1976: 131). Initial Italian military successes were followed by complications, the removal of the commander of the Italian forces, and a successful Ethiopian counterattack in November (Roi 1994: 348). In this context, the Italian government approached the British and French to try to negotiate a settlement. Out of those negotiations came the Hoare–Laval proposals (see above). These proposals ended up becoming public in early December. The

102

international reaction to these proposals was catastrophic to the spirit of collective security. Frank Walters, a League official at the time, writes that the plan seemed to be 'the consecration and reward of aggression, proffered to Mussolini in the name of the League' and that the authority of the Covenant and the potential for collective security had been lost (Walters 1962: 672, 669). Anthony Eden, previously having expressed to his colleagues that 'the proposals were likely to prove very distasteful to some States Members of the League' reported back from Geneva that the 'Impression which Paris proposals have made upon opinion here is even worse than I had anticipated' (Parker 1974: 321–2). A sanctions committee had been expected to meet on 12 December to discuss imposing an oil embargo on Italy in January, hoping to also influence the US in that direction (Baer 1976: 131). However, instead, on 13 December the Hoare–Laval proposals were sent to Council members. The effect on the attitudes of states other than France and England was, generally speaking, that expectations of collective security collapsed. A list of reactions compiled by Baer includes a Greek diplomat who asked Anthony Eden whether this was a shift in policy from opposing aggression to appeasement (Baer 1976: 132). Another reaction was that Romania and Czechoslovakia told Germany that they, along with other Balkan states, would leave the League if the Hoare–Laval proposals were adopted.

Hoare and Laval resigned but the League did not adopt an oil sanction and Italy's military situation improved throughout early 1936 until the declaration of victory in May. On 2 May, Emperor Haile Selassie left Ethiopia. On 9 May, the King of Italy signed an annexation decree, assuming the title of Emperor of Ethiopia. The League Council postponed consideration of the situation, including the question of the continuing sanctions, until 15 June. However, instead Argentina forced a session of the Assembly which met on 30 June. The two issues at hand were the lifting of sanctions and the recognition of the Italian victory. Argentina's intention was to seek the 'widest possible support for the nonrecognition principle embodied in the Saavedra Lamas Pact' (FRUS 1936 III: 156). However, the UK intervened with Argentina and dissuaded it from pressing too hard on nonrecognition. Instead, according to Prentiss Gilbert the US consul to Geneva, in the choice between nonrecognition and appeasement 'the action here will denote a common will for an appeasement' (FRUS 1936 III: 161).

Argentina's representative opened the session with a speech in favour of nonrecognition. Haile Selassie gave a speech, having been admitted as a representative of a League member state. The English representative declared that 'this Assembly should not in any way recognise Italy's conquest over Ethiopia' (LNOJ SS 151 1936: 34). The Ethiopian delegation proposed two draft resolutions on 3 July (LNOJ SS 151 1936: 60), one of which stated that 'The Assembly recalls the terms of Articles 10 and 16, to which it declares its faithful adherence. Accordingly, it proclaims that it will recognise no annexation obtained by force.'[12] As a response to these proposals, an alternative text was drawn up by a committee and adopted by forty-four votes, only Ethiopia voted against, and four abstentions. This text included some language in the preamble relevant to nonrecognition. Section 4 stated 'Remaining firmly attached to the principles of the Covenant, which are also expressed in other diplomatic instruments such as the declaration of the American states, dated August 3, 1932, excluding the settlement of territorial questions by force' (LNOJ SS 151 1936: 65). On the basis that this covered the 'the question which forms the subject of the first draft resolution of the Ethiopia delegation' (LNOJ SS 151 1936: 65), the president of the Council declined to bring the Ethiopia resolution to a vote. When the committee text came to a vote, Ethiopia voted against and then said that Assembly decisions had to be unanimous. The president then said that the text was a recommendation, not a decision, and so a majority was sufficient. So, while nonrecognition was appealed to and technically stated as a part of the League's policy, there was no heartfelt promulgation. That said, Ethiopia was still considered to be a Member of the League, as seen during the next Assembly meeting when a proposal to accept the credentials of the Ethiopia delegation as a Member State was adopted thirty-nine votes to four (LNOJ SS 155 1936: 141). However, it was also decided that economic sanctions were to be lifted and they were on 15 July. The events of July 1936 were not actions of rule maintenance. Instead, 'It was a retreat from collective security by all states, a retreat into neutrality, isolation, regional groupings, or appeasement' (Baer 1976: 298).

After the Italian victory, there was a general sense that the League had failed and that some change was necessary. There was a push for reform of the League. The 4 July text also included a recommendation that 'the Council should invite from the Governments Members of the League any proposals which they might wish to make to improve the application of the principles of the Covenant' (LNOJ SS 151 1936: 65). The Council did that, and received seventeen different suggestions, so a Special Committee was set up to 'Study the Application of the Principles of the Covenant' (Myers 1939: 199). There was broadly speaking two different types of opinion: those who thought that Article XVI, the sanctions clause, should be voluntary, and those who thought states should automatically be under a duty to apply it (van Ginneken 2006: 68). For example, Switzerland formally applied to the Council for the right to be neutral in cases of sanctions under Article XVI, which was granted (LNOJ 1938: 368). In 1938 the Committee considered a report by the British Lord Cranborne who distinguished three types of League: a 'coercive League' where Members would be obliged to impose military and/or economic sanctions; a consultation League where there was a duty to consult but no obligation to impose sanctions; and an 'intermediate' version where Members could use coercion if they wanted to (League 1938: 9–10). These discussions did not lead to much substantive change before the League was dissolved during World War II. What they suggest, however, is that there was little enthusiasm for attempts to maintain the existing system.

Outside the formal League mechanisms, various actions indicated a widespread breakdown in the system of collective security. Several states, in addition to Italy, submitted notice of their intention to leave the League. Honduras and Nicaragua submitted notification in August 1936, immediately after the decision to lift the sanctions regime on Italy. Paraguay and Salvador notified in 1937, Chile and Venezuela notified in 1938, Spain, Peru and Hungary in 1939, and Romania in 1940. One indication of the reasoning behind some of these decisions comes from the main newspaper in Chile, *El Mercurio*, which said that Chile's decision was motivated by the fact that 'the League gradually went to pieces after Italy's conquest of Ethiopia and its subsequent recognition by Geneva'.[13]

Recognition of Italy's conquest, however, did not accelerate until 1938. On 5 January 1938, the Italian bulletin *Informazione Diplomatica* reported that up to that point ten states had given formal recognition to Italy's conquest of Ethiopia: Germany, Switzerland, Austria, Hungary, Yugoslavia, Albania, Spain, Japan, Manchukuo and Yemen.[14] Poland and Ireland were also reported to have given *de jure* recognition (Dart 1938: 361). In addition, several nations had not made a formal statement of recognition, but had addressed the credentials of their ambassadors to the King of Italy as 'Emperor of Ethiopia': Chile, Panama, Guatemala, Ecuador, Ireland and Nicaragua. The Netherlands recognised on 14 February,[15] Bulgaria on 27 March,[16] Turkey and Greece on 4 April,[17] and Czechoslovakia on 19 April.[18] After the League discussion on nonrecognition on 9–12 May (see below), Sweden, Norway, Denmark and Finland recognised.[19] In June, in response to a question in the UK House of Commons, R. A. Butler, the Under Secretary of State for Foreign Affairs, gave a list of recognitions with dates (HC Deb 29 June 1938 vol 337: cc1889–90). These were: Hungary, November 1936; Albania, November 1936; Switzerland, December 1936; Chile, December 1936; Great Britain, December 1936; France, December 1936; Honduras, March 1937; Poland, May 1937; Yugoslavia, November 1937; Ecuador, December

1937; Latvia, January 1938; Netherlands March, 1938; Bulgaria, March 1938; Belgium, March 1938; Rumania, April 1938; Greece, April 1938; Turkey, April 1938; Czechoslovakia, April 1938; Finland, April 1938; Lithuania, May 1938; Panama, May 1938; Eire, May 1938; Estonia, May 1938; Peru, May 1938; Sweden, May 1938; Norway, May 1938; Uruguay, May 1938; Denmark, May 1938; Argentina, June 1938.

However, in May, Butler had distinguished between states who had 'expressly recognised', those who had 'taken action which involves the recognition of Italian sovereignty over Ethiopia', those who had accredited ambassadors to the King of Italy as Emperor of Ethiopia, and those who had recognised de facto (HC Deb 11 May 1938 vol 335: cc1608–9). By the time that the UK and France formally recognised the conquest in November, forty-seven states had given *de jure* recognition to the Italian empire in one form or another.[20] The debate over the distinction between *de jure*, de facto and a partial *de jure* recognition (consisting of the accrediting of envoys to 'Emperor of Ethiopia') ceased to be remarked upon by the end of 1938. The Costa Rican president 'toasted the health of the King of Italy and Emperor of Ethiopia' at a lavish banquet at the Italian embassy, which was 'considered official recognition by Costa Rica of the Italian conquest of Ethiopia'.[21]

The League changes the rules

In May 1938, there was a meeting of the League Council that considered a question put to the Council by the UK in a letter to the secretary-general. The letter raised concern over the

> anomalous situation arising from the fact that many States Members of the League, including no less than five of the States represented on the Council, recognise that the Italian Government exercise sovereignty over Ethiopia or have taken action implying such recognition. (LNOJ 1938: 535)

The meeting was held after the signing of the Anglo-Italian agreement in April, which included the UK's recognition of the Italian conquest. Lord Halifax, now UK foreign secretary, had intended to try for a Council resolution renouncing the duty to not recognise any situation, treaty or agreement brought about by the illegal use of force, and instead making the matter one of individual state's decisions. However, there was such resistance in the preliminary private meetings that the ensuing public discussion was framed as simply a discussion and was not to lead to a vote. Malbone Graham reported that the President of the League of Nations Council, Vilhelms Munters, had said that in the private meeting of the Council in May 1938, he had 'pushed through' the '"decentralization" of policy as regards non-recognition' (Briggs 1940: 95). In the public meeting on 12 May, Halifax said that the UK hoped

> that Members of the Council will share its opinion, that the question of the recognition of Italy's position in Ethiopia is one for each Member of the League to decide by itself in the light of its own situation and its own obligation. (LNOJ 1938: 335)

The Ethiopian foreign minister then read out a statement that explicitly tied the current debate to the nonrecognition rule laid down on 11 March 1932 as well as Article 10 of the Covenant.

Almost all the other members of the Council supported the UK's position in one way or another. Maxim Litvinov, the USSR representative, pushed back and argued against Halifax on the basis that

> It must be clear that the League of Nations has no intention of changing its attitude, whether to the direct seizure and annexation of other people's territory, or to those cases where such annexations are camouflaged by the setting-up of puppet 'national' governments. (LNOJ 1938: 340)

The Chinese delegate, V. K. Wellington Koo, agreed with Litvinov, as did William Jordan, the New Zealand delegate. Jordan argued that acknowledging the freedom of members to decide for themselves on recognition meant abandonment of the 11 March 1932 resolution and Article 10 of the Covenant. He said that, 'It cannot be right to go back on the principles of the Covenant, or to condone acts of aggression' and that allowing individual discretion on recognition was 'a stage further in the surrender to aggression, and will be regarded as one further step in the retreat from collective security' (LNOJ 1938: 345). These dissenters were isolated, however, leading President of the Council Munters to declare that 'since collective action in the Italo-Ethiopian dispute was explicitly abandoned, the question of the consequences arising out of the existing situation in Ethiopia is one for each Member of the League to decide for itself' (LNOJ 1938: 346).

Another interesting indication of the abandonment of the existing rule was the reversal of position after the crisis by a group of seven small European powers: Denmark, Sweden, Norway, Finland, the Netherlands, Spain and Switzerland. All seven states, including Spain and even Switzerland who shares a border with Italy, participated in the sanctions regime. In August 1935, prior to the outbreak of war, the four Nordic powers had issued a joint communique to the effect that they 'support every effort to guard the peace and maintain the legal principles of the League' (van Diepen 2013: 320). However, less than a year later on 1 July 1936, these four states, along with Spain, Switzerland and the Netherlands, made a joint declaration that they would no longer be subject to the authority of the League Council on the question of the application of economic sanctions against aggressor states. As van Diepen comments, 'contemporary observers agreed that this declaration amounted to a virtual break with the system of collective security' (2013: 311). Hans Morgenthau wrote at the time in the *American Political Science Review* that this act was a 'cancellation of the obligations under Article 16 of the Covenant of the League' (1939: 473). A subsequent communique, in July 1938, by the Oslo Powers (Denmark, Sweden, Norway, Finland, the Netherlands, Belgium and Luxemburg), advised the extension of this 'non-compulsory character of sanctions . . . to all members of the League' (Morgenthau 1939: 476). Morganthau argues that this was a rejection of the 'new order' and the 'duty of solidarity in support of the victim of unlawful aggression' and a return to neutrality within a system of balance of power (1939: 478).

Conclusion to the League section

Despite the strong support of a widespread economic sanctions regime against Italy, formally designated as a rule violator, most members of the League did not engage in nonrecognition of the conquest of Ethiopia, nor did they even support the principle of nonrecognition of aggressive gain. Even within the League there were no actions taken constituting active nonrecognition and even some that came close to ambivalence about Ethiopia's status, if not outright recognition. The British, along with most others, agreed that they needed to get League approval or acquiescence in recognising Italian sovereignty over Abyssinia. The eventual formula was that the League was not to formally recognise Ethiopia as Italian, but that the League stated that it was not incumbent upon members not to recognise. This abandoned the previous position as stated on 11 March 1932 in reaction to Japanese actions in Manchukuo, but framed as a general principle. At the same time, the experience during the crisis, both of the Hoare–Laval proposals and the eventual failure of economic sanctions to change Italy's behaviour, led to the abandonment by many states of rhetorical and practical adherence to the principles of collective security. States sought to reform the League and reorient their foreign policies towards appeasement, neutrality, balance of power strategies and regional groupings, rather than a system of collective security.

CONCLUSION

The case of the Ethiopian Crisis provides answers to two different questions. The first relates to perhaps the most notorious element of the crisis: why did so many states, including France and Britain, do a U-turn and acquiesce to Mussolini's colonial conquest when they had previously opposed it so vigorously? Is this seeming hypocrisy proof of the dominance of cynical self-interest over Idealist fantasies, dooming normative considerations to irrelevance? No. The evidence in the case firmly supports the importance of rule maintenance considerations and demonstrates that the turn away from nonrecognition can be coherently explained within the rule maintenance model. There was a tension between the impulse to build a universal collective security system and the threatening growth of German power and revisionism. But there was also a historically contingent sense after Italy's military success in Ethiopia in the face of economic sanctions that collective security was no longer the institutional framework of international society. The rules had changed and so the motivation to try and maintain them had disappeared. Some, like Neville Chamberlain, justified recognition of the Italian conquest in terms of appeasement as a 'new' way of facilitating peaceful change. Others viewed peaceful change as unlikely and were gearing up for a clash with Germany. Either way, few still held to the viability and desirability of a collective security institution in the circumstances. This suggests an important type of departure from the process leading to a rule maintenance action like nonrecognition. If maintaining the rule looks undesirable, then symbolic sanctions aimed at maintaining the rule are unnecessary.

The second question is how the US justified their decision to, unlike most states, persist in their policy of recognition. The available evidence is that the Roosevelt administration stuck to the line, both in internal discussion and in secret and public communication with other states, that nonrecognition was 'to reestablish and maintain principles of international law and morality' (FRUS 1938 I: 121). This shows the utility of the rule maintenance model and demonstrates its applicability outside the Manchurian Crisis case.

NOTES

1. League of Nations Official Journal Special Supplement (LNOJ SS). Referenced with the supplement number, year and page number.
2. League of Nations Official Journal (LNOJ). Referenced with the year and page number.

3. For a small selection, see also Goldman 1974, Hardie 1974, Parker 1993, Roi 1997: 91, Salerno 2002 and Steiner 2011: 562.
4. Foreign Relations of the United States (FRUS). Referenced with the year and volume number, followed by the document number.
5. Goddard (2015: 95) addresses this issue, dividing the literature on appeasement into three schools based on how favourably they view British policies: a 'traditionalist' school, which largely condemns appeasement as irrational; a 'revisionist' school, which sees appeasement as, if not completely effective, a generally rational response to Germany given strategic constraints; and a 'post-revisionist' school, which questions the rationality of appeasement.
6. Such as intelligence collaboration and joint staff conversations including plans for joint operations against Germany (Parker 1974).
7. Documents on British Foreign Policy (DBFP). Referenced with the series, volume and document number.
8. House of Commons Debates (HC Deb). Referenced with date, volume and column number.
9. The following discussion draws on the minutes from this meeting.
10. Franklin D. Roosevelt: 'Statement on the Return of Under Secretary of State Welles from His European Mission', 29 March 1940. Online by Gerhard Peters and John T. Woolley, The American Presidency Project. <http://www.presidency.ucsb.edu/ws/?pid=15926> (last accessed 23 January 2017).
11. Roosevelt, Franklin Delano. *Four freedoms speech*. Project Gutenberg, 1964, <http://www.gutenberg.org/files/5038/5038-h/5038-h.htm#jan1941> (last accessed 4 August 2017).
12. The other resolution, giving 10 million pounds to Ethiopia, was defeated one for, twenty-three against and twenty-five abstentions.
13. 'Chile now out of league: two year notice ended yesterday – press discusses cause', *The New York Times*, 3 June 1940.
14. 'Recognise Italy's empire: ten nations now acknowledge it, Rome journal says', *The New York Times*, 6 January 1938.
15. 'Hague to recognise conquest of Ethiopia', *The New York Times*, 15 February 1938.
16. 'Boris accepts Ethiopia: Bulgarian king recognises Italy's conquest in Ethiopia', *The New York Times*, 27 March 1938.
17. 'Protests are sent by Haile Selassie: he decries Turkish and Greek recognition of Italy's conquest', *The New York Times*, 10 April 1938.
18. 'Italy's African conquest is recognised by Prague', *The New York Times*, April 20 1938.
19. 'More recognise empire: Norway and Denmark prepare to accept Italy's conquest', *The New York Times*, 14 May 1938.
20. 'French envoy gives credentials to Rome: brings total of states recognizing Ethiopian conquest to 47', *The New York Times*, 20 November 1938.
21. 'Costa Rica recognises conquest', *The New York Times*, 13 November 1938.

CHAPTER FOUR

Turkey, Cyprus and the Turkish Republic of Northern Cyprus

INTRODUCTION

In this chapter, I analyse the crisis surrounding the invasion of Cyprus by Turkey in 1974 and the subsequent nonrecognition of an autonomous Turkish-Cypriot entity. This is a positive case of nonrecognition. There are many similarities between the Turkish invasion of Cyprus and the Japanese invasion of Manchuria. In both, a state used force to occupy a portion of a neighbouing state, and then used its de facto control to support the creation of a new state in that territory. In both, there was initial confusion and uncertainty over whether the use of force was illegitimate. Once the international community, that is, a large number of states, the UN Security Council (UNSC) and UNGA, had decided that the invasion constituted aggression, a violation of the norm of the peaceful resolution of disputes, the results of the invasion were not recognised, even though there were few other sanctions imposed on the norm violator. The Turkish-Cypriots have been in a legal limbo ever since. Nonrecognition clearly has been unsuccessful in overturning the results of Turkey's military victory. And yet the UN and every state in the world, except Turkey, persists in this policy. The question is, then, why do they do so? Do they mistakenly see nonrecognition as an effective weapon against norm violators? Are they driven to this ineffective policy by the pursuit of votes at home? As will be shown, these and other alternative explanations for nonrecognition are not well supported in the evidence. Instead, maintaining the illegitimacy of aggression is the crucial justification underpinning the widespread adoption of a nonrecognition policy.

First, I provide a very brief description of the historical context, and the events relevant to the question of nonrecognition. Then I discuss the theoretical implications of the case. This is followed by a detailed analysis of the decision making by the UK, the US and the UN as they are relevant to the adoption of nonrecognition. Of primary interest are the justifications surrounding the adoption of a nonrecognition policy. In this case, arguments against recognising a Turkish-Cypriot state are particularly important as explicit consideration of the issue is usually about deviating from the status quo of nonrecognition.

HISTORICAL OVERVIEW

A British colony since 1878, in 1960 Cyprus became independent after an anti-British terrorist campaign by a Greek-Cypriot national-ist organisation.[1] Independence was agreed upon in the Zurich and London agreements of 1959 and 1960, which laid out a constitution for the new state. Under the new constitution, the two groups on the island, the majority Greek-Cypriots and the minority Turkish-Cypriots, shared power in a single legislature, electing their own representatives. The London–Zurich agreements were also a pact between the guarantor powers, Greece, Turkey and the former colonial power, the UK. The guarantor powers agreed to protect Cyprus' independence, and prevent either the union of the island with Greece (called *Enosis* in Greek) or partition of the island between the two communities (called *Taksim* in Turkish). All three guarantor powers were to station their own troops on the island. Britain retained two military bases, its last in the Mediterra-nean after the loss of Egypt, and Greek and Turkish forces were stationed in the ratio 3:2. The London–Zurich agreements were abrogated in a cri-sis in 1963, which included armed conflict between the two communities and resulted in the deployment of UN peacekeepers, the United Nations Peacekeeping Force in Cyprus (UNFICYP), to the island. Afterwards the Turkish-Cypriots no longer participated in the government.

In July 1974, a group of pro-Greek, and pro-Enosis, military offi-cers led by Nikos Sampson carried out a coup against the President of Cyprus, Archbishop Makarios, in which they tried but failed to assassinate him. In the days following the coup, despite attempts by the US, the UK and the UN to prevent it, Turkey landed troops on Cyprus. After a couple of days of fighting, Turkish troops controlled a very small amount of territory, about 3 per cent, and a ceasefire was announced. The Greek military junta, which was widely suspected of organising the Sampson coup, fell on 23 July and Constantine Karamanlis became interim president of Greece tasked with holding democratic elections. On 25 July the UK, Greece, Turkey, the Greek-Cypriots and the Turkish-Cypriots began peace talks in Geneva. These talks ended on 30 July with a joint declaration on minor issues but no

112

overall settlement. Talks restarted for a second round on 9 August but were broken off by Turkey late on 13 August. Early on the morning of the 14 August, Turkish troops renewed military operations. More successful this time, by 16 August after two days of fighting, Turkish troops had occupied about 37 per cent of the island, up to what was called the Attila line (the Turks called the attack Operation Attila) or the Green Line.

During these two military interventions by Turkey, the UNSC issued seven resolutions (353; 354; 355; 357; 358; 359; 360). While initially, during the first invasion in July, the resolutions were relatively neutral and addressed all parties, by the time of the second intervention from 14 to 16 August, the resolutions were clearly aimed solely at Turkey. Resolution 360 formally recorded the UNSC's 'disapproval of the unilateral military actions undertaken against the Republic of Cyprus'. This was a joint condemnation of Turkey's second use of force.

Negotiations between the various parties continued fitfully and Turkish troops remained in control of the northern part of the island. In the US, the US Congress overrode the objections of Secretary of State Henry Kissinger and the vetoes of President Gerald Ford to place an arms embargo on Turkey, starting from 5 February 1975. On 13 February 1975, the leader of the Turkish-Cypriot administration Rauf Denktash declared a Turkish Federated State of Cyprus (TFSC). Almost immediately, the UNSC issued resolution 367, which regretted the decision. However, the Turkish-Cypriot declaration did not declare a separate state. Rather, it was a separate entity within a federated Cypriot state. In response to the arms embargo, Turkey revoked the Defence Cooperation Agreement of 1969 and other related agreements with the US, resulting in the loss of several important military bases. The embargo was not fully lifted until 1978.

Despite numerous efforts by various parties, including notably UN Secretaries General Kurt Waldheim and later Javier Perez de Cuellar, to facilitate a settlement between the two parties, there was little progress. In November 1983, after a UNGA resolution (37/253) that May calling for the withdrawal of all occupation troops from Cyprus, Denktash unilaterally declared that the TFSC was now an independent state under the name of the Turkish Republic of Northern Cyprus (TRNC). This was followed first by UNSC resolution 541, which deplored the declaration, called it invalid, and called for the nonrecognition of the purported state, and then in May 1984 by resolution 550, which condemned Turkey by name for recognising the TRNC. The TRNC remains unrecognised, except by Turkey, to the current day.

113

Theoretical discussion

The first theoretical task is to establish that this instance of nonrecognition, first of the TFSC and then the TRNC, fits the stages of the model of rule maintenance. Once this is done, we can assess the reasons for adopting a nonrecognition policy.

In the Cyprus case, we have clear evidence of a pre-existing rule against aggression or the use of force for the settlement of disputes. The UN Charter is the most prominent statement of this rule. More recently, the Vienna Convention on the Law of Treaties, Article 52 of which states that treaties concluded under the threat or use of force are invalid, was adopted in 1969. The Declaration of Principles of International Law Concerning Friendly Relations and Co-operation Among States in Accordance with the Charter of the United Nations, in which aggression and the use of force were denounced and the nonrecognition of territorial acquisition was proclaimed, was adopted in 1970. Rhetorical reference to the principle of nonaggression and the peaceful settlement of disputes was also widespread throughout the crisis.

The event which triggered debate over rule violation was the invasion of the island of Cyprus by Turkish armed forces in 1974. The first invasion, in July, was not treated by external states as unjustified aggression. The attempted coup by Greek nationalists and the ensuing threat to Turkish-Cypriots were widely considered extenuating circumstances. However, after Turkey broke off the negotiations of the Geneva Conference in August and seized large parts of the island, their protestations that they were merely protecting the Turkish-Cypriots became untenable. This second use of force was treated by the international community as a norm violation. As Thomas Franck puts it, 'The UN system . . . firmly rejected – and . . . still rejects – the island's forcible partition in violation of the "territorial integrity" endorsed both by the Council and Assembly' (Franck 2002: 120).

For various reasons, the US and the UK did not want to, or were unable to, use force to expel the Turks from Cyprus. While the US Congress did impose economic sanctions, including an arms embargo, on Turkey, as a response to the occupation of Cyprus, these were lifted after four years. Nonrecognition of a Turkish-Cypriot state was thus in the context of a violation of the norm against aggression, profiting from the use of force, and territorial aggrandisement. As the evidence below will demonstrate, nonrecognition was not justified in terms of imposing costs on or hurting Turkey or the Turkish-Cypriots. In general the primary justification given for the policy was that to do otherwise would be to 'condone' or 'legitimise' Turkey's use of force. This is consistent with rule maintenance being the driving motivation of individual policymakers for nonrecognition. There is an even stronger case to be made that rule maintenance was a socially sustainable justification for not recognising a Turkish-Cypriot state. This means that it was the justification that all states as well as the UN could publicly accept.

There were complications. One prominent one was the role of the Greek-American lobby in the US. The US administration, primarily Secretary of State Henry Kissinger and President Gerald Ford, was opposed to economic sanctions on the basis that good relations with Turkey were of geo-strategic importance. However, in the midst of a high-profile campaign by Greek-American interest groups, Congress enacted economic sanctions and pushed them through several presidential vetoes. This complicates inference towards why the executive branch persisted in nonrecognition of a Turkish-Cypriot state. Despite rhetoric of maintaining the rules of international order, there was an awareness of a strong incentive to avoid a domestic backlash against a pro-Turkish policy. On the other hand, there is no positive evidence that Kissinger, Ford, or later President Ronald Reagan or Secretary of State George Schultz, specifically viewed nonrecognition as a cheap way of placating a domestic audience.

Another complication was the rhetorical prominence of the idea that recognition would imperil negotiations between the Greek-Cypriots and the Turkish-Cypriots. After the fighting had stopped, this was sometimes volunteered as a reason for actions including not recognising a Turkish-Cypriot state and condemning Turkey's unilateral recognition. This is an interesting example of how justifications for actions can be nested. Why did it matter if negotiations broke down, a 'peaceful' solution could not be reached and the Turkish fait accompli was accepted? It mattered only because of the implications for the rule structure of international society. If negotiations broke down, then Turkish aggression would have been rewarded. The underlying reason for not wanting to disrupt Cypriot intercommunal negotiations (which have continued sporadically since the beginning of the crisis) was thus to maintain the rule of nonaggression.

States clearly valued a 'peaceful' solution, but they also did not care what that solution was. The solution could have a result identical to the de facto situation on the island, as several actors openly stated. If decision makers do not care about the substance of the outcome, but rather the process by which that outcome is arrived at, then their concern cannot be with the effect of the substantive outcome on their interests. Instead, they must either be concerned with the substance of the process, or the normative and institutional implications of the process.

In this case, the international community insisted on a peaceful resolution, rather than a solution brought about by the use of force. If decision makers do not care about whether Cyprus is united or divided or about how much of the territory either side gets, but instead are primarily concerned that the outcome be decided peacefully, then this is evidence that they are not being driven by their interests in the outcome. They might be concerned about peace qua peace, and value a process with few lives lost. However, once the outcome is relatively fixed, as is the case in Cyprus, this cannot be a reason. Instead, the only reasonable defence of continued concern over the process is that it will have an impact on precedent, or the communal belief in which rules govern the behaviour of members of the community.

THE UK AND NONRECOGNITION IN CYPRUS

Introduction to UK section

The island of Cyprus became a British protectorate after the Ottoman Empire traded it for British support during the Congress of Berlin in 1878, in which the European states dealt with the aftermath of a Russo-Turkish war. Formal annexation in 1914 was followed by the declaration of Cyprus as a Crown Colony in 1925. Until the 1950s, Cypriots had no role in governing the island. After a terrorist campaign by Greek Cypriot Nationalist organisation EOKA (Ethniki Organosis Kyprion Agoniston), and international pressure from Greece and the UN, as well as inter-ethnic violence between the Greek-Cypriots and Turkish-Cypriots, Cyprus became independent in 1960. Under the Zurich Agreement of 1959, the president had to be a Greek-Cypriot elected by the Greek-Cypriots, and the vice-president a Turkish-Cypriot elected by the Turkish-Cypriots. The Treaty of Guarantee of 1960 stated that Britain, Greece and Turkey were guarantors of the territorial independence of Cyprus. A constant theme of UK involvement was that Britain had a special role in Cyprus due to her colonial history.[2]

During the crisis period in 1974–5, UK Prime Minister Harold Wilson was not significantly involved in the decision making for British policy. Instead, Foreign Secretary James Callaghan was relatively autonomous in taking action and was heavily involved, not just in determining British policy, but also personally taking part in many of the negotiations between the Cypriot parties, Greece and Turkey. UK involvement during this crisis was early, sustained and intense. By the early 1980s and the advent of the administration of Margaret Thatcher, attention had waned and there was little interest in the conflict and less action taken towards securing a peaceful solution. However, Prime Minister Thatcher's government did take the lead in pursuing UN declarations of nonrecognition of the TRNC, declared independent in 1983.

British interests

A major British strategic concern in the Cyprus crisis was the status of their Sovereign Base Areas (SBAs). There are two: Akrotiri and Dhekelia. Since the Suez crisis when the UK withdrew from Egypt, these SBAs on Cyprus have been the UK's only military installations in the Eastern Mediterranean. Despite Mallinson's claim that Britain had an 'obsession . . . with the territory that it had taken from Cyprus in 1960' (2007: 503), in November 1974, Callaghan led the Foreign and Commonwealth Office (FCO) in agreeing to withdraw or substantially decrease the British military presence in the form of the SBAs on Cyprus. It was only upon intervention by Kissinger that this decision was reversed (DBPO III, V, 98).[3] This demonstrates that the desire to retain the SBAs cannot have been prominent in the thinking of British political decision makers during the crisis. In particular, while the issue was raised at the beginning of the crisis, Callaghan's attitude towards how to deal with the Turkish invasion and subsequently the declaration of a Turkish Federated State was largely independent of considerations surrounding the retention of the SBAs. There might be an argument that recognition would anger the Greek-Cypriots so much that they would demand withdrawal of the bases (as the recognised rulers of Cyprus only the Greek-Cypriot attitude is relevant). However, the Greek-Cypriots relied on the base areas for injections of money into the local community and anyway needed good relations with Britian for tourism, trade and aid. A desire to avoid angering the Greek-Cypriots does not make sense as a motivation for nonrecognition and in fact this was not something that Callaghan or others in the Foreign Office were concerned about.

Another important issue for the British during the crisis, as it was for the US, was to prevent war between the two North Atlantic Treaty Organization (NATO) allies, Greece and Turkey. Asmussen goes so far as to call this the real aim of British policy during the crisis (2008: 28). In his memoirs, Callaghan puts 'preventing Turkey and Greece from getting at each other's throats' at the forefront of British policy (Callaghan 1987: 339). It was a recurring theme in policy papers and telegrams laying down policy principles. In a memorandum anticipating the first Turkish intervention, Callaghan included the avoidance of 'Greeko/Turkish clashes' as a high priority (FCO 9/1894).[4] Various outcomes of the crisis were sometimes evaluated in terms of the potential for war between Greece and

117

Turkey. For example, the British High Commissioner to Cyprus, Stephen Olver, wrote of the widespread opposition on Cyprus to a partition of the island and linked it to increasing tensions between Greece and Turkey. (DBPO III, V, 52).

Asmussen also highlights the initial desire to avoid Soviet involvement. However, while Kissinger was open about his emphasis on grand strategy, concern with the Soviet angle is conspicuously absent from Callaghan's discussions. In fact, he said that there was only one time during the whole crisis that the Soviets were an issue and this was when they threatened a veto of a UNSC resolution expanding UNFICYP forces. After he explained to them his point of view on the matter, they relented in less than a day, allowing the resolution to go through (Callaghan 1987: 343). In general the Soviets were pretty open about their relative lack of interest and the initial fear of their involvement receded into the background as other factors became more important (Asmussen 2008: 72).

James Callaghan, foreign secretary

Throughout the crisis, Callaghan, who was involved more than any other single external decision maker, consistently demonstrated his concern that the constitutional outcome be determined through peaceful negotiations between the two Cypriot parties. In an internal Foreign Office telegram on 12 August 1974, he said that his view was that 'the responsibility for determining the Constitution of Cyprus in the future must be placed firmly on the Cypriot leaders' (DBPO III, V, 69: 5). Kissinger viewed Callaghan as holding 'strong moral convictions' in the crisis. Initially Callaghan was outraged at the violence employed by the junta in Athens after the coup on Cyprus. Subsequently, however, he became convinced, 'definitively', that Turkey was in the wrong after the second invasion (Kissinger 1999: 209). The British foreign secretary was clearly concerned that aggression should not be rewarded. During the Geneva Conferences, Callaghan frequently warned the Turkish representative, Foreign Minister Turan Gunes, against any further military action. For example, in a conversation on 9 August, he said that if the Conference failed, 'Turkish forces might unilaterally expand their occupied zone' and he 'made it clear that the British Government would take a very serious view indeed of such action' (DBPO III, V, 57: 7). He urged Gunes to realise the widely illegitimate nature of using force to gain the upper hand in negotiations and stated that peaceful negotiations were necessary. On 13 August 1974, in a discussion amongst all the parties to the conference, while discussing the possibility of another military push, Callaghan said that 'If Turkey continued on this course they would have

to defend their action against disapproval from the whole world. . . .
The problem must be solved by agreement not by threat of force' (DBPO
III, V, 76: 31). These preferences over the process by which the territory
was distributed did not mean that Callaghan was blind to the intentions
of the Turkish government. In a telephone conversation with Kissinger
on 14 August, as the second invasion was starting, Callaghan said:

[Callaghan]   I think in military terms, obviously the Turks will carry on
              until they have got this line that they have figured out on the
              map, and cynically, let's hope they get it quickly.
[Kissinger]   I agree.
[Callaghan]   They will then stop, and there will be no political solution.
              (DBPO III, V, 77)

Callaghan advocated for the return of Makarios and was heavily against
the Greek junta initially, and later was strongly opposed to the Turkish
occupation of the north of the island. This could be taken as evidence
that he was driven by a desire to support the Greek-Cypriot claim to
rule the island. However, this interpretation is not consistent with Callaghan's rhetoric in favour of a territorial compromise and his continued push for an agreement at the Geneva Conference that allocated a
substantial amount of territory to the Turkish-Cypriots. Callaghan also
had no particular ties to the Greek-Cypriots nor was he subject to a
noticeable domestic lobby, apart from public opinion in the media that
followed events as much as he did himself. Instead, Callaghan seems to
have been motivated by a genuine dislike of violence and an apprecia-
tion that any durable settlement had to at least have the acquiescence of
both groups on the island. In addition, Callaghan stated both privately
and publicly that he 'recognised that the Turkish-Cypriots had legitimate grievances that needed remedy' (Callaghan 1987: 340).

Callaghan was not the only actor who was opposed to the process by
which Turkish goals were achieved, not by their substance. This position
was common throughout the FCO. For example, the British ambassador to Greece, Sir Robin Hooper, during the Geneva conference, said
that the Turkish 'aim [of achieving a Cyprus in which Turkish-Cypriots
will no longer be second-class citizens] may be a legitimate one but the
means being used to achieve it are not' (WO 386/21).[5]

First Turkish invasion

Prior to the first Turkish invasion of the island, a delegation including
Bulent Ecevit, Turkish prime minister and Hasan Isik, acting foreign

minister, met with the UK leadership in London on 17 July 1974, shortly after the coup removing Makarios from command. The Turks invited Wilson and Callaghan to join in with an intervention into Cyprus under Article 4 of the Treaty of Guarantee. The Treaty allowed for such action as was appropriate to protect and restore the territorial independence of Cyprus, that is, with 'the sole aim of reestablishing the state of affairs created by the Treaty'.[6] In one later exchange, the UK ambassador to Turkey was insistently reminded that Article 4 allowed for unilateral action. Such was the opposition to the Greek deposition of Makarios, Wilson and Callaghan treated the Turkish offer as a reasonable suggestion. Callaghan had already treated Greek actions as if they were illegitimate and aggressive in parliamentary debates (Asmussen 2008: 27). Though the British leaders did repeatedly counsel against a unilateral Turkish intervention, they went so far as to hint at certain measures the UK might take in support of such an intervention, were it to occur. At this point, the British did not condemn of the Turkish position and did not oppose the Turkish characterisation of Greece as 'an aggressor nation'. (DBPO III, V, 25: 13). Wilson later recalled his decision as a 'courteous but declaratory "No"' and said that his 'rejection of [Ecevit's] plan became still more firm' (Wilson 1979: 62). However, this was written in the context of the later Turkish invasions and widespread international condemnation of Turkey. The minutes of the meeting taken at the time do not support the idea that Wilson took as strong a position as he later claimed.

In a minute[7] from 18 July, Sir John Killick (Deputy Under Secretary of State) reported that the use of force by the UK had been considered by Callaghan. This was not mainly in relation to deterring a Turkish invasion. The primary concern at this point was the domestic political situation on Cyprus. One plan was to reinstate Makarios by force, but this was rejected. The British also considered a blockade against Greek reinforcement of their officers already on Cyprus and they saw this as being 'theoretically the same vis-a-vis [sic] Turkey' (DBPO III, V, 27: 11). At this time, Callaghan was also hoping for a UNSC resolution that would back up the diplomatic pressure that the UK and others were putting on the Greeks to withdraw their officers from Cyprus (DBPO III, V, 28). He was, understandably given the meeting on 17 July, aware that the Turkish government was considering a unilateral invasion of the island, but his attitude to it was not that it was unjustified aggression. When discussing tactics with Kissinger, he acknowledged Turkey's 'very strong incentive to act unilaterally' and emphasised the importance of Turkey to Western interests as well as their 'much sounder based government' than the Greek military junta (DBPO III, V, 29).

Callaghan's reaction to the Turkish invasion on 20 July was summarised in a telegram to the Ambassador to Greece Robin Hooper. He laid out the immediate policy goals of the UK government. These included trying to get the Turks 'to issue a statement of intent that they wish to see the return of constitutional rule in Cyprus'. This can be interpreted as both a way of getting information about Turkish intentions, that is, whether the Turks have territorial ambitions, and also a means of expressing to the Turks that such ambitions would be illegitimate. Another stated goal was to prevent the Greek government from getting involved and using force (DBPO III, V, 31).

The sentiment that any particular outcome was acceptable to the UK, as long as it was acceptable to the Cypriots on the ground, was widespread within the UK FCO. During the second invasion, Goodison wrote that 'We believe that a bi-regional federation in Cyprus, on lines advocated by Mr Denktash, but involving an area under Turkish-Cypriot administration rather smaller than 34 per cent of the Republic, offers the best solution' (DBPO III, V, 80: 2). This is almost exactly the de facto situation that was the case after the fighting, and endures today. The constant theme of British policy discussion, throughout the crisis and particularly at the Geneva Conference, is that the actual nature of the outcome, the composition of the government, territorial distribution and so on is unimportant to British interests. In a steering brief for the second stage of the Geneva Conference in August 1974, no particular version of governmental composition or structure is preferred. In fact, it was 'possible to argue that HMG's [Her Majesty's Government] basic objectives could in the right circumstances, be secured by any of the variants of double ENOSIS'.[8] However, the UK should not actually push for double Enosis, because 'There would be severe international criticism if we connived at the extinction – and incorporation into the area covered by the Atlantic Alliance – of a sovereign state which is a member of the United Nations and the Commonwealth' (DBPO III, V, 53).

Thus, the objection that recognition would prejudice the outcome is not because the outcome is of interest in and of itself. We can see from other statements (discussed below) that the main objection is that the gains by the Turkish-Cypriots would then be the result of the unilateral Turkish use of force.

Views on the efficacy of sanctions after the second invasion

Views towards the costs, benefits and likelihood of success of sanctions are vitally important in discovering the motivations for nonrecognition. Even if nonrecognition is not specifically mentioned, if sanctions other than nonrecognition are considered ineffective, or that only highly costly sanctions will work, this is evidence that nonrecognition was not considered to involve the imposition of significant costs on the rule violator or on those imposing the sanctions. In general, diplomatic sanctions were not held to be effective due to their low cost to Turkey. For example, Sir John Killick discussed the various sanctioning options with Kissinger after the conflict and they agreed that the only measure that would be costly enough to work might be the withdrawal of military aid from Turkey (DBPO III, V, 84). Even economic sanctions of this magnitude came under fire. A report by the Joint Intelligence Committee (UK) in February 1975, blaming the Turkish government for a lack of flexibility in negotiations over Cyprus, held that even a withdrawal of US military aid would not greatly affect the Turkish position (DBPO III, V, 105: 3).

The British attitudes towards the effectiveness of sanctions of any sort were almost always negative. They simply did not think that the imposition of sanctions, especially weak, diplomatic ones, would change Turkey's actions. This is indirect evidence that the argument that nonrecognition could be used for coercive purposes is unsupported.

Discussion of nonrecognition

In a meeting in September 1974, long after the fighting had stopped, but before any concrete measures towards formal independence had been taken by the Turkish-Cypriots, Callaghan discussed with other members of the FCO what should be done 'if the Turks declared an independent Turkish-Cypriot Republic as they had threatened'. There was no suggestion of recognition. The debate was about the form of nonrecognition and justification for it. Reaching for precedent, they agreed that they 'should take the line that such a declaration was incompatible with the 1960 Treaty'. However, this formal nonrecognition should not extend to an actual refusal to accept the existence of the Turkish-Cypriots. Goodison makes clear that 'following the Geneva Declaration, [the UK] recognised the existence in practice of an independent Turkish-Cypriot administration' (DBPO III, V, 89: 11). This did not mean that they formally recognised it as ruling a separate state, merely that they were willing to treat the Turkish-Cypriots as a party to negotiations over the fate of the island.

In a letter to Kissinger the same day, Callaghan expressed the hope that there would be no declaration of independence. If it happened, however, he said: 'I am sure none of us can prevent the continued remorseless establishment of a Turkish Cypriot Administration, but it must surely be in the Turkish interest to go about this in the least ostentatious and challenging way' (DBPO III, V, 90: 4).

Here Callaghan is facing up to the impotence of the US, the UK and the UN to change or affect the facts on the ground in northern Cyprus. This does not change his opinion that the administration should remain unrecognised, as the role of recognition here is not coercion. Callaghan also says that the less public the process is, the better for the Turks. Why might this be? The more public the process, the more it is open to international criticism. The more flagrant the norm violation, the more important it is for the community to be seen to oppose it. If Turkey was able to avoid their actions being seen as a violation, then other states would not feel the need to take rule maintenance actions.

In October 1975, after Turkey's February declaration that northern Cyprus was a Federated Turkish State, the UK and US missions to the UN collaborated on strategy concerning a UN response to a unilateral declaration of independence (UDI) by the Turkish-Cypriots. The dominant feeling was that a call for nonrecognition 'would in fact have little effect on states' intended policies towards the so-called state; it might, however, be a useful, if relatively insignificant, weapon in the event of pressure for further action' (FCO 9/2168). Further discussions between the UK and US at the State Department in Washington reveal that both foreign offices felt that a declaration of nonrecognition would have little positive effect and would hurt their relations with Turkey, as well as potentially jeopardising the inter-Cypriot negotiations. Worse, the discussion in the UNSC might escalate to the recommendation of economic sanctions. Mr Ledsky of the State Department asked 'When would we acknowledge political reality?' He was convinced that 'There would either be a separate Turkish-Cypriot state, or the northern part of the island would be incorporated into Turkey, which in some ways would be more satisfactory' (FCO 9/2168: 64A). So, why the need for nonrecognition at all? One indication was the heavy reliance in the discussion on the rest of the international community, who the UK and US policymakers saw as being strongly in favour of nonrecognition. Freeland (UK) said that he 'doubted whether UDI could be treated by us as a non-event when other countries would certainly treat it as something important'. Ledsky indicated that the US position on recognition would change or be re-evaluated 'if 40 or 50 states did recognise' (FCO 9/2168: 64A), although this was not considered to be a realistic possibility in the short term.

This line of thinking was mirrored by others in the FCO. David Lane of the British Embassy to Turkey viewed nonrecognition as irrelevant to the actions of Turkey or the Turkish-Cypriots: 'UDI and northern

Cyprus itself would continue to exist whatever we might say.' He also emphasised the role of the international community. 'Other countries would gradually recognise the new state and at some stage we would presumably have to come to terms with this fact of life' (FCO 9/2168: 53). If this were the case, then the UK would suffer by continuing to withhold recognition. These discussions between foreign offices are interesting given that the world, and the US and UK, has managed to avoid acknowledging political reality for over thirty-five years.

1983 and the Unilateral Declaration of Independence

After Rauf Denktash unilaterally declared the independence of the TRNC in May 1983, there was a reaction in the UK. Not only did Margaret Thatcher's government deplore the UDI but they were the sponsors of two UNSC resolutions declaring collective nonrecognition of the proposed new state. As internal documents from this period remain classified, the main sources for justifications of these actions come from public statements in the media and parliament. Memoirs and biographies of the decision makers, Prime Minister Margaret Thatcher and Foreign Secretary Geoffrey Howe, if they make reference to the UDI at all do not provide any indication of the private reasons for these actions. Publicly, however, they were clear that nonrecognition and condemnation was unlikely to impose noticeable costs on Turkey or the TRNC. The *Washington Post* reported that 'British officials acknowledge there is little in practical terms that can be done to force Denktash to reverse the decision to proclaim the Turkish Republic of Northern Cyprus'.[9]

During parliamentary debates on the subject, the most common treatment of the UDI was in terms of norm violation. The first point to note is that most of the discussion mentioned or was a reaction to the Turkish invasion in some way. On the rare occasion that the speaker supported the Turkish-Cypriots, there was always some justification of why the Turkish invasion was not illegitimate. This shows that the debate about nonrecognition was being conducted in the context of a norm violation. For example, in the House of Lords, Lord Cledwyn of Penrhos took a strong stand in moral terms: 'Many—perhaps most—will assume quietly that the declaration and the new arrangement will drift into permanence. I hope not. That would indeed be a triumph for wrongdoing and for international disorder.' (HL Deb 16 November 1983, 444 c1292).[10] As before, the issue is not the shape of the solution, it is the process by which the solution is reached. Sir Geoffrey Howe, foreign secretary at the time, distinguished between peaceful and non-peaceful solutions, indicating that a peaceful solution was preferable and necessarily depended 'on the attitudes of the communities concerned' (HC Deb 15 November 1983 vol 48: c727).[11] There was no conception that a declaration of nonrecognition of the TRNC, or its continuance, would impose costs on the new state or on Turkey. Many MPs made a point of calling for more stringent measures, or, as Mr. Tom Cox did, contrasting condemnations and nonrecognition with 'meaningful action' (HC Deb 17 May 1984 vol 60: cc589–90).

Legitimizing partition is legitimizing the use of force

In response to the UDI in May 1983, the failure of the previous round of talks, and 'the growing support amongst Members of both Houses for the formal recognition by HM Government of the permanent partition of the island' (UK House of Commons 1987: vii)[12] a Foreign Affairs Select Committee conducted an inquiry and drew up a report on the state and future of British policy towards Cyprus. This inquiry had access to numerous members of the past and current governments of the UK, the Greek-Cypriots, the Turkish-Cypriots, as well as other experts and interested parties, such as the UK pressure groups Friends of Cyprus and Friends of Turkish Cyprus. In amongst consideration of numerous policy issues, such as aid, passports and trade, the Committee explicitly laid out the clearest existing justification for the continued nonrecognition of the TRNC.

The Committee took a clear stand on the legitimacy of Turkey's actions in 1974. With the benefit of hindsight, the Committee stated that the first invasion by itself 'would have come to be seen as a legitimate – and responsible – exercise of her treaty rights and obligations'. However, the second invasion destroyed the possibility of the first invasion being accepted and legitimate because Turkey tried to negotiate a favourable settlement 'from a position of temporary military advantage'. The conclusion of this summary was as follows:

> While the first Turkish invasion of Cyprus in July 1974 could have been regarded as a legitimate and successful exercise of her Guarantor rights in order to prevent Enosis, the subsequent Turkish occupation of the whole of the area north of Nicosia has been, and must be, seen as an illegitimate (but, for the time being, equally successful) attempt to impose partition. In July 1974, Turkey appeared to be acting in support of the 1960 settlement; in August 1974 Turkey was undoubtedly using force to prevent its restoration. (UK House of Commons 1987: xiv)

The Committee did not condemn partition itself. In fact, it said that Turkey had good reason to prefer partition in the face of Greek and

Greek-Cypriot actions. However, putting the partition policy into action 'by purely military means cannot, however, be justified, and was clearly a breach both of general international law and of Turkey's specific obligations under the 1960 treaties' (UK House of Commons 1987: xiv).

In the policy prescription section of the report, the Committee explicitly addressed the reason for continuing the UK's policy of nonrecognition. The section is headed 'The effect of the 1974 invasion' (UK House of Commons 1987: xxvi). The Committee started by saying that there are some fundamental problems with any settlement between the two communities on Cyprus but that the Turkish invasion added a new problem. This new problem concerned foreign governments, not the Cypriots themselves. The UK's position at the time was that 'the Turkish occupation of northern Cyprus in August 1974 and subsequently, was illegal both in terms of the 1960 treaties and in terms of the UN Charter and general international law'. This view was 'shared by most of the international community'. Partition of the island between the two communities had become less acceptable because of the illegality of the means by which the de facto situation was achieved. The Committee inferred: 'Accordingly, permanent and legal partition of the island of Cyprus has become more, rather than less, difficult for other countries to countenance than it might have been before 1974.' The conclusion of the section makes the logic clear:

> To legitimise partition now, however, would be to sanction the rule of force in the settlement of international disputes which the United Kingdom, of all countries, has been most adamant in resisting. It is for this reason, in particular, that we regard Turkey as having needlessly wrong-footed itself in the summer of 1974: permanent and legal partition might well have assumed a respectable place on the agenda of negotiations between the Guarantor Powers in August 1974 if the Turks had *not* sought to impose it by force. By their military actions during that month the Turks have made it much more difficult for this far from irrational conclusion to be officially entertained by the United Kingdom or other interested governments. (UK House of Commons 1987: xxvii, first emphasis added)

Not only is maintaining the rule against aggression an important consideration but it is the main reason, or the reason 'in particular' (UK House of Commons 1987: xxvii). Elsewhere in the report this primacy of rule maintenance is made even more concrete. While discussing the economic dependence of the TRNC on Turkey, the report stated that 'the Turkish military invasion and continued occupation preclude on principle the recognition of northern Cyprus as an independent state' (UK House of Commons 1987: xvi). In the policy recommendations at the end of the report, there are only two reasons given for continuing nonrecognition; 'on principle and as likely to hinder the achievement of the objective of a united Cyprus' (UK House of Commons 1987: xxxiv).

Other recommendations of the report make clear that nonrecognition was not intended to inflict material costs on the TRNC or Turkey. The Committee opposed the embargo imposed on the North by the Southern, Greek-Cypriot state, and recommended an active policy of doing 'everything practicable to facilitate normal trade and other contacts between the Turkish-Cypriot community and the Republic of Cyprus, and with the outside world' (UK House of Commons 1987: xxxiv). This was justified as both weakening the TRNC's economic, political and cultural dependence on Turkey and improving relations between the two Cypriot communities.

In the wake of the report, despite the aforementioned pressures for recognition of the TRNC, the UK government continued to formally reject the legal existence of the proclaimed state.

Conclusion

British decision makers came to view Turkey's second military intervention on Cyprus as a norm violation and treated the unilateral establishment of a Turkish-Cypriot state as illegitimate because it was the result of the illegitimate use of force. Nonrecognition of a separate Turkish-Cypriot Republic was justified in a couple of ways. One important reason was that recognition would 'condone' or 'sanction the rule of force in the settlement of international disputes' (UK House of Commons 1987: xxvii). Another was that, even though the UK did not benefit from nonrecognition, the rest of the international community wanted nonrecognition and it was better to coordinate than to step out of line. Notably absent as justifications were the ideas that nonrecognition would impose deterrent costs on Turkey or that it would deflate domestic pressure for more costly sanctions or other action.

THE US, DOMESTIC POLITICS AND CYPRUS

Introduction to US section

US domestic politics during and after the Cyprus crisis had several important effects on decision making. President Richard Nixon was embroiled in the Watergate scandal and his attention was not focused on Cyprus. Decisions about policy and actions were made primarily by Henry Kissinger (Dallek 2007: 559). Nixon resigned as president on 9 August 1974, right in the midst of the conflict. His replacement, Gerald Ford, was not heavily involved in the Cyprus issue until it became a domestic political issue with the Turkish arms embargo adopted by Congress after the fighting had finished. In an early telephone conversation with his Secretary of State, Ford's contribution to policymaking consisted of saying that he 'would rely on [Kissinger's] good judgement', with Kissinger promising to 'not bother [Ford] with every tactical move' (FRUS 1969-76 XXX: 127).[13] This, as with other crises, made Kissinger the primary formulator of American foreign policy throughout the crisis, although the congressional arms embargo complicated the situation.

The US did not take substantial action during the Cyprus crisis in 1974. Before and after the *coup d'état* on Cyprus deposing President Archbishop Makarios, the US remained content to largely sit on the sidelines, not even strongly condemning the new Sampson administration on Cyprus. Unlike the UK and James Callaghan, Kissinger was not involved in negotiations after the initial Turkish intervention on 20 July 1974, and there was no US presence at the Geneva Conferences. In UN meetings, the US mostly tried to water down resolutions condemning the villain of the moment, especially Turkey. Kissinger did communicate frequently with the participants in the crisis, telephoning and meeting with the main decision makers on a regular basis. His interactions with Bulent Ecevit, the prime minister of Turkey who had been Kissinger's student at Harvard, are particularly interesting as both of them seem to have misunderstood the other's meanings and intentions. The administration's low-key approach was the subject of much domestic criticism in the US, and shortly after the fighting stopped Congress voted to cut off US military aid to Turkey. Kissinger and Ford opposed this, including using several presidential vetoes, but managed only to delay the embargo for a few months. In response, Turkey announced that all agreements concerning US bases in Turkey would be rescinded. It was not until 1978 that Congress lifted the embargo. The US abstained from the UNGA resolution on 20 November 1975. Joseph Sisco, Assistant Secretary of State for Near Eastern and South Asian Affairs said to the Cypriot ambassador that they had abstained because the resolution wasn't acceptable to both sides. One of the big behind the scenes issues was maintaining favour with the Turks, as well as the belief that condemning the Turks would hurt the prospects for negotiations (FRUS 1969–76 XXX: 188). While the US voted for UNSC resolution 541, condemning the establishment of the TRNC, it was the sole abstainer on resolution 550, which was oriented towards condemning Turkish recognition of the northern Cypriot state.

Henry Kissinger

Kissinger's main concerns during the crisis were mostly unrelated to Cyprus itself. As the crisis began, he wanted primarily to prevent a war between Greece and Turkey, both members of NATO, which would make the alliance weak in the Mediterranean and Middle East, and also to prevent the Soviets from potentially extending their influence. In his memoirs, he treats the Cyprus conflict as an intractable 'ethnic conflict', a solution to which was more likely to come from 'the total victory of one side or from mutual exhaustion' rather than anything that external mediation could provide (1999: 202). During the crisis, he was relatively unconcerned with the fate of Cyprus and the Cypriots, being far more interested in how the US appeared to various parties, especially Turkey but also Greece and the rest of the international community. His attitude was very different from James Callaghan's extensive emotional and practical involvement in addressing the crisis and preventing the recurrence of violence. In contrast to the UK, Kissinger did not make much effort to affect the situation on Cyprus. In fact, Kissinger spent most of his time not worrying about Cyprus in and of itself at all. Instead he was trying to steer the line between offending Greece or Turkey. As he said, 'The trick is to diffuse the situation without tilting the present structure' (FRUS 1969–76 XXX: 91).

One tactic used and believed in by Kissinger was to try and obliquely persuade Turkey, and Prime Minister Ecevit in particular, that military intervention was not in Turkey's interests. The difference between this hands-off approach and Callaghan's numerous interventions and near use of force is remarkable. Kissinger's approach is evident in a comment he made in relation to the eventual suspension of military aid to Turkey in October 1974: 'The Turks won't yield to visible pressure. The Turks will yield to pressure with a silk glove that looks like they are yielding on their own initiative' (FRUS 1969–76 XXX: 154). From the lack of any evidence that Kissinger referred to Turkey's actions as illegitimate in some way, it does not seem that Kissinger, unlike Callaghan and others, was convinced that Turkey's actions were illegitimate aggression. Consequently, Kissinger was trying to maintain good relations with the Turkish leadership in the midst of a global swing in opinion against them. A frequent justification for this position was the broader strategic role that Turkey played in US grand strategy. US military bases in Turkey were important both because they were close to the Soviet Union and also because they were close to the Middle East. During the second invasion, Kissinger was far more worried about this than any normative issues about the aggressive or aggrandising nature of Turkish action on Cyprus. For example, he said, the Turks can give us trouble in the next Middle East war. We have to be careful not to get too far separated from the Turks. Do the Turks in New York know we are holding back? Do they know we are not leading any crusade?' (FRUS 1969–76 XXX: 133)

Kissinger's attitude throughout the crisis can be summed up by a statement he made (quoted by Leslie Gelb) on the legal arguments surrounding administration policy towards Cyprus; 'There are times when the national interest is more important than the rule of law' (Gelb 1976: 13).

Views of the constitutional outcome on Cyprus

In a parallel with the British Foreign Office discussion, the general line in the State Department before, during and after the crisis was that the particular distribution of authority on Cyprus was not relevant to US interests (which were seen to largely be good relations with Turkey): 'Our basic position remains that we would welcome any settlement which would be acceptable to the parties involved. We strongly believe that lasting settlement can best be achieved by peaceful (underlined) means' (FRUS 1969–76 XXX: 77).

The emphasis on 'peaceful means' is evidence that while the particular shape of the outcome was irrelevant, the process by which that was reached was important. Further, the crisis was a space in which other interests had to be defended and could be pursued: 'the US does not have fundamental objectives as regards Cyprus itself except in the context of Cyprus' effect on other US interests' (FRUS 1969–76 XXX: 122). The fact that the US are discussing outcomes that include Turkish gains in these terms means that they are not opposed to the actual shape of the outcome in its own right. It also indicates that they are not actually especially worried about imposing costs on the Turks for their actions.

In a lengthy briefing paper written for Kissinger just after the first invasion by Turkey, Assistant Secretary of State for European Affairs Arthur Hartman considered the issues and options available to the US in various scenarios (FRUS 1969–76 XXX: 112). These include numerous different types of military and economic sanctions. Notable by omission is explicit consideration of nonrecognition as a viable sanction. Hartman clearly thought that Turkey would advocate a 'Substantial return to the 1960 constitutional arrangements', on the basis that this would 'defuse adverse international reaction to Turkish military intervention'. It would 'strengthen the Turkish line that their intervention was in strict accordance with the Treaty of Guarantee and was aimed solely at a return to constitutionalism'. Why might this be so? Hartman seems here to be aware of the fact that the general sentiment among the international community is that Turkey's use of force is illegitimate. A plausible reconstruction of the reasoning behind Hartman's claims here is that if Turkey was able to make its actions appear to be aimed at restoring the previously agreed upon constitutional arrangement on the island, then the invasion would not be seen as illegitimate aggression, but instead would be seen as legitimate intervention to enforce the rules.

The second Turkish invasion as a rule violation

Henry Tasca (US ambassador to Greece) expressed the private sentiments of most people, prior to the first use of military force by Turkey, when he said that the terms of the London–Zurich agreements made Greek or Turkish intervention 'legitimate' (FRUS 1969–76 XXX: 89). After the invasion and during the first Geneva conference, the Cyprus Task Force, which was set up by the US administration in response to the crisis, assessed the diplomatic impact of Turkey's actions. 'Diplomatically, by invading Cyprus, continuing to advance after the cease-fire, and stating that Turkey intends to remain on Cyprus in force, the Turks are coming under increasing international criticism.' At this point, 'Turkey's only significant international support now seems to be coming from the US' (FRUS 1969–76 XXX: 97). Even so, the Ford administration publicly 'deplored' Turkey's actions (Gwertzman 1974a).

In the UNSC, sentiment was against the Turks and in particular against the new use of force that was being seen as illegitimate, by Callaghan and the UK, but also by others, notably the Soviet Union and France. The French were pushing a draft resolution in which they emphasised that the outcome of negotiations between the Greek and Turkish-Cypriots 'should not be impeded or prejudged by the acquisition of advantages resulting from military operations' (UNSC resolution 360). Informed of this by William Buffum (US Assistant Secretary of State for International Organization Affairs), who said that 'the Turks are kicking in New York about that', Kissinger approved of the resolution and this language. He justified this by saying 'It could mean there shouldn't be future military operations' (FRUS 1969–76 XXX: 136). This is a display of hope that the expression of disapproval over the use of force to impose political change could alter Turkey's cost–benefit analysis of future military action. This is consistent with Kissinger's tactics of using US approval as leverage on the Turkish leadership.

The Soviet Union, while undoubtedly being pleased by the tension in the NATO ranks, maintained consistently, both publicly and privately, that their opposition to the situation on Cyprus was based on the illegitimacy of the Turkish use of force. During a dinner with Kissinger right after the declaration of the TFSC in February 1975, Gromyko insisted that the Soviets were 'indignant about what has been done in Cyprus'. Not only was what was happening to the Cypriots contrary to 'anyone's interests', but it was a 'violation of the rights of that people with the use of armed force' (DNSA, KT01499).[14] Kissinger responded with an attempt to demonstrate that the US was similarly motivated. One of the things he used as evidence that the US was anti-aggression was that they 'do not recognise the new Turkish state as a state and we will deal with the legitimate government of Cyprus' (DNSA, KT01499). This exchange, conducted in a private setting in which only Gromyko and Kissinger were present, involved the candid discussion of many foreign policy issues and shows the depth of the opposition to aggressive gain and the way that even Kissinger felt the need to appear in accordance with the norm. It also shows the symbolic role of the nonrecognition of the newly declared Turkish Federated State: to represent one's valuation of the norm of nonaggression.

Sanctions

Before the first Turkish invasion, when war with Greece was at its likeliest, Joseph Sisco threatened Turkey with the withdrawal of all military aid in the event of war (FRUS 1969–76 XXX: 105). However, after war with Greece became much less likely with the fall of the junta, economic sanctions were not mentioned. Kissinger was also very dismissive of the UK's flirtation with using military force as a deterrent for a second invasion, calling it 'one of the stupidest things I have heard' (FRUS 1969–76 XXX: 127).

The main approach, of the State Department in general and Kissinger in particular, was to try 'convincing the Turks that military action won't settle the problem on Cyprus or in the area as a whole, and would only invite Greek counter activities' (FRUS 1969–76 XXX: 98). Once the Attila Line had been reached by Turkish forces, there was no sense that symbolic sanctions would have the effect of compelling the Turks to comply. William Hyland, then director of the Bureau of Intelligence and Research, wrote a memo to Kissinger in which he said that 'There are no moral, diplomatic-political pressures that will induce Ecevit suddenly to give up the gains the Turks have made' (FRUS 1969–76 XXX: 143).

Material sanctions were in fact used by the US against Turkey, but they were put in place by Congress and not by the administration. The arms embargo imposed by the US Congress on Turkey was enacted against the public opposition of the Ford administration. Kissinger was livid for several reasons. One reason was that this set a, to him, dreadful precedent of congressionally determined foreign policy against the wishes of the executive. Another was that economic sanctions do not work as a compellent.

> Kissinger: A threat to cut off aid is a weapon; an actual cut-off is not. It will be impossible to conduct the negotiations under these circumstances. Suppose we get the Turks to withdraw 10 kilometers and release 10,000 refugees, and then we restore aid? What do we do two months from now? Cut it off again? It will be on and off like a yo-yo. It can't be done with fixed deadlines. (FRUS 1969–76 XXX: 154)

Publicly, the members of Congress most vocal and active in favour of the embargo justified the action in various terms. A study by the House Committee on Foreign Affairs' Subcommittee on Europe and the Middle East, conducted in 1981 and involving extensive interviews with major participants in the embargo debates, concluded that there were four main reasons for congressional support for the embargo legislation. The first was essentially antagonism over Kissinger's 'seeming disregard for the rule of law . . . barely a month after the Nixon resignation' (US House of Representatives, Committee on Foreign Affairs, Subcommittee on Europe and the Middle East 1981: 19). Part of this idea was the deep hostility towards Kissinger himself, but it also included fears that the foreign policy of the US was being driven by someone who did not share the same principles as those in Congress, and this was an attempt to wrest some control away from him. Second, there were apparently some true believers, those who 'sincerely believed that the embargo could be a strong and effective message to Turkey and could dramatically affect the situation on Cyprus', although it is unclear how widespread this was amongst the political class. However, there was a sense in certain quarters that the embargo was unlikely to work in terms of changing Turkish policy for the better, that is, towards relinquishing control over territory in Cyprus. Support for the embargo in these cases was split between the two final reasons. The third reason was to 'prove to the American people that respect for the rule of law was still a guiding principle', in the face of the Watergate scandal. Finally, some members viewed the 'true value' of the sanctions was to 'show other nations that the United States did not tolerate blatant violation of its bilateral agreements' (US House of Representatives, Committee on Foreign Affairs, Subcommittee on Europe and the Middle East 1981: 22).

However, there are significant instances where the justification of rule maintenance played a part in the public debate over the arms embargo. Edward Kennedy was a senator that played a prominent role both in the attack on the administration's policy during the Cyprus Crisis, and in calling for a Turkish arms embargo. In his criticism of the administration, he used the idea of 'condoning' aggression as a weapon against Kissinger's actions. Kennedy said that the government was suggesting that the invasion 'was understandable, and we must accept, therefore, the "new realities" on the island' (quoted in Watanabe 1984: 103). However, Kennedy was opposed to accepting these realities and the reason for doing so was that it would represent condoning aggression:

Are we to condone the invasion and occupation of Cyprus? Are we to condone ceasefire violations? Are we to condone the nibbling away of an independent state, and a continuing threat of a new offensive in the so-called Turkish 'peace operation'? Are we to condone the failure of our government to condemn the Turkish invasion? Are we to condone the omissions in our diplomacy, and the efforts of our Government to cover up these omissions and the tilt towards Turkey? Are we to stand silent in the face of *these* realities?' (Quoted in Watanabe 1984: 103, emphasis in the original)

Greek-Americans and domestic politics

The Greek lobby, led by the American Hellenic Institute Public Affairs Committee (AHI-PAC), used various arguments in public fora when arguing for a ban on military aid to Turkey. Generally speaking, the most broadly used argument was that Turkish aggression constituted a violation of US law (Watanabe 1984: 112). The Greek lobby also argued that there would be broader implications of US acquiescence to the Turkish invasion. One such implication was that, in future, recipients of US military aid would feel that they also could use those arms to attack their neighbours. Another issue, brought up by Eugene Rossides, chairman of AHI-PAC, was that the imposition of a Turkish arms embargo would condemn wanton aggression of any kind, regardless of the specific circumstances. Rossides also said, 'Even if Turkey had not used US arms in its brutal aggression against Cyprus, it is a basic principle of US foreign policy to oppose aggression.' Similarly, Congressman Riegle claimed that the embargo was necessary to prove 'the fidelity of Congress to an important principle of nonaggression' (quoted in Watanabe 1984: 118). Senator John Brademas also brought up this idea, criticising the administration's 'action and inaction' because it meant that the US 'condoned and . . . [had] given tacit support to these aggressive acts on the part of the government of Turkey' (US House of Representatives, Committee on Foreign Affairs 1974: 81). As Watanabe puts it, 'continued silence in the face of Turkey's military surge and continuing occupation of Cyprus was tantamount to endorsement of these actions' (1984: 121). Whatever the motivations of the individual members of the lobby in favour of the arms embargo, one of the arguments used in the lobbying was rule maintenance. The argument was used at all levels of lobbying activity, privately and publicly. This is evidence that condoning aggressive gain was seen as so bad that it would be a convincing reason to impose an arms embargo.

Kissinger's feelings were out of line with the US domestic political situation and he attempted to use this fact as leverage in his discussions with Ecevit. During the second invasion, he warned Ecevit that 'further Turkish military operations will put the USG [US government] in an impossible position' because of the 'domestic situation in the United States'. If Turkey continued to use force, the administration would 'be obliged to take public steps which would threaten our ability to work together' (FRUS 1969–76 XXX: 138). The specific implications are left implicit, but it must have been clear to Ecevit that explicit condemnations, both bilateral and through the UN, and economic sanctions were being considered in the US public sphere. Kissinger felt constrained by domestic political opinion on actions like US voting on the UNGA resolution 3212: 'We will have a murderous time with Congress, and with the AHEPA [American Hellenic Educational Progressive Association] group, if we don't vote for withdrawal [of the Turkish troops from Cyprus]' (FRUS 1969–76 XXX: 156). Kissinger felt that this put him and the US in between a rock and a hard place. 'But if we do vote for withdrawal, anything that is done in Ankara will not redound to our credit. I don't mean to our personal credit.' Kissinger blames what he calls 'an ethnic pressure group', referring to the Greek lobby, with 'pushing [the US] in a direction that is totally against its interests' (FRUS 1969–76 XXX: 174).

The Turkish arms embargo was an interesting facet of the US reaction to the Turkish invasions of Cyprus. The Greek lobby was very important in publicising and proposing the legislation and arguments in favour, but did not pose such an electoral constraint that Congress heeded its call for more than a few years. In fact, a study of congressional voting in the period shows that there was little support for the influence of the Greek lobby (Hicks and Couloumbis 1977). Surveying the evidence, Rystad argues that ethnic politics was at best one contributing motivation among many, including the opposition to and condemnation of Turkey's aggression (1987). The executive, mainly Kissinger, fought hard against the embargo, argued its counterproductivity and succeeded in getting it overturned. And yet this same executive supported the nonrecognition of the Federated State of Northern Cyprus which led subsequently to nonrecognition of the TRNC for 40 years.

The Unilateral Declaration of Independence in 1983

The US response to Rauf Denktash's UDI[15] of the TRNC in November 1983 was quite different from that of the UK and other members of the UNSC. There were two UNSC resolutions related to the situation. UNSC resolution 541 condemned the Turkish-Cypriot authorities, deplored the UDI and called upon all states not to recognise the TRNC. The US voted in favour of this first resolution. However, the US abstained from a vote on resolution 550, which was aimed, not at the UDI itself, but at the 'purported exchange of ambassadors between Turkey and the legally invalid "Turkish Republic of Northern Cyprus"'. Mirbagheri convincingly argues that President Ronald Reagan's policy of combating Soviet influence in the Mediterranean and the consequent importance of good relations with Turkey contributed to the US decision to abstain on UNSC resolution 550. He also highlights the Reagan administration's scepticism towards the UN as a contributing factor to a lack of support for UN initiatives (1998: 142–4).

In Congress, outrage was the default position on the UDI. The Senate Foreign Relations Committee issued a resolution opposing and condemning the UDI as illegal. This resolution focused its opposition to the UDI in terms of its illegality and made particular reference to 'the presence of Turkish occupation forces on Cyprus' (US CRS 15 November 1983, 32615).[16] The UDI was treated almost universally as a norm violation. For example, Senator Edward Kennedy said that it was 'a contravention of international law that must be strongly resisted by the United States, by our allies, and by all nations in the world community' (US CRS 15 November 1983, 32551). Representative Ed Feighan said that it 'violates the UN Charter, treaty obligations, and the basic norms of international law' (US CRH 17 November 1983, 33298).[17] It was seen as a norm violation largely because of the illegality of Turkey's use of force in 1974. In the House, Rep. Mario Biaggi framed his opposition to the UDI as opposition to Turkish policy. He said that after an 'illegal and unwarranted invasion' Turkey 'illegally occupied almost 40 per cent of Cyprus. They have no right to declare this area as an independent nation' (US CRH 16 November 1983, 33006).

When explicitly justifying the House and Senate resolutions condemning the UDI and asserting continued nonrecognition of the TRNC, there was near unanimity on why this was worth doing and what it might accomplish. Rep. Nicholas Mavroules clearly specified a justification: 'we cannot sanction [i.e. approve of] Turkish aggression and hostility' (US CRH 17 November 1983, 33280). Similarly, Rep. Olympia Snowe pinpointed the reason for the resolution as being that it 'makes clear congressional disapproval of the cavalier disregard for the norms of international law by the Turkish-Cypriots' and that to do otherwise would 'reward Turkish intransigence' (US CRH 17 November 1983, 33300; 33301).

A *New York Times* editorial the day after the UDI summarises the reaction in the US. The editorial blames Turkey for a 'land grab begun by a Turkish invasion in 1974'. Turkey's actions are seen as negative because it used 'its superior force to impose an inequitable division of land'. It lauds the denunciation of the UDI but not because it will induce policy change: 'It is not likely to be undone by mere protest, but the blame for the damage should be understood'.[18]

Conclusion of US section

US Cyprus policy during the 1974–5 crisis and afterwards was crafted and enacted by a variety of actors. Initially, Kissinger was responsible, but unable to have complete control due to congressional action. Domestic pressure against a pro-Turkish policy was intense. Kissinger actively complained about it and stated that it was affecting his decisions. The desire to avoid domestic backlash is a strong contender for the motive for US support for nonrecognition of a Turkish-Cypriot state. However, this did not prevent the US from abstaining on various anti-Turkish UN resolutions. Also, there are indications that Kissinger and others were concerned about keeping US action as similar as possible to that of the rest of international society. Condemnations of the Turkish invasion, the TFSC and the TRNC, as well as support for various UN resolutions advocating nonrecognition, were performed in the context of private insistence on the importance of maintaining the appearance of support for Turkey. Counterfactually, it seems highly plausible that had international sentiment not been as uniformly vociferous in opposition to what was called Turkish aggression, the Ford and Reagan administrations would have been much more inclined to recognise a separate Turkish-Cypriot state. The most likely motivation for US support for nonrecognition policies and actions seems, then, to have been a desire to stay 'in step' with the rest of the international community. However, rule maintenance was still important as a justification. While Kissinger does not seem to have been primarily driven by this consideration, rule maintenance was prominent as both a public and a private justification for not recognising various incarnations of a Turkish-Cypriot state. Rule maintenance was also raised as a reason for the *economic* sanction of an arms embargo against Turkey. Few thought sanctions, especially symbolic ones like nonrecognition, were likely to change the policy of Turkey or the Turkish-Cypriots.

The UN, collective condemnation and nonrecognition

Introduction to UN section

The UNSC has adopted many resolutions on Cyprus. Crucially, UNSC resolution 367 was adopted on 12 March 1975 after discussions following the declaration of the TFSC on 13 February. Subsequent resolutions and discussion in the UNGA and UNSC refers back to this resolution and the principle of the nonrecognition of the results of illegal force. Then, after the Turkish-Cypriot UDI in November 1983, which purported to establish the TRNC, the UNSC issued resolution 541, deploring the declaration, considering it as legally invalid and calling for its withdrawal. This was followed in May 1984 by resolution 550, which specifically condemned Turkey's recognition of the TRNC and reiterated its call for its nonrecognition.

United Nations action during the Turkish uses of force in 1974

UNSC resolution 353 was passed on 20 July, on the same day as the first Turkish troops landed on the island of Cyprus. This resolution was not directed at any particular actors, calling for 'all parties' to stop fighting, for an end to all foreign military intervention and for the withdrawal of all foreign military personnel. As this was in the context of the attempted coup as well as the Turkish invasion, these clauses were not specifically directed at Turkey. At this point, Turkey's action was not seen as unjustified aggression. Numerous states, while deploring the resort to force, made reference to the Greek junta's responsibility for creating the situation. Scali, the US representative, referred to 'the pressures and interventions which contributed to the Turkish action on Cyprus, and for which Greece must bear a heavy share of the responsibility' (S/PV 1974, 1781: 54).[19] The French delegation also noted the 'special responsibility upon the Athens Government for the events that took place' (S/PV 1974, 1781: 62). The USSR went further and claimed that the Greek government was wholly at fault, blaming them for having 'committed aggression against . . . Cyprus' (S/PV 1974, 1781: 73).

The Indonesian and Mauritian representatives made explicit the moral equivalence between the violent actions of 'the military regime in Athens and . . . the military forces of Turkey' (S/PV 1974, 1781: 195). For several weeks and through several resolutions, this moral equivalence was accompanied by acknowledgments that the grievances of the Turkish-Cypriots were legitimate and required some consideration. For example, on 13 and 14 August, France made clear its view 'that the position of the Turkish community on Cyprus requires considerable improvement and protection, as well as a greater degree of autonomy' (S/PV 1974, 1792: 70).

The message of these public speech acts was the same as that communicated privately to other states. The UK ambassador to the UN wrote to Callaghan about 'the attitude of the non-aligned' (DBPO III, V, 50: 6). The non-aligned states were opposed to any intervention, anything which would affect the freedom of the Cypriots to determine the future of the island at this point. They were worried about the consolidation of the Turkish occupation of part of Cyprus. The main factor cited regarding their vote was 'whether or not they could be induced to accept that this was in reality a situation in which Cyprus was trying to control its own destiny and was being frustrated by the invading Turks' (DBPO III, V, 61: 3).

With the Turkish dissolution of the Geneva conference and the advent of the second phase of the invasion, the tide of opinion turned. For example, by 15 August, Austria had changed its position and now 'protested in the strongest possible terms against this violation of international law and this irresponsible act of Turkish armed forces' (S/PV 1974, 1793: 44). By 16 August, there was no question that Turkey's actions were being treated as a norm violation. France had dropped all hint of balance and was formally disapproving of Turkey's 'unilateral resumption of military operations in Cyprus'. This was wrong because it was 'part of an inadmissible practice', that is, 'the ultimatum approach'. Turkey was 'seiz[ing] advantages in the island'. France held that 'No war, no attempt to use force, can ever settle political problems.' So, the international community had to 'propose guidelines for the settlement' (S/PV 1974, 1794: 15–30). Here the French delegation are opposing Turkey's action solely on the basis that aggressive gain was illegitimate and that reaffirmation of the principles of nonaggression and peaceful settlement of disputes was important to show everyone involved what the boundaries of legitimate action were. Other members of the UNSC were also now opposing Turkey's actions and referring to them as 'the violation of principles enshrined in the Charter'. The Costa Rican representative asked whether there was a risk that 'irreparable damage has

. . . been done to the principles upon which international order is based'. The Cyprus case had important implications for 'what might happen if an era were to come in which, because it was not strictly abided by, that Charter was weakened, thrusting the world back once again under the reign of force' (S/PV 1974, 1794: 36–9). UNSC resolution 360 was passed on 16 August and included a formal disapproval of Turkey's actions. The resolution also urged an outcome that was not 'impeded or prejudged by the acquisition of advantages resulting from military operations'. This became a central theme of discussion during Turkey's second invasion and has dominated discourse surrounding a potential settlement ever since. During UNGA discussions in November 1974, the UK ambassador to the UN reported that the main sticking point was 'the indefinite maintenance of a large body of Turkish troops in Cyprus' (DBPO III, V, 97: 2).

Precedential reasoning was paramount. Action, in the sense of resolutions of condemnation and calls for withdrawal of troops, was justified in terms of protecting principles. After the fighting had ended, during discussion of UNSC resolution 361, the French representative went further and stated his rationale for supporting the wave of resolutions during the crisis. He said that 'The foundations of a just peace and a safer order must be defined' (S/PV 1974, 1795: 164). This is a clear reference to rule maintenance: France is saying that unless the UNSC collectively defines the rules of proper behaviour, the current circumstances will cast doubt on which rules are seen as accepted.

Nonrecognition of the Turkish Federated State of Cyprus, 1975

Rauf Denktash, the leader of the Turkish-Cypriots, declared the autonomy of the Turkish-Cypriot Administration on 13 February 1975, at a meeting of the Autonomous Turkish Administration Assembly of Cyprus. This declaration was not intended to create an independent state. Regardless, the declaration was treated by the Greek-Cypriots as an attempt at formal partition of the island. The declaration was discussed in the UNSC in February 1975, leading to the adoption of resolution 367 on 12 March 1975. The operative clause of this resolution was a complicated navigation through several shoals of meaning:

> 2. Regrets the unilateral decision of 13 February 1975 declaring that a part of the Republic of Cyprus would become 'a Federated Turkish State' as, inter alia, tending to compromise the continuation of negotiations between the representatives of the two communities on an equal footing, the objective of which must continue to be to reach freely a solution providing for a

political settlement and the establishment of a mutually acceptable constitutional arrangement, and expresses its concern over all unilateral actions by the parties which have compromised or may compromise the implementation of the relevant United Nations resolutions.

The primary issue under discussion was whether the declaration represented 'an attempt to dictate and impose a solution at gun-point' (S/PV 1975, 1813: 38). USSR Ambassador Malik linked the 'unilateral actions of the leadership of the Turkish community [i.e.] steps to create a separate state structure' with the fact that northern Cyprus was 'controlled by Turkish troops' (S/PV 1975, 1813: 38, 126, 177). The presence of Turkish troops became an important sticking point. This was used as the main reason that the actions of the Turkish-Cypriots could not be justified under the banner of self-determination. In further discussion on 24 February, numerous states argued that reaching 'freely a mutually acceptable political settlement' (S/PV 1975, 1815: 19) was only possible if negotiations were not 'conducted under duress' (S/PV 1975, 1815: 23). The presence of foreign forces on the territory of the Republic of Cyprus (i.e. Turkish troops) meant that the Turkish-Cypriots were trying to use the advantages gained from military victory to impose a settlement. As the UK representative later pointed out, the declaration

> prejudges the intercommunal talks, since the concept of such a State contains elements which, if the Greek-Cypriot side could accept them, would render the intercommunal talks almost superfluous. To that extent, that action represents an attempt to obtain by declaration objectives which, in our view, should properly be the subject of negotiation between the two sides. (S/PV 1975, 1818: 11)

While the fate of Cyprus itself was referenced, much of the justificatory discourse was oriented around the future and setting a precedent. The Bulgarian representative identified the problem.

> If the international community permits this threat to materialise, it may prove to be a most dangerous precedent, particularly for certain non-aligned countries in the vicinity and for more distant countries, with very serious consequences for their independence, sovereignty and territorial integrity. (S/PV 1975, 1813: 126)

For the Cameroonian representative, 'the principle of the non-acquisition of the territory of a State by force should be unambiguously reaffirmed in the present case' because otherwise the case of Cyprus would imply that 'all the small Powers Members of the Organization that wish to live in freedom and independence', might '[fall] prey to the whims and aggression of countries that are militarily and technically better equipped than they are' (S/PV 1975, 1816: 37).

Nonrecognition of the Turkish Republic of Northern Cyprus, 1983

Intercommunal talks between the Greek-Cypriots and Turkish-Cypriots continued sporadically until 1983. In May 1983, the UNGA passed a resolution (37/253) which 'reaffirm[ed] the principle of the inadmissibility of occupation and acquisition of territory by force', deplored unilateral actions that promoted fait accomplis, and called for the immediate withdrawal of occupation troops. Resolution 37/253 also included a clause in which it 'consider[ed] that the *de facto* situation created by the force of arms should not be allowed to influence or in any way affect the solution of the problem of Cyprus'. This demonstrates again the extent to which the results of the use of force were not recognised as valid. The process by which the outcome of the conflict was reached was the key element in the illegality and illegitimacy of the unilateral declaration of a separate administration by the Turkish-Cypriots.

Soon after this UNGA debate and resolution, Denktash told the London *Times* that he saw this latest manifestation of global opposition to his cause as the 'last drop' driving him to seek whatever advantage in negotiations he could. Specifically, he decided to declare an independent state that could seek international recognition (Necatigil 1989: 166). Then, on 15 November 1983, the TRNC was proclaimed by the unanimous vote of the Legislative Assembly of the hitherto TFSC.

The UNSC immediately considered the issue after requests to do so from Cyprus, Greece and the UK. The Cypriot representative, Iacovou, explicitly compared Northern Cyprus to Manchukuo, amongst other examples of 'puppet' regimes that were 'the fruits of aggression' and argued that 'Situations resulting from invasion and occupation should not and could not be recognised (S/PV 1983, 2497: 38).

These themes were repeated and not challenged by third-party states, except Pakistan. In a typical speech, the Nicaraguan representative claimed the root cause of the Cyprus conflict was 'violation of article 2(4) of the United Nations Charter', and that the UDI by the Turkish-Cypriot leadership was a violation of the principle that 'the de facto situation created by force can have no influence or effect on the political solution'. He only provided one clear substantive reason why condemnation and nonrecognition would be useful: the setting of precedent and the maintenance of international law: 'We must not permit the status of Cyprus as a unified and an independent State

142

to be altered unilaterally. To do so would be an extremely danger-ous precedent.' The UDI 'must not have any international legal effect whatsoever' (S/PV 1983, 2498: 48).

Most other states followed the line of Nicaragua and made links to nonaggression. The Guyanan representative made the goal of the resolu-tion under consideration (341) clear:

> The Security Council has an obligation to discourage the use of force in international relations. This Council must be unequivocal in its rejection of international lawlessness. It must so respond that military adventurism, intervention, and occupation are clearly seen as unacceptable and as unlaw-ful practices, and peaceful settlement is more frequently and more actively pursued. (S/PV 1983, 2500: 3)

Here the concern is with the existence of a norm. He is saying that the UNSC's actions are oriented towards ensuring the continuance of the norm or rule against aggression.

Backstage discussion of the UK's draft resolution included a call for a stronger condemnation of Turkey's actions in 1974 as 'foreign aggression'. Resisting this, the British agreed to call it 'legally invalid' (Bernstein 1983). According to Sir John Thomson, the UK ambassador to the UN who wrote and negotiated both UNSC resolutions 541 and 550, the UDI was opposed because 'it looked as if it was breaking the only means that all of us saw of ever getting a solution to this problem'.[20] The problem was getting a settlement without restarting a war or acquiescing to the Turkish-Cypriot fait accompli backed by Turkish troops. Thomson also pointed to a ten-sion between wanting to make the resolution 'stronger' (i.e. more condem-natory of Turkey and the Turkish-Cypriots) and wanting to avoid giving the Turkish-Cypriots a reason to reject the entire UN-based peace process driven by the Secretary General Perez de Cuellar. But the UDI had to be resisted as otherwise a peaceful settlement would not have been possible. A peaceful settlement was important because once one use of force was seen as profitable, all the parties involved, including Greece and Turkey, would try to use force to 'resolve' the situation.

Conclusion UN section

Both the public and private terms of debate in UNSC and UNGA discus-sions revolved around whether Turkey's intervention in Cyprus should be opposed as a norm violation. Once Turkey dissolved the Geneva peace negotiations in order to occupy over a third of the island, this meaning was settled upon. A major theme of the justifications for the condemnations of Turkey and the nonrecognition of a Turkish-Cypriot state was that the norm of nonaggression was under threat and should be maintained. Another central theme was the role of the continued occupation of Cyprus by Turkish troops in whether negotiations could be represented as being free or under duress.

CONCLUSION

The TRNC has occupied a legal limbo for over thirty years. It has remained unrecognised throughout vast changes in the international environment and the domestic political and economic situations of both Greek and Turkish Cypriots as well as the US and the guarantor states of Greece, Turkey and the UK. Almost the only constant has been the circumstances surrounding the birth of the Turkish-Cypriot state, and the continued presence of Turkish troops on its soil. The case of the nonrecognition of the TRNC demonstrates the applicability and utility of the rule maintenance model. The five stages, from rule violation to absence of effective sanctions to uncertainty over the rule, to symbolic sanctions aimed at maintaining the rule, to the reestablishment of the rule, play out in this case and allow us to account for the contrived and artificial situation of the international community's rhetoric adherence to the fiction of a united Cyprus in the face of decades of de facto governance. Once again, paying attention to norm dynamics and the institutional context of nonrecognition provides vital insights into decision making. IR theories that ignore the need to reproduce norms and rules will fail to explain a wide range of international phenomena.

Alternative explanations of nonrecognition in this case mostly fare poorly. Few involved in the nonrecognition decision thought that the symbolic act would impose such costs on Turkey that it would change its course, or that other states would tremble at the prospect of facing a similar sanction in the future. Coercion or signalling resolve are not relevant here. While emotions ran high for some, such as James Callaghan, actors from outside the island were not blinded by spite or even acting purely out of a sense of the rightness of the sanction. Instead, prospective nonrecognition of a Turkish-Cypriot state was used to indicate the attitude of the international community towards Turkey's (second) use of force on Cyprus. Then, once a de facto entity had been established via the invasion, that entity was not opposed because of the impact of that de facto situation on the private interests of third-party states. The dominant sentiment was that the shape of the actual outcome was irrelevant; the process by which it was reached was the crucial point. The

TRNC was the fruit of aggression and so could not be allowed to enter the ranks of the international community.

There was a complicating factor. US domestic politics during the crisis lends initial plausibility to the claim that nonrecognition was driven by a desire to avoid domestic opprobrium. The prominent role of the 'Greek lobby' and the hijacking of foreign policy by Congress destroys the image of an autonomous foreign secretary steering the ship of state and making decisions based on the social conventions of international society. And yet Kissinger and Ford did not avoid a backlash; they suffered and bitterly opposed Congress on the arms embargo. At the least, then, nonrecognition was driven by a desire to remain in step with other states, and there is a strong case to be made that an important justification was to avoid 'condoning' Turkey's second invasion. The key counterfactual here is what Kissinger would have done had Congress not forced through economic sanctions against his wishes. It is highly implausible that he alone of all states would have recognised the TRNC. Even in the 1980s when the Reagan administration abstained from a UNSC resolution condemning Turkish recognition of the TRNC, in order to maintain US–Turkish relations, that same administration full-throatedly rejected the TRNC's declaration of independence and reaffirmed with the rest the inadmissibility of conquest.

The utility of the model in accounting for nonrecognition in the Cyprus case suggests that the processes it highlights are recurrent in international politics and especially in the use of symbolic sanctions like nonrecognition. The Cyprus case is also useful as it provides some suggestions as to sources of variation. The model identifies the social construction of the situation as a norm violation as a crucial step in the process leading to rule maintenance. If, however, something were to disrupt the construction of the use of force as a case of aggression, then rule maintenance would not be necessary. An important feature of this construction appears to be the extent to which an alternative justification for the use of force is publicly available and how believable it is. In the Cyprus case, the first Turkish invasion of the island was seen to be justified by the violent coup and subsequent attacks on Turkish-Cypriots, as well as the agreement from 1960 that authorised the guarantor states to use force in some situations. These alternative justifications meant that the Turkish invasion was ambiguous enough that few at the UN treated it as aggression. After Operation Attila and the occupation of a third of the island the alternative justifications were no longer seen as credible. However, a lot of significance was placed on the presence of Turkish troops. Had Turkey withdrawn from Cyprus, say under guarantees by UNFICYP to protect the Turkish-Cypriots, the status of the TRNC as the fruits of aggression would have been harder to sustain. Had the two communities come to an agreement, Turkey's intervention would have achieved its goals but without challenging the norm against aggression and so rule maintenance would have been unnecessary. The next case, the emergence of Bangladesh, provides more insight into these dynamics.

NOTES

1. This overview draws on several secondary sources: Asmussen 2008, Dodd 2010 and Mirbagheri 1998.
2. Dodd (2010) provides an overview of the conflict, covering the period from 1878 to 2004, although there is understandably little room for sustained analysis of particular episodes.
3. Documents on British Policy Overseas (DBPO). Referenced with the series, volume, and document number.
4. FCO refers to the Foreign and Commonwealth Office Archives. Referenced with the piece reference.
5. WO refers to the War Office and Ministry of Defence Archives. Referenced with piece reference.
6. Treaty of Guarantee, 1960, <http://www.mfa.gov.tr/treaty-concerning-the-establishment-of-the-republic-of-cyprus.en.mfa> (last accessed 4 August 2017).
7. That is, a short memorandum of conversation.
8. Enosis was the Greek word used to indicate union of the section of Cyprus ruled by Greek-Cypriots with Greece. Here double Enosis is used to mean the union of both sections of Cyprus with their respective ethnic homelands.
9. 'Britain, former ruler of Cyprus, launches campaign to end crisis', *Washington Post*, 17 November 1983.
10. House of Lords Debates (HL Deb). Referenced with date, volume, and column number.
11. House of Commons Debates (HC Deb). Referenced with date, volume, and column number.
12. This report was compiled by the UK House of Commons Foreign Affairs Select Committee on Cyprus.
13. Foreign Relations of the United States (FRUS). Referenced with the year and volume number, followed by the document number.
14. Digital National Security Archive. Referenced with document number.
15. Denktash apparently viewed the UDI as a bargaining chip in the latest round of intercommunal negotiations (Necatigil 1989: 166).
16. US Congressional Record, Senate (CRS). Referenced with date and paragraph number.
17. US Congressional Record, House of Representatives (CRH). Referenced with date and paragraph number.
18. 'Turkish land grab in Cyprus, *The New York Times*, 16 November 1983.
19. S/PV (S: Security Council and PV: *procès-verbal*) refers to the United Nations Security Council Official Record. Referenced with year, meeting and paragraph number.
20. Interview conducted 27 February 2012.

CHAPTER FIVE

The independence of Bangladesh

INTRODUCTION

In this chapter, I analyse the crisis surrounding the Indian invasion of East Pakistan in 1971 and the subsequent recognition of East Pakistan as the new state of Bangladesh in 1972. Certain important features of this crisis are the same as other cases. One state used premeditated military force against the army of a neighbouring state. The victorious invader then occupied a portion of the territory of the neighbouring state and supported the creation of an alternative government recognising it as ruling a new state. This description could be used of the Japanese invasion of Manchuria and the Turkish invasion of Cyprus. However, in the Bangladesh case, the new state was recognised by most states and eventually the UN accepted Bangladesh as a member nation.

The primary question for this case is why actors felt that recognition of Bangladesh would not entail the unravelling of the norm of nonaggression. Even though India's use of force did achieve the political goals of her leadership, including the dissolution of her primary rival as well as the return of millions of refugees to Bangladesh, other actors did not collectively condemn India. They also did not refuse to accord legitimacy and legality to the results of that use of force. In this chapter I analyse the actions and statements of key decision makers to find out what they were doing, thinking and saying about the recognition of Bangladesh.

HISTORICAL OVERVIEW

In 1970, Pakistan was slated to hold its first democratic elections since independence from Britain and partition from India in 1947. The elections were delayed due to a devastating cyclone in East Pakistan in November, but were held in December 1970. West Pakistan, the traditional seat of political power, was dominated by Zulfikar Ali Bhutto's Pakistan Peoples Party, who won 81 of 138 parliamentary seats in the western region (out of a national total of 307). However, East Pakistan overwhelmingly favoured Awami League candidates: 167 of 169 eastern seats were taken by Sheikh Mujib-ur Rahman's Bengali nationalist party. The Awami League technically had a majority of seats in the parliament, but they were prevented from forming a government by existing ruler President General Yahya Khan, who also controlled the military, in collusion with Bhutto. Negotiations ended in a stalemate and a repressive crackdown on Bengali political opposition by West Pakistani armed forces starting in March 1971. The pacification operation resulted in widespread killings and a massive outpouring of refugees, especially of Bengali Hindus, across the border into Indian Bengal. In April, the Awami League issued a declaration of independence in an attempt to form a new state of Bangladesh. This was initially ignored internationally. Soon, however, the amount of refugees in India was being estimated to be in the millions and Indira Gandhi, prime minister of India, decided to prepare for a military intervention into East Pakistan (Kux 1993: 290). As part of this, she supplied and trained an impromptu paramilitary force, called the Mukti Bahini (Liberation Army), in guerrilla campaigns against the Pakistani military (Sisson and Rose 1990: 185–93). As more evidence of West Pakistan's lethal activities emerged, international opinion turned against Yahya Khan's regime; numerous states condemned the atrocities and the US House of Representatives suspended all aid to Pakistan in August (Kux 2001: 195). Looking for ways to shield India from the diplomatic fallout of unilateral military action, Gandhi then signed the Indo-Soviet Treaty of Peace, Friendship, and Cooperation with the USSR. The treaty convinced US President Richard Nixon and his National Security Advisor Dr Henry Kissinger that the situation in the subcontinent had wide-ranging global geopolitical implications (Kissinger 1979: 913).

In October, increasing its support of the Mukti Bahini, the Indian Army began launching artillery strikes and hit and run attacks into East Pakistan. By late November, Indian units were holding their positions well inside East Pakistan's territory (Sisson and Rose 1990: 213). According to Indian Army Chief General Sam Manekshaw, India planned to launch an all-out assault on East Pakistan on 4 December 1971 (Kux 2001: 199) However, unwilling to suffer the undeclared attacks any longer, Pakistan struck major Indian air bases in north-western India on 3 December, leading India to declare war in self-defence. On 5 December, the USSR vetoed two UNSC resolutions calling for a ceasefire and a withdrawal to internationally recognised borders, and India recognised the Bangladesh government. Stalemate in the UNSC led to the near-unanimous (104 to 11 with 10 abstentions) UNGA resolution 2793, which duplicated the resolutions vetoed by the USSR in the UNSC. Indian military success continued as the USSR vetoed another UNSC resolution on 13 December and the next day, Pakistani forces in East Pakistan proposed a ceasefire which India accepted.

After the end of the war, the Bangladeshi leader Sheikh Mujib publicly welcomed the presence of Indian troops and signed an agreement with India about a timetable for their withdrawal. The Bangladeshi leadership also requested recognition of the status of Bangladesh as a new state. Between 11 January and 14 February 1972, thirty-six states recognised Bangladesh, including the UK, and nine others on 4 February (Keesing's Record of World Events 1972: 25113). The US did not recognise Bangladesh until 4 April, several weeks after President Nixon had completed his trip to the People's Republic of China (PRC), re-establishing relations between the two countries after a diplomatic freeze going back to the end of the Chinese Civil War in 1949. Bangladesh applied for UN membership later that year, but a UNSC resolution admitting the new state was vetoed by China in August. Bangladesh was admitted to the UN in 1974.

THEORETICAL DISCUSSION

The events of this case show that one of the features of the practice of nonrecognition of aggressive gain, then, is that it appears to be inconsistently applied. In particular, there are cases where it seems that aggression[1] occurred, the aggressor state achieved some of its objectives and yet there was no collective nonrecognition of those results of the use of force.

Evidence from analysis of the case of the recognition of Bangladesh demonstrates that the rhetorical trope of the illegitimacy of aggressive gain was used by several actors in the crisis to bolster their positions. Pakistani leaders, particularly Zulfikar Ali Bhutto, argued against recognition of Bangladesh, both publicly and privately, on the basis that such an act would constitute the legitimation of aggression. Similarly, the newly admitted state of the PRC condemned India's invasion as aggression. China also vetoed the admission of Bangladesh to the UN for several years after widespread bilateral recognition had taken place, justifying its action in terms of the illegitimacy of aggressive gain. Other states were also concerned about the effects of allowing, or seeming to allow, a state to profit from the use of force by recognising Bangladesh. So, even though nonrecognition of aggressive gain did not take place, the rule was still relevant in the crisis.

149

Towards the end of the crisis, India publicly committed to the withdrawal of Indian troops from Bengal. The new Bangladeshi government also approved of the temporary presence of the troops before they were to be withdrawn. These reasons were the most prominent ones given for why recognition of Bangladesh was acceptable even though force had been used to bring about the de facto independence of East Pakistan. This has theoretical implications for arguments about variation in the use of nonrecognition. Rule violations are not self-evident; they are to a considerable extent socially constructed. Some actions that could be construed as rule violations can instead be excused, for example through the provision of some extenuating circumstances or by a redefinition of the implications of the rule. In the discussion over the recognition of Bangladesh as a state, recognition was tied strongly to the withdrawal of Indian occupation troops, as is shown below. It appears that actors external to the crisis were trying to disassociate recognition from approval or legitimation of India's aggression. If nonrecognition of aggressive gain is used as a symbolic sanction for rule maintenance, then in cases where the rule is not under threat, nonrecognition is unnecessary. Apart from India's public commitment to troop withdrawal, there were other justifications given by actors in the crisis for why the results of India's use of force should not be resisted as illegitimate. The democratic election of the Awami League, which became the ruling party in Bangladesh, in the Pakistani elections of December 1970, and the fact that the Awami League declared Bangladesh independent *before* India's intervention undercut the potential illegitimacy of India's military intervention. The military repression of Bengalis in East Pakistan from March 1971 by West Pakistani forces was also occasionally mentioned. When India denied that they pursued territorial aggrandisement and they committed to withdrawing their troops from Bangladesh, these were held to be sufficient reasons that the rule against aggression was not under threat. The contrast with the Turkish invasion of Cyprus is instructive. As shown in Chapter 4, despite repeated demands from the UN and other states, Turkey refused to withdraw troops from the island or even reduce troop levels without major concessions in negotiations with the Greek-Cypriots. The Turkish-Cypriot leaders were elected and held referenda on major decisions like declaring the independence of the TRNC. Unlike Bangladesh, however, these declarations came only after the use of force by an outside power.

There are other potential sources of variation that could explain the difference in outcomes between the cases of widespread nonrecognition and the Bangladesh case. Unlike Manchukuo and the TRNC, Bangladesh was a large state, with a population of around 70 million at the time. Policymakers privately referred to the large population of East Pakistan before India's use of force as a reason why the eventual independence of Bangladesh was 'inevitable'. However, this was not cited in public, or in private government-to-government communications, as a justification for recognition of Bangladesh after India's invasion. Similarly, the geographical separation of West Pakistan from East Pakistan (they are on opposite sides of India's territory) seems in the abstract that it might make separate statehood more reasonable, but this was not explicitly used as a reason why recognition of Bangladesh was justifiable.[2]

NIXON, KISSINGER, SUPPORTING PAKISTAN AND OPENING CHINA

Introduction to US section

The South Asia Crisis of 1971 can fruitfully be divided up into three time periods. First was the period between the elections in Pakistan in December 1970 and the outbreak of war in December 1971. India formally declared war on Pakistan on 3 December 1971, but there had been substantial cross-border military operations beginning in October. US action in the first period was characterised by attempts to prevent the outbreak of hostilities. The second period was during the war, through a ceasefire in East Pakistan and a unilateral ceasefire by India on the western front, up until 21 December when the UNSC passed resolution 307. During this period the US concentrated on condemning India for its aggression and trying to formulate a UNSC resolution that would call for a withdrawal of forces back to status quo international borders. The third period concerns the official recognition of Bangladesh as a sovereign state. The US recognised Bangladesh on 5 April 1972 but UN membership was vetoed by China (PRC) on 25 August and it was not until September 1974 that Bangladesh was formally admitted to the UN, although it was given membership in many specialised UN agencies prior to that.

The two most important formulators of foreign policy during the Bangladesh Crisis were President Richard Nixon and his assistant for national security affairs, Dr Henry Kissinger (Kissinger 1979). Nixon and Kissinger had a grand foreign policy plan that involved initiating relations between the US and the PRC. Previously, after the Chinese revolution ended in 1949, the US had continued to support the Guomindang, or Nationalist Party, after it retreated to the island of Taiwan in virtual defeat. Since then, the US had not recognised the PRC as the

151

legitimate ruler of China and did not conduct regular diplomatic relations with the communist state. Kissinger and Nixon viewed the opening of relations as a potential foreign policy public relations bonanza, as well as a way to shift the global balance of power away from the USSR and towards the US. This is generally referred to as a case of Triangular Diplomacy (Hanhimaki 2004). In Kissinger's memoirs (1979), he underlines the importance of US actions in the Bangladesh crisis in terms of how they would affect the US relationship with China, with a particular view to protecting the trip to China in 1972. It is also clear from contemporary records that Kissinger, and Nixon although it often seems that Nixon took his cues from Kissinger in this respect, was especially concerned with the impact of actions in the crisis on wider geopolitical goals. This is a consensus position in the secondary literature (e.g. Kux 1993, 2001; Hanhimaki 2004). Even though others in the administration were oblivious to these concerns (the State Department did not know about the proposed China trip for much of the crisis), these linkages were frequently cited by both Nixon and Kissinger in their discussions on policy towards India and Pakistan.

All indications are that the US administration, even Nixon and Kissinger who were actively supporting Pakistan (i.e. West Pakistan) during the crisis, viewed independence or at least substantial political autonomy for East Pakistan as inevitable. Conflict management measures, such as economic and diplomatic sanctions, were justified by a variety of reasons. The US used the withdrawal of economic aid to deter India from initiating hostilities (Kux 1993: 302). Diplomatic sanctions before and during the early part of the war were not justified in terms of specific deterrence (as I will show in the more detailed discussion below). The practical utility of sanctions, in terms of deterrence, was frequently questioned. Kissinger linked them with signalling generalised resolve. He often said that a particular policy option was needed or the US would appear weak, or that other states would see what the US did as setting a behavioural precedent. One particularly high-profile action that Kissinger took in order to demonstrate resolve, that is, an unwillingness to back down, was the dispatch of an aircraft carrier group to the Bay of Bengal. Nixon justified actions in multiple terms during the war, but the motivation that was cited most frequently by far for a public condemnation of India's aggression was a value-rational opposition to aggression as 'evil'.

Maintaining the international rule against aggression was repeatedly cited explicitly by key decision makers as a reason for taking certain actions during the crisis. In particular, decision makers argued against both a UNSC resolution that called for or acknowledged a transfer of authority from Pakistan to Bangladesh, and official US recognition of Bangladesh, on the basis that these actions would legitimise aggression. For example, Kissinger railed against a potential clause in UNSC resolution 307 advocating the transfer of authority to Bangladesh in exactly these terms. In fact, this is the only reason he gives. This is in spite of his advocacy of a 'political settlement' that involved complete Bangladesh independence. The desire to avoid appearing to bless or reward aggression was also relevant in two ways to US recognition of Bangladesh. First, Kissinger cited it directly as one reason of three to delay recognition. Second, members of the administration were working on the assumption that relations with the Chinese government were sensitive to this issue because the Chinese were so publicly and consistently opposed to legitimising aggression.

Views on an independent Bangladesh

US decision makers frequently expressed the view that the political independence of East Pakistan or Bangladesh was inevitable. This position was a consistent feature of discussions amongst Nixon, Kissinger and others in the Nixon administration throughout the crisis, starting from well before the war began. As early as March 1971, a National Security Council (NSC) memo recommended immediate recognition of Bangladesh if it were to secede, even if this secession were contested by West Pakistan or India (FRUS 1969–76 E-7: 123).[3] The members of the Washington Special Action Group (WSAG; an advisory group set up by Kissinger to deal with crises) were agreed on 26 March that in practical terms independence for Bangladesh would come 'fairly quickly' but that the US should 'drag its feet' on recognition so that it could not be blamed for breaking up the country (FRUS 1969–76 XI: 11).

Two weeks later, in the midst of the fighting and before the Pakistan forces in the East had accepted a ceasefire, Nixon declared 'The partition of Pakistan is a fact' (FRUS 1969–76 XI: 168). After military action had ceased in East Pakistan, Nixon and Kissinger were concerned with the integrity of West Pakistan as a unit but, despite delaying recognition of Bangladesh until April 1972, remained convinced that the independence of Bangladesh from Pakistan was inevitable.

Kissinger was not opposed to the goals of the Indians, including autonomy for Bangladesh, but he was objecting to the use of force in attaining them: 'If they would cooperate with us we could work with them on 90% of their problems, like releasing Mujibur or attaining some degree of autonomy for Bangla Desh, and these steps would lead eventually to their getting it all' (FRUS 1969–76 XI: 159).

In late November, Kissinger summed up the attitude of the administration towards the independence of Bangladesh:

Mr. Sisco:	[Yahya] has three options: do it directly with Mujib; do it through the UN; don't do it at all. If East and West Pakistan can't get together, the U.S. can live with an independent East Pakistan.
Mr. Kissinger:	We don't give a damn. (FRUS 1969–76 XI: 198)

Economic sanctions and deterrence

Prior to the outbreak of war between India and Pakistan, the US was engaged in efforts to prevent the use of force. Some of these efforts involved threats designed to deter one side from initiating hostilities. Economic sanctions were prominent in this regard. For example, both Nixon and Kissinger seemed to think that using the leverage of the threatened cut-off of aid would deter the Indians from initiating hostilities against East Pakistan. In October, before Indian armed forces started conducting take and hold actions across the border in Bengal, Kissinger asked:

Dr. Kissinger:	Let's get this completely clear. Do the Indians really understand that we will cut off aid if they go to war?
Mr. Van Hollen:	Yes, the Secretary (of State) told them that.
Dr. Kissinger:	This is of the utmost importance. The Indians must understand that we mean it. The President has said so. In fact, he tells me every day. Are you sure the Indians got the message? (FRUS 1969–76 XI: 159)

Diplomatic sanctions: 'I think we need some symbolism' (Nixon)

When managing the conflict, apart from economic sanctions, the primary measures considered were a UNSC resolution and the explicit condemnation of one side as an aggressor. Attitudes towards these two varied but at almost no time was there any sense that either of these two actions would have an effect on the prospects for peace. The motivation behind these sanctions was thus not specific deterrence.

In a WSAG meeting on 12 November 1971 (FRUS 1969–76 XI: 183), Kissinger and Sisco, Assistant Secretary of State for Near Eastern and South Asian Affairs, were discussing what to do 'if war breaks out'. Sisco suggested that the US 'move into the UN Security Council and seek some sort of restraining order'. Perhaps surprisingly, he immediately declared, 'I am under no illusion about the practical effect of such a resolution or that it will be an easy exercise.' Given that such a resolution would be both unhelpful and difficult to get, what could be Sisco's reason for performing this action? Initially he says that he thinks 'it is important to go public before the balloon goes up' and that it is a 'preempting move'. However, Kissinger then asked him to elaborate:

Dr. Kissinger:	What would be the operational significance of a UN resolution?
Mr. Sisco:	I don't overestimate the significance. Of course it can't prevent a war.
Dr. Kissinger:	What about timing? At what point would we say we have made all the moves?
Mr. Sisco:	That could come later.
Dr. Kissinger:	A Security Council resolution doesn't do a damned thing. What could it do?
Mr. Sisco:	It would draw world attention to the situation, expose the facts, including what is happening militarily, and clarify where the responsibility lies.

Here, the posited function of a UNSC resolution calling for a ceasefire is not to bring the ceasefire about. Both Kissinger and Sisco hold the practical effect to be very low. In fact, Sisco goes on to say that 'the practical result of SC debate is likely to be nil in terms of practical deterrence'. However, clarifying where the responsibility lies is a crucial task if actors are to come to a judgement over whether and how rules are being broken. Christopher Van Hollen, deputy to Sisco, reiterated this justification, saying that the resolution would mean that, 'The public would be made aware that it is Indian forces which are continually crossing an international border.' This statement only makes sense if made against a background where the cross-border use of force is against the rules, or illegitimate. The intended purpose of a UN resolution here is to name the rule-breaker.

Kissinger's scepticism over the use of a SC resolution seems to have conditioned Sisco's policy advice. On 22 November, Sisco justifies a move to the UN by saying there are two purposes to it. One is to involve the UN in offering good offices for mediation. The other is to 'try to get some form of restraining order from the Security Council which hopefully would arrest or slow down further deterioration of the situation' (FRUS 1969–76 XI: 194). This is inconsistent with his assertions a week earlier of the practical uselessness of such a restraining order (FRUS 1969–76 XI: 194). Nixon had a similar mixed attitude. In a meeting on 24 November, after Rogers had discussed the symbolic role of the UN, Nixon was torn between his impulse to punish India and the advice given to him that it would not be effective at deterring India:

Nixon: Now I know it can be said that it won't do any good, and we
          don't have any leverage, and it's only symbolic and the rest. But
          on the other hand, I want you to look into what we could do
          that is symbolic because I think we need some symbolism . . .
          But if there's a breakout of war, you can forget United States aid
          to India. And I feel that we ought to do something symbolic, I
          really feel it.
Rogers: Yeah, there's no problem there.
Nixon: That I think something symbolic might have an effect, might
          have an effect, on restraining India. That – I don't know. Many
          people think it won't? (FRUS 1969–76 E-7: 156)

Diplomatic sanctions: Nixon and condemning India

Although he did not say this directly to Nixon, Rogers in fact did think
that something symbolic, like a condemnation of India, would have an
effect, but not the one Nixon was looking for. On the day that India formally declared war, Rogers argued with Kissinger about Nixon's desire
to publicly condemn India.

K: The President does want to act. Wants to take a line to condemn the
      Indians.
R: It's not a matter of condemning or blaming. It's trying to stop it. If we
      blame India a general war will break out.
K: In the subcontinent.
R: We are short-sighted if we think our general approach is castigating
      India. It's to bring a ceasefire.
K: And withdrawal.
R: If we say let's condemn India, what does that do? We are trying to bring
      about ceasefire.
K: That's what we want to do but in order to get that we have to make
      clear who started action. (FRUS 1969–76 E-7: 158)

Here Rogers is worrying that condemnation will increase tensions
and make a ceasefire harder to broker. However, along with Kissinger,
he does seem to agree that declaring the rule-breaker is an important
action. This concern with 'naming and shaming' is also present in the
cases of Manchuria and Cyprus. Such a concern is consistent with the
rule maintenance model. Clarifying blame and trying to reduce uncertainty over whether the use of force is legitimate or illegitimate is a
major concern of actors in all of the cases studied in the book. Rogers'
position in the above quotation is that this should be done in the collective forum of the UNSC. Again, this is consistent with a need to create

an intersubjective meaning, or common knowledge of the attitudes of state representatives.

By the time that war was formally declared, Kissinger had conceived of a new reason for pressing ahead with action through the UN, changing US domestic public opinion.

Dr. Kissinger: It's a question of whether we want a fan-dance or want to position ourselves. We want the resolution tabled. We know it won't come out as it goes in. Having bitched around for the last two weeks, the only thing we want now is to make our position clear. Everyone knows we will end up with Indian occupation of East Pakistan. It will be interesting to see how all those people who were so horrified at what the Paks were doing in East Pakistan react when the Indians take over there. The only thing we want to achieve is to make our position clear. We want that resolution tabled. (FRUS 1969–76 XI: 224)

Even though the end state is Indian occupation of East Pakistan, Kissinger is adamant that the UNSC resolution be put to a vote in order that the US position is made clear. That it is to be made clear to the US public is elaborated upon in a telephone call to Nixon later that day where Nixon, after being informed that there is a full-scale war going on, asks about the UNSC.

HAK: At the Security Council, the Indians and Soviets are going to delay long enough so a resolution cannot be passed. If it was, the Soviets would veto. UN will be impotent. So the Security Council is just a paper exercise— it will get the Post and Times off our backs. And the Libs will be happy that we turned it over to the UN. The damage won't show up for a few years. At the moment we retrench around the world, this proves that countries can get away with brutality. (FRUS 1969–76 XI: 225)

It seems likely here that by saying 'brutality' Kissinger is referring to the Indian invasion in and of itself. This makes more sense given that there is no actual evidence of Indian mistreatment of Bangladeshis (especially compared to the very public and violent West Pakistani repression), and that he is talking about a UN resolution opposing the invasion. Further, Nixon then agrees that UN action is to make the press see the point and 'to talk as though the Indians are the aggressors'.

By 12 December, only two days before Pakistani forces in East Pakistan sought a ceasefire, after there had been several vetoed resolutions in the UNSC and a UNGA resolution, Nixon and Kissinger had a detailed conversation in which they considered returning to the UNSC for another attempt to get a resolution. Nixon is convinced that condemning India as an aggressor will help to build world public opinion against India and that this will undercut India's bargaining position (FRUS 1969–76 E-7: 177. The quotations in the rest of this section are from this document).

> Nixon: —[unclear]. The world opinion thing is going to affect the Indians. We've just got to get, it's got to get out the fact that they've been condemned in the press and that they rejected a majority vote. That's got to be said. Get the word to State and everybody in every statement that India has rejected an overwhelming vote of the General Assembly. That has to be said.

Nixon here seems very concerned with the effect of world opinion on the Indians. This theme is premised on a view of Indians as unusually vulnerable to this kind of pressure.

> Nixon: . . . we're going to make certain diplomatic moves. I don't know what they are, but if this Indian action against the West continues against the overwhelming weight of the world public opinion, then I will have to make a public statement labeling India as the aggressor, as a naked aggressor. . . . You see the thing I feel is that the Indians are susceptible to this world public opinion crap. They're susceptible to it because they have lived on it for so long.

Here Nixon views taking a strong public stand against aggression as efficacious, partly because it will shame India into changing its behaviour. However, there were other considerations. After going over the wording of such a statement with Kissinger, Nixon helpfully outlines his reasoning:

> Nixon: But anyway, what I'm getting at is, now, having said all this, what purpose does this serve to put out something labeling India as—the purpose as I see it, it serves, well it serves three purposes. It helps with our Chinese friends. Second, it puts a little bit of heat on the Russians. Third, it puts some heat on the goddamn Indians.
>
> Kissinger: Right.
>
> Nixon: World opinion. Fourth, it helps us with our own domestic situation here at home, only to the extent that we're taking a beating. I'm not concerned about it.

Nixon's emphasis in the discussions is on the condemnation's effect on India. Kissinger agrees with Nixon's reasons, saying that, 'We have to do a public statement to impress the Russians, to scare the Indians, to take a position with the Chinese.'

Nixon and anti-aggression

In his interactions with other states, whether in person or in official communications, Nixon frequently urged that force not be used to solve the problem. Together with Kissinger, he also was very concerned with shaping public opinion and assumed that calling India an aggressor would be an effective term of condemnation. Kissinger displayed a similar concern with affecting public opinion during the Cyprus crisis. On 11 December he discusses 'the PR side of it', resolving to tell his consultant John Scali

> RN: We ought to hit that very, very hard—this is against the overwhelming weight of world opinion—we happen to have world opinion on our side this time for whatever it is worth—that point should be made and particularly the UN has to be used right to the hilt—everything [that] is done it has got to be with the UN overwhelmingly on our side and India in effect continuing its aggression against the mandate of the UN—I think that is the PR side of it. (FRUS 1969–76 XI: 277)

When discussing the withdrawal of aid from India, he says, 'I don't think the American people want to aid a country that is an aggressor.' However, in the same conversation he also treats India as if they are actually the aggressors. For example,

> P: I don't think even you, Henry, [know] how tough I feel about that aid business. We are not going to aid countries that engage in aggression and then don't do a goddamn thing when we ask them to get out. (FRUS 1969–76 XI: 230)

Here, deterrence is not the issue. For Nixon, India has engaged in aggression and he intends to punish them by cutting that aid. Aggression for Nixon is a 'horrible thing': 'P: . . . we are not going to roll over after they have done this horrible thing. They [We] are not going to roll over and say, "Now, India, everything will be like it was and we'll come help you again."'

Nixon insisted that India being a democracy does not make its use of aggression acceptable. 'Nixon: By God, we just don't do it that way. I mean, it doesn't make, an evil deed is not made good by the form of government that executes the deed' (FRUS 1969–76 E-7: 171).

Kissinger and signalling generalised resolve

During the most intense period of the war, Kissinger, unlike any other figure in the administration, was preoccupied with the effect that US behaviour would have on other states' perceptions of US intentions, specifically in terms of keeping commitments. That is, he was concerned with the effect on the reputation of the US. In particular, he put forward the view that if the US allowed an ally, Pakistan, to be defeated and then dismembered by a state supported by the USSR, then other states would view their alliances with the US as less reliable. Kissinger used this to justify several policies: not voting for a Soviet-sponsored UN resolution, recognising Bangladesh in response to a ceasefire on the border between India and West Pakistan, and, most prominently, sending an aircraft carrier task force from east of the Straits of Malacca into the Bay of Bengal.

However, Nixon was unclear about the logic behind this position and needed an explanation of Kissinger's reasoning behind both resistance to a compromise and the sending of an aircraft carrier into the region.

Nixon: You see those people welcoming the Indian troops when they come in. [unclear]. Now the point is, why is then, Henry, are we going through all this agony?

Kissinger: We're going through this agony to prevent the West Pakistan army from being destroyed. Secondly, to maintain our Chinese arm. Thirdly, to prevent a complete collapse of the world's psychological balance of power, which will be produced if a combination of the Soviet Union and the Soviet armed client state can tackle a not so insignificant country without anybody doing anything.(FRUS 1969–76 E-7: 168; 9 December)

Sisco rather bluntly challenged this sort of linkage, saying, 'I don't see the implication for the rest of the world that you draw' (FRUS 1969–76 XI: 255). In an article published as a response to Kissinger's memoirs, Christopher Van Hollen, Deputy Assistant Secretary of State for Near Eastern and South Asian affairs during the crisis, criticised Kissinger's raising 'the Bangladesh regional crisis to the level of geopolitics' as 'unnecessary and unwise' (Van Hollen 1980: 340).

UNSC resolution 307 and legitimising aggression

A UNSC resolution passed after the fighting had ended could hardly serve as an effective deterrent. During the war, Yahya and the US had pushed for a resolution as they expected that it would come out in Pakistan's favour. After it was clear that East Pakistan had been

160

separated from West Pakistan, there was new concern about the effect of a resolution. Apart from calling for a ceasefire in the West, Kissinger reported in a memo to Nixon that: 'The Pakistanis have shown a new turn of attitude. They now seem to feel that, since East Pakistan is lost, a UN resolution which "legitimises" the Indian seizure may be unacceptable' (FRUS 1969–76 XI: 310).

Kissinger expressed his concern over a resolution which legitimised aggression by calling for the transfer of political authority to Bangladesh, that is, recognising Bangladesh as a legitimate state, to Yuli Vorontsov (a Russian diplomat at the Soviet Embassy in Washington) on 15 December.

> I said I wanted him to know that we would not agree to any resolution that recognised a turnover of authority. There was a question of principle involved. It was bad enough that the United Nations was impotent in the case of military attack; it could not be asked to legitimise it. However, as I pointed out, we were prepared to work in a parallel direction. (FRUS 1969–76 XI: 312)

Kissinger railed against this proposed resolution later the same day in a conversation with Nixon:

> K: Now the Indians are unbelievable. The Indians are demanding the UN agree for the turnover of authority to the Bangla Desh. Now that would make the UN an active participant in aggression. I don't think we can agree to this.
> P: No. (FRUS 1969–76 XI: 315)

Several days later, after India and Pakistan had agreed to a ceasefire and a proposed Soviet resolution had been thrown out of the SC, Kissinger was still complaining that a potential SC resolution 'legitimises aggression' (FRUS 1969–76 XI: 324). The UNSC resolution 307 that was eventually passed on 21 December did not include a clause that called for or acknowledged a transfer of authority to Bangladesh.

It was clear to everyone involved that Bangladesh was going to be an independent state sooner or later, and sooner rather than later. Given this it seems unlikely that the motive for not advocating the transferal of authority to Bangladesh in an SC resolution was preventing Bangladeshi independence. Kissinger here seems primarily concerned with, as he puts it, legitimising military attack. This makes sense if Kissinger viewed the recognition of Bangladeshi authority as creating a precedent, that is, that a state could use military force for political gain. UNSC resolution 307 did not include a call for the transfer of authority. This nonrecognition of Bangladesh in resolution 307 seems to have been motivated within the US administration by a desire to avoid jeopardising the illegality of aggressive gain.

This theme would also be prominent in the justifications put forward for delaying formal US recognition of Bangladesh until April.

Delaying recognition of Bangladesh

After the end of the war, the US government had to face the issue of the recognition of Bangladesh. There had been consideration of this question by the NSC and State since the electoral crisis in early 1971, but the urgency increased as recognition was granted by other states, beginning with India during the war and continuing with the UK on 4 February 1972. Yet the US did not recognise Bangladesh until early April 1972, months after the UK and other countries had done so. What reason could there be for delaying something that was both inevitable and that many other countries had already done? In a 16 February memo to Nixon, Kissinger lays out what he calls the 'three main considerations in delaying our recognition'.

—President Bhutto when he was here in December asked for a month to begin sorting himself out. He has now had almost two months and has himself suggested that we recognise.

—We did not want to move too quickly in blessing the fruits of India's action. However, one could argue now that this is perhaps properly handled in the pace with which we rebuild our relationship with India rather than in our relationship with Bangladesh since our argument is with the Indians rather than the Bengalis. In any case, Indian troops are scheduled to be withdrawn by March 25.

—Having told the Chinese at earlier steps how we planned to proceed and having cooperated through the crisis at the United Nations, we judged that it would be appropriate to explain our thinking to the Chinese before changing our course, especially since your trip was so close. (FRUS 1969–76 E-7: 396)

The third argument is a complex one. Nixon and Kissinger were very concerned with China's attitude towards their actions throughout the crisis. In a secret meeting between Kissinger and China's ambassador to the UN Huang Hua during the war, Hua made China's position on recognition through the UN very clear:

Ambassador Huang: In fact, it means legalizing of the new refurbishment of another Manchukuo, that is, to give it legal status through the UN, or rather through the modalities of the UN. This goes against the desires of the people in Pakistan, against the desires of the peoples of the world that was expressed in the voting of the General Assembly on this issue. (FRUS 1969–76 XI: 274)

Delaying recognition of Bangladesh until after Nixon's trip to China was partly based on the reasoning that the Chinese might object to it and hence that this might endanger the trip. Kissinger commented that he wanted 'to be sure that a move towards recognition doesn't jeopardise a larger objective with China' (FRUS 1969–76 E-7: 210). The NSC staff asserted that 'the new US relationship with China requires that the US not appear to foresake Pakistan or reward India for its recent aggression' (FRUS 1969–76 E-7: 207). Here, relations with China are a reason for not appearing to reward aggression.

The second reason for delaying recognition is that it would constitute 'blessing the fruits of India's action' (FRUS 1969–76 E-7: 396). Kissinger is again worried that recognition would involve the legitimisation of aggression. However, he provides two reasons that recognition would not actually do this. One is that withholding recognition from Bangladesh would hurt Bangladesh and not India, so instead action that hurts or appears to hurt India should be used. The other is that if Indian troops are withdrawn across the border, recognition will not bless Indian aggression. This issue of troop withdrawal was of widespread concern in the administration. The NSC linked 'Resumption of normal programs in India' with 'withdrawal of Indian forces on both eastern and western fronts' and 'withdrawal from East Bengal' with 'recognizing Bangladesh since its government might well be considered not in control as long as Indian occupation continues' (FRUS 1969–76 E-7: 207). Director of the CIA Richard Helms also raised concern over recognition while Bangladesh was occupied by Indian troops.

> Mr. Helms: I would like to mention one thing right away about recognition. Seventeen countries now recognise Bangladesh, and it looks as though fourteen more are getting ready to do so. I think we must ask ourselves if the U.S. really wants to recognise Bangladesh while Indian troops in effect occupy the country. (FRUS 1969–76 E-7: 220)

The relevance and irrelevance of domestic audiences

Nixon and Kissinger did not make a significant effort to appeal to domestic public opinion during the crisis through their foreign policy actions. While their conversations display much concern with public opinion, their attitude is always about how to shape it with their own propaganda. There is no indication that any of their foreign policy actions were taken with a view to reacting to pressure specifically concerning the condemnation of India as an aggressor or recognition of Bangladesh. In contrast to the Cyprus case, there were no ethnic pressure groups that mobilised the press and members of Congress to advocate for one particular side in the crisis. For the bulk of the crisis, at least until it became publicly clear that India was using force in East Pakistan, Nixon and Kissinger stood relatively isolated both from opinion in the press and their own State Department in their pro-Pakistan position. Kux reports that a poll showed that public opinion in the US was 'two to one against administration policy' (1993: 302). However, Harris polls taken after the war in late 1971 and early 1972 show a more complicated picture (Harris 1972). By 42 per cent for to 16 per cent against, the public agreed with the proposition that 'India was wrong to invade another country, East Pakistan, no matter how wrongly West Pakistan may have been in the way it ruled East Pakistan.' This indicates the extent of the public opposition to aggression. At the same time, 55 per cent for to 5 per cent against said 'the people of East Pakistan should rule their own country, so their getting their independence is a good thing'. One question asked was which country, India or Pakistan, respondents felt more sympathy for. India received 14 per cent of the vote, Pakistan 23 per cent and the rest answered no preference. Another question focused on Nixon's performance, asking respondents what their view was on the president's handling of the war. Of the voting, 24 per cent said not sure, 23 per cent said poor, 25 per cent said fair, 23 per cent said pretty good and 5 per cent said don't know/non-response. Generally, there was high levels of ignorance or ambivalence, demonstrating that much of the American public did not know or care about the crisis.

The force of the domestic audience conjecture is that domestic constituencies demand action in pursuit of their goals and decision makers fear domestic political repercussions if they do not at least appear to perform some such act. This does not characterise Nixon and Kissinger's attitudes. Despite relatively strong and widespread condemnation in the media of their refusal to take action against the repression in East Pakistan, they maintained what was described as a pro-Pakistan position throughout.

Conclusion of US section

US decision makers viewed Bangladeshi independence as likely or inevitable long before India invaded East Pakistan. They used economic sanctions to try and deter India from using force, and viewed diplomatic sanctions, like UN resolutions condemning India, as useless for deterrence purposes. Even so, Nixon was anxious to condemn India as an aggressor. He justified this both strategically for building support for Pakistan but also apparently genuinely from a sense of military aggression as illegitimate. Kissinger was primarily concerned with how US actions appeared in a geopolitical sense to China and to other states in general. However, he opposed the inclusion in UN resolution 307 of the advocacy of the transfer of political authority to the Awami League because it would legitimise aggression. He also justified delaying recognition of Bangladesh until the act would not appear to bless the fruits of India's action. He saw the withdrawal of Indian troops from Bangladesh as removing this concern. Domestic audiences were largely irrelevant to Nixon and Kissinger's decisions surrounding the recognition of Bangladesh.

BRITISH 'NORMAL CRITERIA' AND TRADING INTERESTS

Introduction to UK section

The British decision not only to recognise Bangladesh, but to recognise early, was justified primarily in terms of three issues: the fulfilment of international legal criteria for recognition; British trading interests in East Pakistan; and the avoidance of retaliation by West Pakistan. Underlying the decision making was a complete absence of any belief or attitude that India's actions had been an instance of aggression, the illegitimate use of force or norm-breaking in general. This is notably different from the attitude of Nixon, and to some extent Kissinger, in the US. Whereas Nixon frequently expressed concern over the Indian use of force, explicitly using the term 'aggression' to describe it, British decision makers did not use this word, and did not treat the use of force as illegitimate. It is important to note here that this is another reminder of the non-essentialist nature of 'aggression'; rather than being a fact about an action (i.e. it is not a natural kind [Hacking 1999]), aggression is a concept that actors apply to an action. In cases where there are prominent alternative characterisations, like this case, different actors have different reactions. A key part of the rule maintenance model is the contestation of critical descriptions or framings. Indeed, as I show below, British government actors actively tried to legitimate India's military intervention to other actors. The terms of this legitimation centred on the withdrawal of Indian troops from the new state of Bangladesh, and the absence of territorial aggrandisement or aggressive gain.

165

The British referral to the withdrawal of Indian troops as an important factor in the timing of recognition implies that had the Bangladesh authorities not publicly accepted the Indian Army and called for a time-table for their withdrawal, agreed to by Prime Minister Gandhi, then recognition would have been constrained. There were several reasons that deflected the charge of territorial aggrandisement by India: the violent repression by the West Pakistanis; the overwhelming electoral victory by the Awami League; and the acceptance of the Indian troop presence as temporary, both by the Bangladesh administration and by the UK.

The main actors in the UK during the Bangladesh crisis were Prime Minister Edward Heath, Foreign Secretary Alec Douglas-Home, and various foreign office civil servants from the South Asia Division.

Legal requirements

In general, the UK government used international legal criteria in deciding whether to recognise the Bangladesh administration and especially when to do so. In an analysis of the reasoning behind the UK's recognition decision, Musson writes that 'the principle' of whether to recognise 'rested almost entirely on the fulfilment of international criteria' (2008: 139). These were not the only considerations, but they were the most frequently stated. These criteria, as interpreted by the British government, were laid out in numerous briefing memos:

> The British Government's criteria for recognising a new State are that it should have achieved its independent position with a reasonable prospect of permanency.
>
> The view of the British Government is that a revolutionary government is entitled to de jure recognition as the Government of the State as soon as it may fairly be held to enjoy, with a reasonable prospect of permanency, the obedience of the mass of the population and the effective control of much of the greater part of the national territory. (Briefing notes for press conference, FCO 37/902)[4]

In discussions with other states, British diplomats consistently referred to 'normal criteria', which meant the international legal criteria. For example, in a meeting with the German ambassador to the UK on 31 December 1971, the Permanent Under Secretary of State said that the normal criteria applied 'and that the presence of large numbers of Indian troops in East Bengal complicated the situation at the present time' (memo by Daunt FCO 37/902). Stanley Tomlinson (South Asian Department) informed the Vietnamese ambassador that recognition 'would not be feasible while the maintenance of order depended on the presence of the Indian Army' (memo 5 January 1972, FCO 37/1019). By 18 January 1972, Tomlinson was telling the Yugoslavian ambassador that recognition could go ahead because

> It seemed to us that the normal criteria for recognition were just about fulfilled and we did not regard the presence of Indian troops, particularly given what had been said in public by Sheikh Mujib about their status and their eventual withdrawal, as a serious obstacle. (FCO 37/1020)

This position was taken when communicating with the belligerent states as well as those not directly connected to the crisis. Douglas-Home advised the consulate in Dacca to communicate unofficially with the new Bangladesh administration:

> Your aim should be to convince them that we are not deliberately snubbing the Bangladesh authorities by not granting immediate recognition. We therefore suggest that you should say that our non-recognition does not imply that we disapprove of the Bangladesh Government but the fact is that we have certain objective criteria for recognition and so far these have not been met. As the acting president has pointed out the question is connected with the speed with which the rule of law can be established in the country. (Telegram Douglas-Home to Dacca, FCO 37/902)

Internal deliberation centred on the issue of legal criteria and effective control. FCO South Asian department policy memos by R. T. Fell and P. F. Walker (FCO 37/902) and D. Slater (FCO 37/1019) use effective control as the main criterion for recognition. In a memo of 13 January 1972 intended for general distribution amongst UK embassies, Douglas-Home discussed the criteria for recognition. The only issue he cites is that 'Sheikh Mujib's Government evidently has the support of the people and reports indicate that the country is under reasonable control.' However, he then addressed the 'fact that the Indian army is still in the east'. He dismissed this because Mujib had arranged with Gandhi that the Indians would withdraw. 'The important thing is that they are there with the consent and by the will of the indigenous government' (FCO 37/1020).

Other states

Third-party states generally focused on the issue of whether the Indian Army controlled Bangladesh. Speaking privately, the Director of Asian Affairs in the French Foreign Ministry gave control of territory as one of

167

four issues to be taken into account when considering recognition (Ewert-Biggs telegram 11 January 1972, FCO 37/1019). He also raised the issue of the Indian presence. The most important point was that 'Indian forces were there with the consent of the Dacca Government: It was not a Prague situation' and that 'they would not stay longer than the Bangla Desh Government wanted'. Soviet Premier Brezhnev's public position was that a political settlement should be reached 'without interference of any kind from outside forces' (Ewert-Biggs telegram 11 January 1972, FCO 37/1019). UK ambassador to the USSR John Killick argued that Soviet recognition of Bangladesh was likely to be delayed 'at least while Indian forces are so dominant and perhaps until they are withdrawn' (telegram 22 December 1971, FCO 37/902). Remember that the USSR vetoed UNSC resolutions that criticised the Indian invasion and called for the withdrawal of troops. Yet the USSR still would not recognise Bangladesh until Indian troops were withdrawn (or until there was a public commitment by India to a timetable of withdrawal). This is evidence that an important goal for the USSR was to maintain the common knowledge that force should not be used for profit or to affect political change.

The Canadian position as expressed to the UK was particularly hard line on the issue of the withdrawal of Indian troops from Bangladesh. The director of the Canadian Foreign Ministry's South Asia division said privately that Canadian recognition would only be forthcoming if Indian troops were withdrawn and Mitchell Sharp, Minister of Foreign Affairs, effectively committed himself to that position in a press conference (telegram from Ottawa, FCO 37/1020). Prime Minister Trudeau expressed the same doubts to Heath at the end of January. Trudeau asked for more concrete information on Mujib's plan for a withdrawal of Indian troops and the disarmament of the Mukti Bahini; 'If we and other countries could obtain firm information about such a plan, it would no doubt assist us in our evaluation of the situation' (letter 21 January 1972, PREM 15/751).[5]

Garvey telegram

The most complete and reflective record available of decision making on the recognition question is a long memo sent by the High Commissioner in Delhi, Terence Garvey (Garvey telegram 7 January 1972, FCO 37/1019). Breaking down his reasoning into sections, he lays out the arguments for and against recognition. The two main points in favour were British trade interests, which were greater in East than West Pakistan and needed to be protected, as well as that recognition would help to bolster the Bangladesh administration who were not pro-Soviet, which was seen as a good thing. The arguments against recognition were that the legal criteria were 'not conspicuously fulfilled', Indian troops were not withdrawn, and that recognition might either undercut Bhutto's domestic legitimacy or provoke him to engage in anti-British retaliation. Elaborating, Garvey refers to the importance of the restoration of law and order. His comments on the presence of Indian troops in Bangladesh are revealing. Indian troops were 'likely, on balance, to be a help rather than a hindrance to evolution of new state in direction favourable to our material and political interests'. However, contrary to British interests, the UK 'should no doubt wish to see prospect of substantial withdrawal of Indian troops, and beginnings of progress towards this end'. Why could this be? Garvey notes that 'This is of greater importance presentationally than in fact.' The indications are that while direct British interests would be served by the retention of Indian troops, their withdrawal is more in line with some important international social norms.

Jute, tea and British trading interests in East Pakistan

There is considerable evidence that domestic economic interests were important in the decision to recognise Bangladesh. Not only do decision makers often refer to trading interests, but there was public and private political pressure to protect British businesses in East Pakistan.

Garvey reported on 28 December that even before the UK recognised the Bangladesh government, a 'British trade and industrial delegation representing jute and tea interests is expected to visit Dacca' (FCO 37/902). Jute is a fibre with numerous uses, especially in textile manufactures. Around the same time, Douglas-Home authorised the consulate in Dacca to address resuming the export of jute (FCO 37/902). Later, in January, a group of MPs visited the Secretary of State to advocate for recognition of Bangladesh in order to protect the Dundee jute industry (memo by Slater, FCO 37/1019). In a meeting between Heath and Sheikh Mujib in London on 8 January 1972, the British specifically mentioned the jute trade. Mujib explicitly linked UK recognition of Bangladesh to his cooperation restarting bilateral trade (PREM 15/751). The Deputy High Commissioner in Dacca, Rae Britten, while advocating for early British recognition, noted that 'The tea gardens here [in Bengal] were by far our most valuable asset in undivided Pakistan' (PREM 15/751).

Resistance from West Pakistan

Bhutto publicly denounced the international legal recognition of Bangladesh and specifically argued against UK recognition in communications with

Heath and Douglas-Home. British decision makers were very concerned with potential retaliation by Bhutto against British trading interests in West Pakistan. So, they set out to coordinate multiple states to recognise Bangladesh at the same time. Collective action by the international community meant that Bhutto would find it harder to retaliate against all of them; if all recognised Bangladesh at once, Pakistan could not threaten to sever relations or retaliate. This collective action was only possible if there was general acceptance that Indian action did not count as aggression.

Interpreting the insistence on the withdrawal of Indian troops

Once the decision to recognise Bangladesh had been made, Heath and Douglas-Home set out to legitimate it to various audiences. President of Pakistan Bhutto had sent Heath a letter complaining about Britain's actions and arguing against recognition of Bangladesh by the UK. In line with his performances at the UN, the main theme was that recognition of Bangladesh would legitimate aggression:

> this will be the first instance of Britain accepting and endorsing the dismemberment of a Commonwealth country achieved through aggression.
> . . . The intended recognition of 'Bangladesh' by Britain would . . . put a seal of respectability to an aggression against a Commonwealth country and set a dangerous precedent for the future. (Letter 19 January 1972, PREM 15/751)

In a series of telegrams sent in reply to Bhutto, Heath directly countered this argument with the claim that Mujib's administration was in control of the country, it was 'not under foreign control' and that 'The Indian forces are there at his behest and the Indian Government has undertaken to withdraw them at his request' (telegrams of 24 and 29 January 1972, PREM 15/751).

This delinking of the Indian intervention from aggressive gain was also a prominent feature of British efforts to build support for collective recognition of Bangladesh. In personal messages to the French President and the West German Chancellor Willy Brandt in mid-January 1972, this was Heath's only justification for recognition. That the country of Bangladesh was 'behind' Mujib meant that:

> whatever view is taken of the manner of its creation, a new national entity is coming into being whose Government appears to command the general acceptance of the majority of the people. The maintenance of law and order is still, in the last resort, dependent upon the Indian Army, but their presence is accepted by the Government in Dacca and Mujib told me that, on

his return, he would formally request the Army's withdrawal in accordance with a phased and agreed plan. (PREM 15/751)

The reference to the manner of Bangladesh's creation can only refer to the potentially illegitimate use of force. Heath is trying here to frame recognition as a separate issue from India's military intervention; the withdrawal of Indian troops means that the use of force is not being rewarded. This reasoning was duplicated in communications with all other states (Douglas-Home telegram 21 January 1972, PREM 15/751).

As is clear from the above discussion on British reliance on normal legal criteria, the issue of effective control and the role of Indian troop presence was a central factor both in decision making and in legitimating recognition to other states. Internally, the issue appears to have been the extent to which the Mujib regime was a 'reality'; whether the adminis- tration had the power to control the population for the indefinite future. The UK position, across all members of the government who expressed an opinion on the topic, was that the Indian intervention was not a case of aggression. So, they did not need to evaluate the extent to which India was profiting from its use of force. Externally, the insistence on the with- drawal of Indian troops, or at least on the appearance of free consent on the part of Mujib and the Bangladesh government to a temporary troops presence, served two purposes in the debate. First, the interna- tional legal position for recognition was premised partly on effective control of the territory, with a reasonable prospect of permanency. If Mujib's regime was dependent on the Indian Army for the maintenance of law and order, then this criterion would have been unfulfilled. British diplomats frequently appealed to this consideration when deliberating internally as well as externally on whether and when to recognise. Sec- ond, West Pakistan and other critics of India's actions were attacking the intervention on the basis of the illegitimacy of aggression and territorial aggrandisement. If Indian troops were effectively occupying Bangladesh and the Bangladeshi government was under the control of India, then the intervention could be perceived or represented as being a case of the illegitimate use of force. Public commitment by Mujib and Indian Prime Minister Indira Gandhi to a timetable of Indian withdrawal undercut the aggrandisement criticism.

Conclusion of UK section

UK decision makers did not hold India's intervention to be illegitimate or contrary to the rule of nonaggression. Their reasons given explic- itly for recognising Bangladesh were the international legal criterion of effective control of territory, and the protection of British trading inter-ests in Bengal. There is then a contrast with British attitudes towards a Turkish-Cypriot state in the Cyprus crisis. Whereas the British opposed the recognition of the TRNC on the basis that such recognition would 'condone' or 'legitimise' aggression, they did not oppose the recogni-tion of Bangladesh on this basis. Internally and in private, the British government did not ever treat the Indian use of force as aggression. While legitimating the recognition decision to other international actors, Britain used a rhetorical strategy of delinking recognition from the issue of India's use of force. The British did not see the recognition of Bangla-desh as constituting a threat to the rule against aggression. They justified this with reference to what they said were extenuating circumstances. One prominent excuse was the public willingness of the Indian govern-ment to withdraw troops from Bangladesh. The British said, effectively, that this meant the Indian government was not using its military victory for personal gain.

THE UN DEBATES ON AGGRESSION AND WITHDRAWAL

Introduction to UN section

The UNSC was not involved in the crisis in the India–Pakistan subcon-tinent until 4 December 1971, the day after India formally declared war on Pakistan. There were two phases of discussion in the Council during the war. The first, 4–6 December, ended in a stalemate with the Soviet Union twice vetoing a resolution. The second, 12–21 December, ended in the passing of UNSC resolution 307. A third phase relevant to the questions asked in this book was 10–25 August 1972. This concerned the formal admittance of the state of Bangladesh to the UN, and ended in China vetoing a resolution recognising Bangladesh as a UN member.

Debating a resolution

The main axis of contention in the arguments over a UNSC resolution in December 1971 was whether a clause calling for a ceasefire should be accompanied by another clause advocating a political settlement based on the transfer of authority to Bangladesh, or, instead, an appeal for the withdrawal of the armed forces of both sides behind international borders. The US, through Ambassador George H. W. Bush, proposed a draft resolution (S/10416) that included a withdrawal clause: '2. *Calls for* an immediate withdrawal of armed personnel present on the terri-tory of the other to their own sides of the India-Pakistan borders.'

The withdrawal was linked by numerous representatives to the principle that political advantage should not be obtained through the exercise of force. Huang Hua (China) strongly linked withdrawal with aggression.

> The Chinese delegation is of the view that in accordance with the Charter of the United Nations the Security Council should surely condemn the act of aggression by the Government of India and demand that the Indian Government immediately and unconditionally withdraw all its armed forces from Pakistan. (S/PV 1971, 1606: 240)[6]

He then explains this position more fully in the meeting on 5 December:

> The demand for only a cease-fire in place by the two sides, without a demand for withdrawal of Indian troops, is in effect tantamount to conniving at and encouraging aggression and to recognizing the Indian aggressor troops remaining in Pakistan as legal. (S/PV 1971, 1607: 75)

There is clear concern with the legality of the situation and with interpretation of what ceasefire and withdrawal means for the legitimacy of the actions taken. Huang Hua cites the 1967 Arab–Israeli war as a precedent.

> Just as the representative of Somalia said yesterday, have not the resolutions passed by the United Nations on the question of the Middle East, which failed to demand the immediate withdrawal of Israeli aggressor troops from Arab territory but only called for a cease-fire in place, resulted in legalizing the fruits of aggression and imposing them on the Arab countries and people and in creating in the Middle East the danger of aggression and war on a still larger scale? (S/PV 1971, 1606: 240)

The Pakistani representative explicitly denounced the USSR's and Indian position against demanding withdrawal in terms of rule maintenance: 'By not dealing simultaneously with the question of withdrawal together with that of cease-fire, the Council would legitimise military occupation and perpetuate it' (S/PV 1971, 1608: 113).

The US draft resolution did not include a clause explicitly calling for a political settlement of the East Pakistan issue. There was a clause directed towards 'the creation of a climate conducive to the return of refugees to East Pakistan' (S/10416), but this clause did not obviously advocate political autonomy or independence for East Pakistan. The Soviet draft (S/10418), on the other hand, consisted in its entirety of two clauses: one calling for a political settlement in East Pakistan, and the other calling on Pakistan to 'cease all acts of violence by Pakistani forces in East Pakistan which have led to the deterioration of the situation'. This was effectively a condemnation of Pakistan for its actions and an attempt to frame Pakistan as the guilty party.

Both the US draft resolution and an eight-power resolution put forward by Argentina, Belgium, Burundi, Italy, Japan, Nicaragua, Sierra Leone and Somalia, which also included calls for mutual withdrawal, were vetoed by the USSR. Both received eleven votes in favour and two against (the USSR and Poland), with two abstentions (the UK and France). The USSR draft resolution only received two votes in favour, and so was not carried.

Perhaps sensing that directly denouncing the West Pakistani repression of East Pakistan was not a convincing angle, the USSR argued in a new draft resolution (S/10426) that

> the question of a cease-fire should be inseparably linked with a demand that the Government of Pakistan should simultaneously take effective action towards a political settlement in East Pakistan, giving recognition to the will of the East Pakistan population, as expressed, clearly and definitely, in the elections of December 1970. (S/PV 1971, 1608: 52)

The obvious stalemate prompted the Somalian representative to introduce a draft resolution that referred the matter to the UNGA under the Uniting for Peace resolution 377 A(V) of 3 November 1950.

The UNGA resolution

The UNGA considered the matter the next day, 7 December. A resolution very similar to that proposed by the US in the UNSC was introduced and passed with 104 in favour, eleven against and ten abstentions. This was UNGA resolution 2793 (XXVI). It included a call for withdrawal of armed forces to international borders and a call for bringing about conditions necessary for the return of refugees to East Pakistan. Notably, it did not call for a political settlement. A USSR draft resolution calling for a political settlement based on recognition to the will of the East Pakistan population as expressed in the elections of December 1970 was not put to a vote. The axis of debate was very similar to that in the UNSC meetings.

A second round of debate and an eventual resolution

During the second phase of debate, 12–21 December, India tried to deflate some of the criticism levelled at its position in the previous phase. One prominent theme was that India was not aiming at what it called 'territorial aggrandizement' (S/PV 1971, 1611: 69). The Indian representative repeatedly framed India's unilateral formal recognition of Bangladesh as proof of India's intentions:

> we wanted to make it absolutely clear that the entry of our armed forces into Bangla Desh was not motivated by any intention of territorial aggrandizement. (S/PV 1971, 1611: 99)

> we have no intention whatsoever of acquiring any part of West Pakistan or of Bangla Desh by conquest or otherwise. Our recognition of the People's Republic of Bangla Desh makes it quite clear that we have no territorial designs on Bangla Desh. (S/PV 1971, 1611: 221)

Foreign Minister of Pakistan Zulfikar Ali Bhutto, as the Pakistan representative, spiritedly continued the themes from the earlier debate. The illegitimacy of profiting from or creating rights via the use of force dominated his rhetoric. He insisted that UNSC action would mean creating precedent and potentially legitimising aggression:

> If the Security Council wants me to be a party to the legalization of abject surrender, then I say that under no circumstances shall I be . . . I will not take back a document of surrender from the Security Council. I will not be a party to the legalization of aggression. (S/PV 1971, 1614: 58)

> This is gunboat diplomacy in its worst form. It makes the Hitlerite aggression pale into insignificance, because Hitlerite aggression was not accepted by the world. If the world is going to endorse this aggression, it will mean a new and most unfortunate chapter in international relations. A new chapter may have begun in India and Pakistan, but please do not start a new, dreadful, chapter in international relations. (S/PV 1971, 1614: 74)

> Impose any decision, have a treaty worse than the Treaty of Versailles, legalize aggression, legalize occupation, legalize everything that has been illegal up to 15 December 1971. I will not be a party to it. (S/PV 1971, 1614: 84)

A few sentences after the last statement, Bhutto stormed out of the UNSC chamber.

Few rhetorical positions changed in the second phase. Most states were open to a political settlement of the Bangladesh issue, but refused to endorse one without a withdrawal of forces. The Argentinian representative, Carlos Ortiz de Rosas, put it succinctly:

I do not know how the Security Council is going to ask one country to find a political settlement while negotiating under the occupying forces of another foreign country. No Member State of the 131 Member States in the United Nations would accept such a settlement. It is obvious that a political settlement is needed. It is logical and indispensable that a political settlement be sought. But first things first; and first there must be a cease-fire and withdrawal of troops. (S/PV 1971, 1615: 97)

Here it is clear that he doesn't have a problem with the settlement itself, which is probably going to be independence at this point; rather his issue is with the idea that the UNSC and international society more widely approve, that is, grant legitimacy to, a political situation that was brought about by the use of force.

Once West Pakistan forces in East Pakistan surrendered, the USSR (and Poland) acquiesced and abstained from, instead of vetoing, UNSC resolution 307. India's disavowal of territorial ambitions was noted by several participants and cited as a positive contribution. Resolution 307 contained no clause even remotely advocating the transfer of political authority in East Pakistan to a new entity.

Admitting Bangladesh to the United Nations

After the sense of crisis had dissipated and numerous states had given formal bilateral recognition to the new state of Bangladesh, including the US in April 1972, Bangladesh made an application for membership in the UN. This was considered in three meetings, the first on 10 August 1972, where China opposed membership. After consideration by the Committee on the Admission of New Members, two more meetings on 24 and 25 August 1972 ended with China vetoing a resolution (S/10771) admitting Bangladesh to the UN. During the debates, there was widespread consensus that recognition of Bangladesh was of benefit to world order and that Bangladesh met the criteria for a sovereign state. Bangladesh's peace-loving and democratic nature and intentions were cited approvingly. Supporters of membership also repeatedly appealed to the sheer size of Bangladesh's population. There was no mention of the role of aggression in bringing about the current state of affairs by states other than China.

China's stated objections included reference to the non-fulfilment of UNSC resolution 307 and UNGA resolution 2793. Huang Hua claimed that

As everyone is aware, it is precisely the Soviet and Indian Governments that have committed aggression against another country by the use of force as mentioned in this connexion. It is again they who are trying to impose 'Bangladesh' upon the United Nations by forced arguments in wilful distortion of the Charter. (S/PV 1972, 1660: 78)

They are deliberately taking advantage of the consequences of the war of aggression and refuse to withdraw all the Indian troops of aggression and are detaining the more than 90,000 prisoners of war and civilians as hostages, for the purpose of blackmailing Pakistan and pressuring the United Nations. (S/PV 1972, 1660: 79)

Conclusion of UN section

The public terms of debate in UNSC and UNGA discussions included contestation over whether Indian actions constituted aggression and whether Bangladesh's recognition as a state should be compromised by the use and threat of force. Many states held the withdrawal of Indian troops from Bengal to be the central condition for the legitimacy of the official existence of Bangladesh. China continued nonrecognition of Bangladesh, and the use of its bureaucratic position to prevent Bangladesh's admission to the UN, was framed primarily in terms of not legitimising aggressive gain.

CONCLUSION

The creation of Bangladesh can easily be described in terms which make it largely equivalent to the establishment of Manchukuo or the TRNC. And yet its independence was recognised relatively quickly. What, then, are the implications of this case for the model of rule maintenance, and can the model be useful in this case?

First, the Bangladesh case shows the plausibility of one of the sources of variation in nonrecognition, and rule maintenance actions, suggested by the rule maintenance model. In stage two of this model, the members of the community interpret the action that is potentially a norm violation (see Figure 1.2). This interpretation may or may not be strategically motivated, and there may never be complete consensus over whether the action is or is not justified. However, if the action is redefined or excused or socially constructed so that it does not represent a threat to the rule, then rule maintenance is unnecessary. India's invasion of East Pakistan could have been construed as a violation of the rule against aggression and hence a threat to the intersubjective understanding that there is such a rule. If it were such a threat, then rule maintenance would not only make sense but might be necessary to prevent states from thinking that

177

there is no longer a general agreement that force cannot be used at will. However, as we have seen in the Bangladesh case, action that might have been generally accepted as aggression can instead be excused, for example through the provision of some extenuating circumstances or by a redefinition of the implications of the rule. There were several ways that India's invasion was rhetorically distinguished from aggression. First, there was the often implicit argument that the declaration of a state of Bangladesh was an act of self-determination. Actors referred to the democratically elected nature of the East Pakistani government, or indirectly referenced it with terms like the 'Government appears to command the general acceptance of the majority of the people' (Heath letter 15 January 1972, PREM 15/751). For example, this was part of the British argument that the Bangladeshi government fulfilled the international legal criteria for recognition. It seems plausible as well as that the fact that East Pakistani independence was originally declared prior to India's invasion would have played a role in this perception. Although the reasoning behind this argument was not explicitly spelled out, we can understand it. If the new Bangladeshi government had instead been the result of a military coup, say, then the argument that it constituted a case of self-determination would have been less convincing.

India's repeated public commitments to withdrawing their troops from Bangladeshi territory also undercut the status of the Indian invasion as a case of aggression. This was the most frequent and prominent reason given, across all external actors but especially by the British, for why recognition of Bangladesh would not be a case of legitimising aggression. While again the logic is not laid out formally, a plausible interpretation is that India's commitment to withdrawing troops meant that it would not be formally gaining territory nor would it be in a position to control the Bangladeshi government de facto once its troops were out of the country. So, even if you could make the argument that India had profited in various ways, for example the division of its major rival into two states now antagonistic to each other,[7] India had not gained in the basic and direct form of political control over territory or population. It also makes sense that in a hypothetical case of malicious, premeditated, acquisitive aggression, the aggressor would not agree to withdrawal of troops. Requiring the withdrawal of troops could function as a coarse-grained test of aggressive intentions.

So, regardless of whether British decision makers in particular were partially motivated to recognise Bangladesh because of British tea and jute interests, arguments about withdrawal of troops were necessary in order to avoid opposition to Bangladesh on the basis that it represented the fruits of aggression. Given that the Indian invasion then did not count as aggression, there was no need to engage in rule maintenance. An interesting counterfactual here would be if India did not promise to withdraw troops and instead pressured or replaced the elected Bangladeshi government. Recognition of Bangladesh would have been much harder to justify in this hypothetical situation and probably would have meant a much bumpier road to recognition or even support for sanctions against India. This counterfactual is strengthened when Cyprus is used as a comparison. The withdrawal of troops from the invaded territory was one of the main demands of the international community in both cases. Turkey's refusal to do so has remained one of the main sticking points in negotiations over the status of the TRNC for decades.

A second way in which the model of rule maintenance is relevant to the Bangladesh case is that there are several features of the case that are illuminated by the model. If a Bangladeshi state was going to be recognised anyway, and almost everyone involved in the US, UK and UN viewed this as the eventual outcome, why was there such contestation over the status of the new state? Under the model of rule maintenance, because there was uncertainty over whether India's actions constituted aggression, there was still the possibility of opposition to Bangladesh's independence. The frequent concern, by Kissinger and Bhutto among others, that various actions might legitimise aggression shows the relevance of the model to the situation and in explaining why other paths were not taken (or the importance of off-the-equilibrium-path outcomes).

So, the recognition of Bangladesh does not invalidate the rule maintenance explanation of nonrecognition. Instead, it is consistent with the overall model of rule maintenance. It also shows that actors can take into account rule maintenance considerations even when they eventually decide that rule maintenance is not necessary. More generally, this case is yet another demonstration of the importance of the dynamics of normative or institutional systems in driving outcomes in international politics.

Notes

1. Here, the issue is not whether India's invasion was aggression in some transcendental or essentialist sense, but that it is describable in terms which make it similar to other uses of force that have been seen as aggression.
2. We might also note that the PRC was not recognised by various states despite its size. Also, the state of Hawaii is geographically distant from the rest of the US but if Russia invaded I doubt that this would be seen as a convincing reason for recognition.

3. Foreign Relations of the United States (FRUS). Referenced with the year and volume number, followed by the document number.
4. FCO refers to the Foreign and Commonwealth Offices Archives. Referenced with the piece reference.
5. Premier's Archives (PREM). Referenced with the piece reference.
6. S/PV (S: Security Council and PV: *procès-verbal*) refers to the United Nations Security Council Official Record. Referenced with year, meeting and paragraph number.
7. Also remember that this division had effectively occurred with the breakdown of the 1970 election and the declaration of Bangladesh's independence by the Awami League in early 1971, well before India invaded East Pakistan.

CHAPTER SIX

The uncertain fruits of victory: variation in nonrecognition

An important concern of models built on a few historical case studies, no matter how deep and robust the evidence in those cases, is whether they apply to other cases. In order to assess whether the model of rule maintenance can explain variation in nonrecognition, I now look at the broader range of cases where the cross-border use of force resulted in political change militarily asserted by the victorious state. Given the case selection criteria (see below) there are twenty-one relevant cases since World War I. While these cases cannot all be studied to the same depth as the few historical cases considered earlier in this book, they can give a preliminary sense of the direction of the evidence. In this chapter, the goal is to use the rule maintenance model to explain some of the variation we see in the broader universe of cases where nonrecognition was up for debate and also to use this broader universe of cases to improve the model by adding more content and identifying more specific mechanisms by which cases exit the ideal-typical process leading to a rule maintenance action like nonrecognition. I first define relevant concepts and specify case-selection criteria, before identifying some sources of variation in whether nonrecognition was adopted. Finally, I investigate the case of Russia's 2014 annexation of Crimea in more detail to see whether the model has relevance to the present day.

CONCEPTS AND CASES

A case is a candidate for a nonrecognition debate when three conditions obtain:

1. at least one state uses military force against another state, that is, across international borders;

2. there is some de facto 'spoils of war', that is, political change of some sort asserted by the militarily victorious state; and

3. the cross-border use of force is not collectively authorised by an international organisation.

The first condition excludes many cases of civil war or of secession. Some cases include elements of both interstate and intrastate violence. One example is the conflict surrounding the independence of Bangladesh, formerly East Pakistan, from Pakistan. Severe violence, perhaps rising to the level of genocide, was inflicted on the East Pakistanis by the West Pakistanis. However, India entered the conflict, going to war with Pakistan in both the West and the East. This cross-border use of force was the subject of the crisis, and the debate over recognition of Bangladesh was centred around India's invasion and not the internal violence. In other situations, like the Vietnam War, it is not clear-cut whether there were two states fighting over each other's territory, or two factions fighting for control of a single territory.

The definition of 'military force' employed here is relatively expansive, including cases like Crimea where there was no overt, formal invasion, as well as Italy–Ethiopia, which involved a massive, extended, military campaign. The criterion that there be force used by states across borders excludes some liminal cases, including the case of Abkhazia. During the war between the Georgian government and the Abkhaz separatists in 1992–3, there was an influx of fighters to the Abkhaz side from a variety of places, including Russia. However, Boris Yeltsin's Russian government policy was in support of Georgia, not the Abkhaz, so this cannot be classed as a case of Russian use of force. One interesting case is that of South Africa–Namibia. South Africa was awarded the League of Nations mandate over South-West Africa after World War I. As South Africa had had military forces in the territory we now know as Namibia and had acted in a de facto governmental capacity for decades, the use of force was not a single action. In the 1960s various guerrilla actions by, for example, the South West African Liberation Army were resisted in a violent counterinsurgency campaign by the South African army. Dugard suggests that the proximate triggering action for much of the collective response to the occupation was the trial of thirty-seven South West Africans under South African law. The UNGA (resolution 2324, 16 December 1967) condemned the trial and the UNSC called it an 'illegal' trial (UNSC resolutions 245, 25 January 1968; and 246, 14 March 1968), for the first time implying that South Africa's mandate was terminated. Whatever the legal technicalities, Dugard argued that this 'strengthened the view outside South

Africa that South Africa's right to administer the Territory has been terminated' (1970: 20). Subsequently, UNSC resolution 269 (12 August 1969) stated that the Council

> Decides that the continued occupation of the Territory of Namibia by the South African authorities constitutes an aggressive encroachment on the authority of the United Nations, a violation of the territorial integrity and a denial of the political sovereignty of the people of Namibia.

A particularly interesting aspect of this case is, then, that even though the violence did not fit the archetype of an aggressive invasion, the international community effectively defined it as such.

As noted in Chapter 1, the interest in this study is in cases where recognition was in doubt and as such, there must be some *lingering contestation* of the results of the use of force. The 'lingering' criterion excludes cases where the results of the use of force are relatively fleeting. The 'contestation' criterion excludes cases where the political issues are redistributed by mutual consent, such as in a peace treaty or other agreement. For example, in 1948, Israel won its independence in a war against a coalition of Arab States. The territorial outcome of the war was mutually agreed upon in Armistice agreements in 1949 between Israel and Egypt, Lebanon, Syria and Jordan. In 1950, the US, Britain and France guaranteed these borders against revision by force. So, while the territorial settlement was not either side's ideal point, this case does not rise to the level of contestation that for example the 1967 war did (where there were no peace agreements), and so it is not included. A similar case is the 1992–5 war in Bosnia which involved a territorial redistribution (including the creation of Republika Srpska and Republika Srpska Krajina) as a result of force used by the Federal Republic of Yugoslavia (Serbia and Montenegro). However, because the outcome was a product of the Dayton Agreement which was supported and guaranteed by the international community, including the US, UK, Russia, France and Germany, the results were not contested enough to be classed as a recognition debate.

Similarly, the outcome of the dispute between the Netherlands and Indonesia over West New Guinea was not sufficiently contested to count as a case of a nonrecognition debate. The conflict resulted in the transfer of West New Guinea from the Netherlands to a UN Temporary Executive Authority and thence to Indonesia after a plebiscite. Dutch agreement to this plan came after the limited use of force by Indonesia and the threat of a full-scale war that Dutch decision makers 'felt they could not win' (Saltford 2000: 18). However, as both parties to the dispute agreed to the transfer in UN-mediated peace negotiations, there was no contestation constituting a nonrecognition debate.

This study is also only interested in cases where the use of force is at least potentially considered to be a norm violation. This excludes from consideration uses of force that are not norm violations but are instead instances of the community enforcing a norm or otherwise authorising the use of force. So, when the US and others' troops invaded Kuwait in 1991 and used force to change the political situation on the ground (i.e. expel Saddam Hussein's forces), this was not a norm violation because it was authorised by the UN. The spirit of this criterion also excludes the use of force by NATO against the Former Republic of Yugoslavia (Serbia) in Kosovo in 1999. Even though there was no UNSC resolution explicitly authorising military force, there were resolutions (such as UNSC 1199) invoking Chapter VII of the UN Charter, and a resolution introduced by Russia demanding the immediate cession of force against the Federal Republic of Yugoslavia was rejected by a vote of twelve to three.

Related reasoning also excludes the numerous cases of conquest during World War II. By the time of Nazi Germany's invasion of Poland, there had ceased to be global norms. International order was in an extreme crisis and arguably did not exist.

These conditions produce a list of twenty-one cases (Table 6.1).

Nonrecognition status

The outcome of interest here is 'nonrecognition status'. The underlying concept is the extent of acceptance of the situation as legitimate by the international community. The concept ranges from complete collective recognition at one end to complete collective nonrecognition at the other. An example that would be close to the recognition end would be the case of the Indian conquest of the enclave of Goa in 1961. There are no outstanding claims that Indian sovereignty over Goa is illegitimate and no state maintains a nonrecognition policy towards Indian Goa. Near the other end, an example of complete nonrecognition is the TRNC, which is recognised only by one state, Turkey, and numerous states and international organisations explicitly maintain a nonrecognition policy of the TRNC. Perhaps the purest example of nonrecognition is the establishment of the Republic of Nagorno-Karabakh, declared on 2 September 1991 and reaching its current situation after Armenian military victory and a ceasefire in 1994. No UN member state recognises the Nagorno-Karabakh Republic, not even Armenia. Overwhelmingly, the expressed attitude has been that the results of the Armenian military victory in the conflict should not be recognised.

Table 6.1 List of cases of nonrecognition debates

Case	Date
China–Japan (Manchukuo)	1932
Italy–Ethiopia	1935
Pakistan–India (Kashmir)	1947–8
India–Hyderabad	1948
North/South Vietnam	1954–75
India–Portugal (Goa)	1961
Dahomey–Portugal	1961
China–India (Aksai Chin)	1962
Ethiopia–Eritrea	1962–91
South Africa–Namibia	1966–89
Israel–Arab States	1967
India–Pakistan (Bangladesh)	1971
Iran–United Arab Emirates (Hormuz Islands)	1971
Turkey–Cyprus	1974
China–Vietnam (Paracel Islands)	1974
Indonesia–East Timor	1975
Morocco–Spanish Sahara	1975–2000
Iraq–Kuwait	1990–1
Nagorno–Karabakh	1991–2
Russia–Georgia (South Ossetia)	2008
Russia–Ukraine (Crimea)	2014

Coding recognition status as either 'recognition' or 'nonrecognition' is problematic for several reasons. Primarily, collective nonrecognition status is not in fact binary, as the example of Morocco–Spanish Sahara shows. Western Sahara is in practice divided between Morocco-occupied territory and the Sahrawi Arab Democratic Republic (SADR). The UN recognises the sovereignty of neither Morocco nor the SADR and many states do not recognise either Moroccan sovereignty or an independent Western Saharan state. Some states recognise the SADR but many do not.[1] The SADR is a member of the African Union (and Morocco withdrew membership in protest). However, the Arab League has not admitted the SADR as a member and instead supports Moroccan territorial integrity. India, one of the most prominent states to recognise the SADR, allowed a Saharan embassy from 1985, but withdrew its recognition in 2000 (Dasgupta 2000). Western Sahara is a case where there is genuine dissension in international society broadly as to the legitimacy of the various claims involved. That said, the balance is in favour of nonrecognition of Morocco's conquest, although this does not translate into support for the SADR's claims.

An additional problem is that recognition status changes. After Italy defeated Ethiopian Emperor Haile Selassie's forces and claimed the conquest of Ethiopia and its annexation into the Italian Empire, numerous states, as well as the League of Nations, maintained a nonrecognition policy for several years. However, by the end of 1938, when appeasement and rearmament were replacing collective security as the international conflict management system, a clear majority of states recognised Italy's possession of Ethiopia.

What sorts of evidence are relevant to determining whether states have not recognised a situation? Despite our desire for a clear, precise and exhaustive characterisation of the sorts of actions that count as relevant to recognition, the indeterminacy of the concept of 'nonrecognition', integral to all social facts, means that a variety must be taken into account. No less an authority than International Court of Justice Judge Krzysztof Skubiszewski, in a dissenting opinion on the judgement made on the East Timor case brought by Portugal against Australia, after listing states who had 'granted their recognition, in one way or another, sometimes de facto only and without committing themselves to confirming that self-determination took place', notes that 'there is room for hesitation with regard to some of the States enumerated above' (International Court of Justice Reports 1995: 233). Perhaps the clearest demonstration of nonrecognition is UN, or League of Nations, resolutions. For example, several UNSC resolutions constitute collective declarations of nonrecognition with regard to Israel's territorial gains in the 1967 war. Resolution 242 (22 November 1967) states that the Council, 'Emphasizing the inadmissibility of the acquisition of territory by war', holds that peace should include 'Withdrawal of Israel armed forces from territories occupied in the recent conflict' and affirms the necessity 'For guaranteeing the territorial inviolability and political independence of every State in the area.' After Israel took various steps with regard to Jerusalem, the Council issued resolution 252 (21 May 1968), which reaffirmed 'that acquisition of territory by military conquest is inadmissible' and considered 'that all legislative and administrative measures and actions taken by Israel, including expropriation of land and properties thereon, which tend to change the legal status of Jerusalem are invalid and cannot change that status'. Perhaps even more explicitly, in 1981, after Israel appeared to formally annex the Golan Heights, resolution 497 stated that the Council, on the basis 'that the acquisition of territory by force is inadmissible', decided 'that the Israeli decision to impose its laws, jurisdiction and administration in the occupied Syrian Golan Heights is null and void and without international legal effect'.

Not all cases involve such clear examples of collective nonrecognition. Some actions are close to a UNSC resolution but diverge in one way or another. For example, in 2014, a draft UNSC resolution (S/2014/189) stating that the Council 'Reaffirm[ed] that no territorial acquisition resulting from the threat or use of force shall be recognised as legal' and that called

> upon all States, international organizations and specialised agencies not to recognise any alteration of the status of Crimea on the basis of [the 16 March 2014] referendum and to refrain from any action or dealing that might be interpreted as recognizing any such altered status

was put up for a vote. It would have passed, but for a Russian veto. This is clearly evidence of nonrecognition, to us as scholars as well as the international community, even though legally it is not the same as an adopted resolution.

In this study I make a summary judgement as to whether a case involved collective nonrecognition or not (Table 6.2). I also include a 'mixed' category where there is no overwhelming trend. The only case where a summary judgement does not seem reasonable is the conflict between Pakistan and India over Kashmir. In 1947, the Maharaja of Jammu and Kashmir initially decided to remain independent and not to join either Pakistan or India. However, Pakistani forces engaged in fighting and, in response, the Maharaja decided to accede to India on 26 October 1947. Indian troops entered Kashmir and a small war was fought. India appealed to the UNSC on the basis that Pakistan had committed aggression against Indian territory. However, despite repeated Indian appeals, there was no formal condemnation of Pakistani aggression by the UN. UNSC resolutions 47 and 49 called for withdrawal of troops but did not place the blame on either party. One of the issues in the negotiations during 1947–9 held under the auspices of the United Nations Commission for India and Pakistan (UNCIP) was whether Pakistan should be treated as an aggressor or whether there should be parity. UNCIP tended towards parity (Korbel

Table 6.2 Nonrecognition status

No nonrecognition	Nonrecognition	Mixed
Italy–Ethiopia 1935	China–Japan (Manchukuo) 1932	Pakistan–India (Kashmir) 1947–8
India–Hyderabad 1948	China–India (Aksai Chin) 1962	
India–Portugal (Goa) 1961	South Africa–Namibia 1966–89	
Dahomey–Portugal 1961	Israel–Arab States 1967	
North/South Vietnam 1954–75	Turkey–Cyprus 1974	
Ethiopia–Eritrea 1962–91	Indonesia–East Timor 1975	
India–Pakistan (Bangladesh) 1971	Morocco–Spanish Sahara 1975–2000	
Iran–United Arab Emirates (Hormuz Islands) 1971	Nagorno-Karabakh 1991–2	
China–Vietnam (Paracel Islands) 1974	Russia–Georgia (South Ossetia) 2008	
Iraq–Kuwait 1990–1	Russia–Ukraine (Crimea) 2014	

1949, 1953). Both at the time and since, states have generally not taken formal stances on whether Kashmir should be part of India, part of Pakistan or should be independent.

Another marginal case is the war between China and India in the Himalayas in 1962. China occupied some territory in Aksai Chin (Calvin 1984). The Chinese invasion was condemned by the US and Britain – who openly supported the Indian cause. As a result of the conflict, the US recognised, on 26 October 1962, the McMahon Line as the international boundary line. This was a change from the previous policy in favour of India (Devereux 2009). The British, apart from reconfirming the validity of the McMahon Line, took a step further than even the US position when the then Foreign Secretary Lord Home told the Foreign Press Association that 'we have taken the view of the government of India on the present frontiers and the disputed territories belong to India'. This statement of support was later reiterated by Lord Home at the UN (Kalha 2012). Some other countries also openly denounced

China's actions but many expressed neutrality or indifference. India did not refer the dispute to the UN (perhaps because the Soviets hinted that they would be obliged to support the Chinese [Retzlaff 1963: 99]) so there was no discussion in that forum on the issue. However, nonaligned nations (Ceylon, Burma, Cambodia, Indonesia, the United Arab Republic and Ghana) did hold a conference in Colombo in December 1962. There was no unequivocal condemnation of China and instead the conference recommended bilateral negotiations over the border. However, when China rejected the recommendations of this conference, various countries become more openly sympathetic, particularly the United Arab Republic (Abadi 1998: 24). No states have explicitly recognised China's territorial claims to Aksai Chin. Thus, while the overall balance is on the side of nonrecognition, it is only marginally so.

SOURCES OF VARIATION

Consideration of the cases where there was no nonrecognition reveals that there are several reasons why the international community did not decide to impose a symbolic sanction in order to maintain the rule. There are three points at which events diverge from the ideal-typical process leading to nonrecognition: 1) there might be ambiguity over whether the action should be classified as a case of conquest or aggressive gain, 2) effective material sanctions might be imposed or 3) the international community might decide that the rule is not worth maintaining after all.

Ambiguity

That an action is or is not a violation of a norm is not given by nature. It is socially constructed. This means that there is room for strategic contestation of the legitimacy of an action, that is, whether it really qualifies as a violation, and for subconscious reinterpretation of a situation so as to excuse it or justify it in alternative terms. Shannon, while explaining the psychological processes involved in norm violation, points out that while norm violation might be motivated by self-interest, actors must face the constraints and opportunities that come with 'one's ability to define a situation in a way that allows socially accepted violation' (2000: 300). When an act or situation appears to potentially represent a norm violation, actors attempt to justify it, both to themselves and to outside audiences. This involves 'creative, subconscious interpretations of one's normative environment' (ibid.: 303).

So, even though an action is potentially classifiable as a case of 'spoils of war', that does not mean that it automatically will be. Actions have to be interpreted in light of the norms that actors deploy. Sometimes states are able to make a clear judgement about a situation, but sometimes there is ambiguity over what type of action they think it is or think it should be treated as. Eight of the ten cases of no nonrecognition involve a failure to conclusively determine or agree that the use of force is a case of aggression and hence a violation of the norm against aggression and hence a threat to that norm. I identify here four different types of ambiguity: 1) conflicting norms, 2) status of entities, 3) unclear sovereignty claims, and 4) consent.

Conflicting norms

The same action is potentially justifiable in alternative terms, with the audience's judgement determining which justification or interpretation works. One of the most potent norm complexes in the twentieth century is that surrounding self-determination. An important element of this norm complex is the delegitimation of imperialism and colonialism. Some violence has been justified under the banner of fighting for freedom or of supporting decolonisation efforts. The relevant point for this study is that if a use of force were used to conquer territory that could be framed as an imperial possession, then that use of force could be redefined away from aggression and instead legitimated under the banner of self-determination. This is what we see in the India–Portugal (Goa) case. After 451 years under Portuguese governance, the territory known as Portuguese India (more commonly as Goa but also including Daman and Diu) was annexed by India via an armed military invasion on 18–19 December 1961. The attack included heavy air, sea and land strikes with little resistance from the Portuguese side. Both sides suffered fatalities, but the Portuguese faction was outnumbered and forced to surrender. Goa, Daman and Diu were annexed, with Goa becoming the twenty-fifth Indian state in 1987. There was a split in opinion on the normative status of the Indian invasion. One group hailed it as liberating Goa from Portuguese colonialism and the other regretting that India had used force. For example, in the UNSC on 19 December 1961, in response to a complaint from Portugal that India was guilty of aggression in occupying the Portuguese territories of Goa, Daman and Diu, a draft resolution calling for a ceasefire and withdrawal of Indian forces from the territory was vetoed by the Soviet Union (and voted against by three other members). Another draft resolution rejecting the Portuguese complaint and calling upon that country to terminate hostile action and to cooperate with India in the liquidation of its colonial possessions in India was defeated by the votes of seven states including the US, the UK, France and China (Wright 1962: 617). Public statements deploring India's resort to force were made by some states including the UK, the US, Canada, Australia, New Zealand, Pakistan, France, the Netherlands, Spain and Western Germany. However, full support for the Indian action was expressed by the Soviet Union and all Soviet-bloc countries, Yugoslavia, the Arab States, Ghana, Ceylon and Indonesia (Keesing's Record of World Events 1962). There was thus no collective determination that India's conquest and annexation was a violation of the norm against conquest. The UNs' acquiescence in India's annexation of Goa was due to the feeling in many states, including the Soviet Union, 'that it was a legitimate act in the anti-colonial and anti-imperialist struggle and that colonialism was such an evil that the use of force to eliminate it should be tolerated' (Korman 1996: 274).

In the early 1960s there was a ferment of anti-colonialist sentiment as many new states were formed out of former colonies and territories. One famous expression of this sentiment was, in 1960, the UNGA resolution 1514 Declaration on the granting of independence to colonial countries and peoples. Also, the UNGA passed resolutions 1541 and 1542 concerning (under article 73e of the UN Charter) the submission of information regarding the economic, social and educational conditions of colonies ('territories whose peoples have not yet attained a full measure of self-government'). Portuguese territories including Goa and dependencies were specifically singled out as not being in compliance. The connotation of this was that the conditions in Portuguese colonies were so bad that they were especially illegitimate. On 19 December 1961, the second day of the invasion, the UNGA passed resolution 1699, condemning Portugal for not fulfilling its obligations and requesting member states to 'deny Portugal any support and assistance which it may use for the suppression of the peoples of its Non-Self-Governing Territories'. This was the context in which India annexed Goa under the banner of decolonisation.

Another similar situation is the Dahomey–Portugal 1961 case. Dahomey (now Benin) armed forces seized the Fort of Sao Joao Baptista de Ajuda, a Portuguese possession, on 31 July 1961, just seven months after Sao Joao was included in UNGA resolution 1542. 'Dahomey's action, despite involving a straightforward violation of Article 2(4) of the UN Charter, which prohibits the use of force against the territorial integrity of another State, appears to have drawn no significant international condemnation' (Trinidad 2012: 972). As Trinidad argues, this is a case where the international community favoured decolonisation as such, completely divorced from any considerations of self-determination of peoples, as the Fort had no permanent population (and was only

191

1 square kilometre in size). The strength of decolonisation as an idea was such that after the 1974 Portuguese revolution, Portugal itself recognised Indian sovereignty over Goa and Dahomey's sovereignty over the Fort.

Decolonisation was one way in which uses of force were reframed and legitimated, but not the only one. As we have seen in a previous chapter, the invasion of Pakistan by India in 1971 resulted in the de facto independence of the declared state of Bangladesh comprising the Eastern half of Pakistan. While India's use of force was initially vociferously condemned by most states, Bangladesh ended up being recognised. The Bangladeshi administration had been democratically elected and India rapidly withdrew its troops from the territory in order to demonstrate that the new state of Bangladesh was both not a puppet and that it could keep order on the ground by itself. Here the more general norm of self-determination seems to have been operating rather than specifically decolonisation.

Status of entities

Another type of ambiguity was over the status of the entities involved in the fighting. The norm against aggression and conquest has states as its subjects. The archetype of conquest involves one state declaring war, crossing borders and annexing occupied territory. In several cases of nonrecognition debates, there was serious ambiguity over whether the entities involved constituted separate states. This is not to say that there was consensus that the entities were conclusively substate or non-state, but that a substantial group of actors retained enough doubt that the situation was a case of interstate conquest.

The first such case was the India–Hyderabad case. In September 1948, India invaded the state of Hyderabad with military force and occupied the territory from the Nizam's rule. Following the Indian Independence Act of 1947, Hyderabad decided to accede to neither of the two newly independent states, and instead remained independent. India though did not accept this position, and insisted on integrating Hyderabad. The annexation of Hyderabad was carried out by the Indian Military Forces over a five-day period before the Nizam surrendered (Eagleton 1950). There was no UNSC resolution or any collective or widespread declaration that India's action was aggression. There were also several reasons why there was pervasive ambiguity over whether Hyderabad's annexation was a case of conquest. Primarily, the status of Hyderabad was unclear. Despite the legal technicality that the 'paramountcy' of the British Empire was not transferred to the new states of India and Pakistan, it merely lapsed,

192

there was a feeling that the princely states had to choose one or the other. Also, while Hyderabad had not formally acceded to either state, prior to the invasion by Indian forces, there had been an agreement, called the 'Standstill Agreement', signed on 29 November 1947, Article 1 of which stated:

> Until new arrangements in this behalf are made, all agreements and adminis-trative arrangements as to the matters of common concern, including External Affairs, Defense and Communications, which were existing between the Crown and the Nizam immediately before August 15, 1947, shall in so far as may be appropriate, continue as between the Dominion of India (or any part thereof) and the Nizam. (Das 1949: 71)

There was thus serious doubt that Hyderabad constituted a separate state entity.

Another example of ambiguity over the status of the entities involved was the conflict in Vietnam. For two decades after the end of the French colonial administration of Indochina in 1954, entities in North Vietnam (the Democratic Republic of Vietnam, DRVN) and South Vietnam (the Republic of Vietnam, RVN) fought a war that ended in the defeat and occupation of the South by the North in 1975. Many countries recog-nised only one Vietnam as having sovereignty over the entire territory. After the Paris Peace Accords between the DRVN and the US in 1973, many countries that had previously not recognised the DRVN did so. However, once North Vietnam conquered South Vietnam and incorpo-rated it into its territory, the Socialist Republic of Vietnam (SRV) com-prising both territories was declared on 2 July 1976 with Hanoi (the capital of North Vietnam) as its capital. Despite the fact that some have argued that recognising the DRVN implied the existence of two separate states (e.g. Crawford 2006: 476) there was little sense that this was a case of one state annexing another state and instead that it was an 'inter-nal' matter of two claimants to the same territory. For example, even though the UK stated that it recognised the DRVN 'as the Government of a State whose territory lies north of the provisional military demar-cation line laid down in the 1954 Geneva Agreements' (Talmon 1998: 99), it was also a party to the Act of the International Conference on Vietnam of 2 March 1973, an adjunct to the Paris Peace Accords. This Act throughout refers to the unity and territorial integrity of Vietnam. For example, Article 4 states 'The Parties to this Act solemnly recognise and strictly respect the fundamental national rights of the Vietnamese people, i.e., the independence, sovereignty, unity, and territorial integ-rity of Viet-Nam, as well as the right of the South Vietnamese people to self-determination.' The SRV was admitted as a member of the UN in 1977. A few countries delayed recognition of the SRV, with the US not recognising until 1995.

Finally, Ethiopia's annexation of Eritrea in 1962 led to thirty years in which Eritrea was a province of Ethiopia until armed guerrillas won a war of independence and then a referendum leading to a separate existence as a sovereign state. In November 1962, Ethiopian troops stationed in Eritrea were ordered to take positions at the main points of Asmara, and other Eritrean towns and members of the Eritrean Assembly were, by force of arms, ordered to meet and dissolve the Federation of Eritrea and Ethiopia (Haile 1987: 15). There was no sense in the international community that the annexation had taken place against a sovereign state, despite the UN having guaranteed Eritrean autonomy during the process of creating a federated state of Ethiopia and Eritrea in 1952.

Unclear sovereignty claims

In a couple of cases, there was ambiguity over whether the spoils of war were actually spoils at all. In international politics, there is variation over how firmly a piece of territory is considered to be under the sovereignty of a state. While no one would doubt that Paris is part of France, numerous territories in the world suffer from conflicting sovereignty claims that are at least minimally plausible. One type of such situations is relatively uninhabited littoral islands. Both the Iran–United Arab Emirates (UAE) Hormuz Islands case and the China–Vietnam Paracel Islands case involve this type of islands.

On 29 November 1971, Iran and the Emir of Sharjah announced an agreement calling for Sharjah to maintain sovereignty over the island of Abu Musa and for Iran to station military forces on the island. Oil revenues from the oil fields surrounding the island would be shared. On 30 November, Iran sent military forces to Abu Musa, in accordance with its agreement with Sharjah, but then also took control of the two nearby Tunb islands (Caldwell 1996: 52–3). Algeria, Iraq, Libya, the People's Democratic Republic of Yemen, Kuwait and the UAE took the dispute to the UNSC on 9 December 1971 and called the occupation of the two islands of Tunb 'a blatant aggression not only against Ras Al-Khaima alone, but against all the Arab people in all their countries' (S/PV 1971, 1610: 4).[2] However, despite continuing opposition by the Arab states, including statements by the Gulf Cooperation Council[3] and the Arab League,[4] when Iran took steps to assert control over the entire island of Abu Musa in 1992, there was no nonrecognition by the international community. There was no sense that the norm of non-aggression had been violated. There was genuine ambiguity over who had pre-existing title to sovereignty over the islands and there was an agreement between the parties leading to the new situation, and so most states treated the issue as one of a border dispute rather than a clear-cut norm violation. On 9 December 1971, the UNSC effectively rejected the claims of aggression by Iran by deferring consideration of the matter to a later date, referencing the possibility of a third-party mediated negotiated solution (S/PV 1971, 1610: 24).

Similarly, a clash over some islands in the South China Sea in 1974 did not result in nonrecognition of the result. On 19 January 1974, South Vietnamese troops landed on an island in the South China Sea. Chinese troops opened fire. A naval engagement was fought and then the next day China bombed and occupied three more islands. Generally, there was little sense outside Vietnam that there had been a case of clear-cut aggression. For example, John F. King, State Department Spokesman, commenting on the capture of a US civilian by China in the attack, referred to the islands as 'disputed territory' (Markham 1974). *The New York Times* commenting on the story described the situation as 'China and South Vietnam have claimed sovereignty over the islands' (Gwertzman 1974b).

Consent

A fourth type of ambiguity concerns whether or not the spoils of war were conceded willingly or not. In some cases, there is a change of heart, or at least of rhetoric, by the supposedly aggrieved party. In both the Hyderabad and the Paracel Islands cases, the entity who raised the issue that the use of force constituted a rule violation subsequently withdrew their complaint. While it can plausibly be argued that they did so under duress, their official position was respected by the community.

In 1948, subsequent to India's conquest, the Nizam of Hyderabad sent a telegram to the UN withdrawing the case from before the Council, and also made public statements that he had decided to accede to India and asserting that he was not under any coercion (Eagleton 1950: 295). In 1974, in a series of letters to the president of the UNSC, South Vietnam protested that China had claimed sovereignty over the Paracels and Spratleys and then that there had been heavy casualties in a fight between a Chinese landing force and Vietnamese troops (United Nations 1974: 187). However, on 24 January 1974, Vietnam cancelled their request for an urgent meeting of the UNSC. The reason given was because China had a veto and so there was no hope for constructive debate or positive action (United Nations 1974: 188). However, US opposition to creating a major international issue, including Kissinger's studied limiting of his comments to regretting that force had been invoked, also seems to have played a role (Gwertzman 1974a).

Effective material sanctions

On 2–4 August 1990, Iraq launched an invasion of Kuwait, occupying the entire country in two days. On 8 August 1990, Saddam Hussein installed his cousin, Ali Hassan Al-Majid, as the governor of Kuwait and Iraqi state radio claimed that it had achieved 'a comprehensive and eternal merger' with Kuwait and declared it the nineteenth province of Iraq. There were initial measures constituting nonrecognition of the annexation. For example, on 6 August 1990, the UNSC issued resolution 661 which included a call 'upon all States: . . . Not to recognise any regime set up by the occupying power.' Also, on 9 August 1990, resolution 662 included the following:

> Gravely alarmed by the declaration by Iraq of a 'comprehensive and eternal merger' with Kuwait, . . . Decides that annexation of Kuwait by Iraq under any form and whatever pretext has no legal validity, and is considered null and void . . . Calls upon all States, international organizations and specialised agencies not to recognise that annexation and to refrain from any action or dealing that might be interpreted as an indirect recognition of the annexation.

However, the nonrecognition of Iraq's annexation of Kuwait was short-lived because by 28 February 1991 a US-led coalition of forces authorised by the UNSC had expelled Iraqi forces from Kuwait and reinstalled Jaber Al-Ahmad Al-Sabah as Emir of Kuwait. Thus, the reason why the international community do not currently engage in nonrecognition of the Iraqi conquest is that they instead used effective military sanctions to enforce the rule against aggression, expel Iraq and re-establish the previous government in Kuwait.

Abandoning the rule

When Italy invaded Ethiopia in 1935, the League of Nations imposed collective economic sanctions on Italy in order to enforce the rule against resorting to force in violation of the League Covenant. However, after Italy's military victory, within a few years, almost all states had recognised Ethiopia as a part of the Italian Empire. The recognition of Italian sovereignty over Ethiopia was not an isolated affair, but instead was part of a much broader institutional shift away from the existing, albeit incipient, rules, principles and practices that constituted interwar peacemaking. For example, according to Baer,

> When it became clear, in the course of the Ethiopian affair, that the status quo in Europe would not be effectively defended, future possibilities for a collective security system or even for an arrangement other than appeasement to accommodate peaceful change, disappeared. (1972: 178)

The reason why many states switched from initial resistance to Italy's conquest to acceptance and recognition was because they were abandoning the embryonic collective security system and resorting to alternative approaches to conflict management, of which appeasement is the most famous.

Table 6.3 shows that all of the cases where there was no nonrecognition imposed by the international community can be explained by the model of rule maintenance.

Table 6.3 Sources of variation in nonrecognition

Case name	Reason for no nonrecognition	
India–Portugal (Goa)	Ambiguity	Conflicting norms
India–Pakistan (Bangladesh)	Ambiguity	Conflicting norms
Dahomey–Portugal	Ambiguity	Conflicting norms
China–Vietnam (Paracel Islands)	Ambiguity	Unclear sovereignty, consent
Iran–United Arab Emirates (Hormuz Islands)	Ambiguity	Unclear sovereignty
India–Hyderabad	Ambiguity	Status of entities, consent
North/South Vietnam	Ambiguity	Status of entities
Ethiopia–Eritrea	Ambiguity	Status of entities
Iraq–Kuwait	Effective material sanctions	
Italy–Ethiopia	Rule abandoned	

THE ANNEXATION OF CRIMEA

The most recent example of a debate over nonrecognition occurred during the writing of this book: the collective nonrecognition of Russia's annexation of the Ukrainian province of Crimea. In the aftermath of the Ukrainian revolution in 2014, a series of armed pro-Russian protests in the Simferopol and Sevastopol areas of the Crimean peninsula led to the seizure of Crimea's parliament and other buildings in February 2014. A new de facto prime minister was elected by the parliament who appealed to Russian President Vladimir Putin for assistance and later held a referendum on self-sovereignty for Crimea. This referendum was held on 16 March, the official result of which was a vote to rejoin the Russian Federation. On 21 March the Russian government approved a treaty of accession of the Crimea to the Russian Federation. Apart from a few states, like Syria, Venezuela, Afghanistan, Cuba and Nicaragua,[5] the vast majority of the international community does not recognise Russia's annexation of Crimea.

To what extent do the events in this case fit the rule maintenance model? First, Russia's actions were declared a norm violation. Even before the Crimean parliament and the Russian government went through the process of treaty ratification, Western states had issued harsh condemnations. The President of France issued a statement that the

> referendum in Crimea . . . is illegal under Ukrainian and international law. I condemn this decision [to integrate Crimea into Russia]. France recognises neither the results of the referendum held in Crimea on 16 March nor the incorporation of that region of Ukraine into Russia.[6]

UK Prime Minister David Cameron said that, 'It is completely unacceptable for Russia to use force to change borders, on the basis of a sham referendum held at the barrel of a Russian gun.'[7] German government spokesperson Steffan Seibert said that the 'referendum violates the Ukrainian constitution and is a breach of international law [and it] is illegal in our view'.[8] US President Barack Obama told Putin personally that 'the referendum in Crimea was a clear violation of Ukrainian Constitutions (ph) and international law, and it will not be recognised by the international community'.[9]

In the UNSC, a draft resolution introduced by a coalition of forty-two states called for reaffirming Ukraine's sovereignty and territorial integrity and for all states 'not to recognise any alteration of the status of Crimea on the basis of this referendum' (S/2014/189). Thirteen members of the council voted in favour, China abstained and Russia vetoed it. As the Australian representative Gary Quinlan noted, despite the veto, 'the message from Council members and the wider international community has been overwhelming' (S/PV 2014, 7138). A similar resolution was proposed in the UNGA (A/RES/68/262) and was passed with 100 in favour, fifty-eight abstentions and eleven in against. While the large amount of abstentions points to some irresolution, it seems reasonable to say that at this point Russia's actions have been declared a norm violation by the international community.

In accordance with the next stage of the rule maintenance model, despite the imposition on Russia of sanctions by various states and international organisations, like the US, the EU, Canada, Australia and Japan, there has been no reversal of the de facto incorporation of Crimea into the Russian Federation.

What about the stage of uncertainty concerning the status of the rule? Eighty years after Stimson proclaimed his doctrine and seventy years after the founding of the UN, is the rule against aggression sufficiently institutionalised not to be threatened? While there have been no calls to change formal international law, Russia's actions prompted a slew of commentary by various people that points towards a state of uncertainty over the status of the rule. US President Barack Obama, speaking to an EU audience in March 2014 about how it was a 'moment of testing for . . . the international order' said that Russia's annexation

> is challenging truths that only a few weeks ago seemed self-evident, that in the 21st century, the borders of Europe cannot be redrawn with force, that international law matters, that people and nations can make their own decisions about their future.[10]

Speaking to the UNGA later that year, Obama said that 'Russia's actions in Ukraine challenge this post-war order.'[11] NATO Secretary-General Anders Fogh Rasmussen, in a speech to the Brookings Institution said that 'we live in a different world than we did less than a month ago' and described Russian action as an attempt to 'rewrite or simply rip up the international rule book' (Dews 2014). In an article titled 'The new world order' in *The Economist* (2014) it was written that 'Mr Putin has driven a tank over the existing world order.' Other articles were titled things like, 'Is the "liberal international order" dying?' (Harris 2014), 'Europe's shattered dream of order' (Krastev and Leonard 2015) and 'The new world disorder' (Ignatieff 2014), and some spoke of 'Putin's puncturing of the post-Cold War order' creating a post-Crimea world (Shevstova 2014). There is, therefore, some indication that there is some sense of uncertainty over the status of the rule against using force to gain territory, making the rule maintenance action of nonrecognition worthwhile.

So, the Crimean crisis does seem to fit the rule maintenance model. We cannot yet delve into the private and classified communications that would give us more evidence of reasoning behind nonrecognition decisions. However, there are some indications that rule maintenance considerations have been important in sustaining the collective impetus towards nonrecognition of the Crimea annexation. After Russia's veto of the draft resolution S/2014/189 (see above), several comments in the UNSC pointed towards reaffirmation of principles as the primary or only justification for the resolution. Mark Lyall Grant of the UK said that the draft resolution was 'to reaffirm core United Nations principles' (S/PV 2014, 7138). Gary Quinlan (Australia) said, 'Its purpose was to reaffirm the fundamental principles and norms governing relations between States in the post-1945 world.'[12] The Lithuanian representative, Raimonda Murmokaite, framed her response purely in terms of 'saying yes' to various 'internationally accepted rules of behaviour based on the norms and principles of international law'. Sylvie Lucas, the president of the UNSC and representative of Luxembourg, said that 'the draft resolution was intended to recall the purposes and principles of the United Nations'. Outside the UNSC, President Obama, while speaking to a NATO/EU audience about the international system and international laws and rules, mentioned that 'those rules are not self-executing. They depend on people and nations of good will continually affirming them', and justified condemnation of 'Russia's violation of international law' as necessary 'because the principles that have meant so much to Europe and the world must be lifted up'.[13]

This brief consideration of the Crimean crisis is not dispositive, but does point towards the central role of rule maintenance considerations in at least the public discussion, justification and legitimation of the nonrecognition of Russia's annexation. The prospects for the generalisability of the rule maintenance model to the broader universe of cases of nonrecognition seems a promising topic for future in-depth research.

NOTES

1. Talmon lists seventy-seven states as having announced their recognition of the SADR with four subsequently withdrawing that recognition before 1998 (1998: 308–9). Talmon adds that 'in most cases it is not clear in what capacity the SADR has been recognised' (1998: 309).
2. S/PV (S: Security Council and PV: *procès-verbal*) refers to the United Nations Security Council Official Record. Referenced with year, meeting and paragraph number.
3. 'GCC condemns Iranian annexation measures in Abu Musa Island', 14 September 1992, Middle East Energy News, <https://mees.com/opec-history/1992/09/14/

gcc-condemns-iranian-annexation-measures-in-abu-musa-island/> (last accessed 23 January 2017).

4. 'Arab League backs UAE in dispute over Abu Musa', 21 September 1992, Middle East Energy News, <https://mees.com/opec-history/1992/09/21/arab-league-backs-uae-in-dispute-over-abu-musa/> (last accessed 23 January 2017).

5. Rosenberg 2014; 'Nicaragua recognises Crimea as part of Russia', Kyiv Post, 27 March 2014, <http://www.kyivpost.com/content/ukraine/nicaragua-recognises-crimea-as-part-of-russia-341102.html> (last accessed 23 January 2017).

6. 'Ukraine – Communiqué issued by François Hollande, President of the Republic, 18 March 2014', <http://www.diplomatie.gouv.fr/en/country-files/ukraine/events/article/ukraine-communique-issued-by> (last accessed 2 February 2016).

7. PM statement on President Putin's actions on Crimea, 18 March 2014, <https://www.gov.uk/government/news/pm-statement-on-president-putins-actions-on-crimea> (last accessed 23 January 2017).

8. 'German government condemns referendum', 17 March 2014, <http://www.bundesregierung.de/Content/EN/Artikel/2014/03/2014-03-17-krim-statement-sts.html> (last accessed 23 January 2017).

9. 'Transcript: Obama announces sanctions after Crimean referendum', 17 March 2014, <https://www.washingtonpost.com/world/transcript-obama-announces-sanctions-after-crimea-referendum/2014/03/17/b000e574-ade4-11e3-9627-c65021d6d572_story.html> (last accessed 23 January 2017).

10. 'Full transcript: President Obama gives speech addressing Europe, Russia on March 26', 2014, <https://www.washingtonpost.com/world/transcript-president-obama-gives-speech-addressing-europe-russia-on-march-26/2014/03/26/07ae80ae-b503-11e3-b899-20667de76985_story.html> (last accessed 23 January 2017).

11. 'Remarks by President Obama in address to the United Nations General Assembly', 24 September 2014, <https://www.whitehouse.gov/the-press-office/2014/09/24/remarks-president-obama-address-united-nations-general-assembly> (last accessed 23 January 2017).

12. Which were 'respect for the sovereignty and territorial integrity of all States, the obligation to refrain from the threat or use of force against the territorial integrity or political independence of any State, the illegality of the acquisition of territory through the threat or use of force and the obligation to settle disputes by peaceful means'.

13. 'Full transcript: President Obama gives speech addressing Europe, Russia on March 26', 2014, <https://www.washingtonpost.com/world/transcript-president-obama-gives-speech-addressing-europe-russia-on-march-26/2014/03/26/07ae80ae-b503-11e3-b899-20667de76985_story.html> (last accessed 23 January 2017).

Conclusion

The conventional wisdom in international relations is that symbolic sanctions like nonrecognition of the results of force are either a waste of time because they do nothing to enforce compliance to the rule or that they are a cynical ploy by decision makers to appear to be doing something without paying the costs of doing anything stronger. By contrast, this book has argued that nonrecognition is a means of maintaining the rule of nonaggression. It does this by creating common knowledge, through collective public declaration, that states still consider the rule to be the rule. In other words, nonrecognition recreates the illegitimacy of aggression. How do we know this? Are decisions to engage in nonrecognition actually driven by rule maintenance considerations? In Chapters 2 and 4, I find that not only was rule maintenance one of the reasons given for the nonrecognition of Manchukuo and the TRNC, but that for many of the actors it seems to have been the main or the only justification for the policy. In both cases, public collective debate over the issue, in the League of Nations and the UN, was based on rule maintenance reasoning. Further, in Chapter 3, I find that the US, one of a small minority to persist in nonrecognition of the Italian conquest of Ethiopia, justified its policy in terms of rule maintenance.

The findings of the Manchurian Crisis case in Chapter 2 provide the clearest indication that nonrecognition is a symbolic sanction aimed at maintaining the rule against aggression. The reasoning behind the decision is often revealing and explicit. By the end of the process of deliberation over the League's adoption of the Lytton Report, the only surviving justification for not recognising Manchukuo was that such nonrecognition was an act of 'the maintenance of the principles of peace and right' (LNOJ 111 1933: 39).[1] However, some of the features of the case provide a more complicated picture than that portrayed by the model presented in Chapter 1. One complication is that the definition of Japan's actions as aggression was vastly more fraught and fragmented than the phrase 'interpreted as a violation' seems to indicate. Initial perceptions of the actions of the Japanese military in the US and the League Council were mixed. Even after the League dispatched the Lytton Commission to determine who was acting in self-defence and whether aggression had occurred, the report issued by that Commission did not definitively classify the situation as one of aggression. Despite this ambiguity, the League Assembly voted unanimously (minus Japan) to adopt the policy of nonrecognition of Manchukuo. This suggests that concern for the stability or continuity of a rule might result in maintenance actions even when there is only a threat of an action being interpreted as a violation.

A similar ambiguity over the 'definition' of a norm violation was present in the debate over Turkey's invasion of Cyprus, detailed in Chapter 4. Turkey's first use of force was not considered by the US, the UK and the international community as a case of aggression. The Turkish-Cypriots were widely considered to have legitimate grievances, especially in the face of the Greece-backed coup on Cyprus. However, when Turkey abandoned the negotiations in Geneva and restarted military action, there was no plausible justification for their actions except improving their bargaining position through the use of force. The UN's collective condemnation of Turkey, including a change in the language used in UNSC resolutions, and the switch to treating the invasion as illegitimate was much quicker and ultimately less ambiguous than in the Manchurian case. Again, rule maintenance considerations were not only prominent, they were dominant for UK policymakers and in UN discussion. The main complication in this case was the US. Kissinger was far more concerned with maintaining friendly ties with Turkey than with bothering about international law. Even a domestic backlash leading to congressional imposition of economic sanctions was eventually overturned. However, the US did keep in step with the rest of the international community on nonrecognition of the TRNC, using similar rhetoric, and some of the US domestic political debate included concern over 'condoning' aggression.

One of the biggest issues, constantly referenced in UN debates over Turkish action, was the withdrawal of Turkish troops from Cyprus. The withdrawal of troops would have been an important sign that Turkey was not looking to 'profit' or use their de facto military victory as bargaining leverage. Chapter 5 shows that one of the key features of the recognition of Bangladesh was that India publicly committed to withdrawing its troops from Bangladeshi soil. This 'negative case of nonrecognition', that is, a case of recognition, thus suggests one avenue for variation in the imposition of symbolic sanctions like nonrecognition. If a use of force is redefined or excused or socially constructed so that it does not represent a threat to the rule of nonaggression, then rule maintenance is unnecessary. This insight was both reinforced and expanded in Chapter 6. Ten cases of a nonrecognition debate did not result in nonrecognition and eight of those involved a failure to conclusively determine that the use of force constituted a rule violation. This failure took several forms. In some cases, the norm of decolonisation or self-determination overrode the norm against conquest. In others, there was ambiguity over whether the actors in question were really states, or whether they had had sovereignty over the territory in the first place. Finally, in a couple of cases, the conquered formally acquiesced to their change in status. This finding suggests that the politics of collective interpretation of actions as rule violations is an important future topic for more detailed research.[2]

Another source of variation was revealed in Chapter 3's analysis of the Ethiopian crisis. The recognition of Italy's conquest of Ethiopia was not a decision isolated from considerations of norm dynamics and rule maintenance. The switch by the League and many of its members was part of a strategy to enlist Italian support against Nazi Germany, which was increasingly indicating that it was not intending to abide by the new rules of peacemaking. However, this switch happened in the context of a more general abandonment of those new rules, the incipient system of collective security, in favour of varied versions of appeasement policy. Once the rule was no longer valued or seen as realistic, decision makers saw no need to continue maintaining the rule.

THEORETICAL IMPLICATIONS

Understanding the role of nonrecognition of aggressive gain has several broader implications. Before writing this book, I had found that the substantive topic of the delegitimation of the spoils of war was unaddressed in the still burgeoning literature on the norms of war. Furthermore, existing theories in IR did not provide a satisfactory explanation of why states would resist a clearly established new balance of power, but not actually take action to change that balance. This was especially puzzling given that I could find no explicit rationale for doing so and many arguments against such a seemingly idealistic policy. The case of the nonrecognition of Manchukuo was particularly problematic as the historical literature almost universally condemns this as useless and a serious mistake in the run up to World War II. So, I looked further afield for explanations. One of the revelations of my book research has been that the boundaries separating different disciplines in social science hide or obscure deep parallels in the study of human behaviour. Norms, rules and institutions are the focus of inquiry across the fields of political science, sociology, economics, philosophy, legal studies, evolutionary biology and social psychology. Differences in terminology, starting assumptions and explanatory goals and methods can make for confusion, but the questions of norm formation and enforcement are central in all of these literatures.

Game theoretic work provides a starting point into some of the basic strategic dilemmas faced by social actors. However, despite Harsanyi's advances in transforming games of incomplete information into games of imperfect information, game theory and rationalist scholarship based on its insights relies on the irreducible concept of common knowledge.[3] The creation of common knowledge turns out to be an incredibly important part of how the beliefs of individuals take on a life of their own and become 'intersubjective'. Intersubjectivity is a crucial part of constructivist theoretical discourse. These ideas are thus right at the intersection of the two main theoretical strands in IR, and are an important point of complementarity between them. In this book, I have used the idea that collective public 'rituals', or acts or declarations, create common knowledge of actors' beliefs[4] to explain the use of symbolic sanctions that have little or no coercive effect. These symbolic sanctions create common knowledge, with the result that actors then believe that there is a norm, that there is an intersubjective entity. They then treat this norm as existing objectively. They have to orient their behaviour around it, even if they individually do not believe in it.[5] Symbolic sanctions are worth doing because of this effect on actors' expectations and interpretations. They also then become the site of political contestation; it may be in your interests to facilitate, or foil, the creation of such intersubjective understandings.

The findings of this book thus suggest that we need to think more about the creation and manipulation of common knowledge in international politics. These dynamics occur frequently, in international politics and in other areas of social and political life, and yet they are usually ignored in analyses of state behaviour in the IR literature. It is my hope that the findings of this book prove fruitful in the sense of motivating others to take seriously the creation and contestation of common knowledge both as a driver and an effect of state behaviour.

In terms of rule maintenance more specifically, several avenues of future research suggest themselves. Rule maintenance actions are a means to mutual reassurance that the rule is still the rule, but undoubtedly there are numerous factors contributing to actors' beliefs and expectations about others' behaviour. In particular, it seems likely that the longer a rule has existed and the more it has been reproduced, not only the more that individuals treat it as normal and taken for granted (internalisation), but also the more people will expect others to act in accordance with it and take it into account when deciding how to act. This implies that rule maintenance actions are more important, more effectual and more necessary for the rule to continue, in the earlier stages of a rule's development. New rules might be more fragile and need maintaining, whereas old rules might be more robust and thus require less attention. This is an important question that would have consequential policy implications for statesmen who want to help or hinder the development of international rules.

Another issue is the extent of the participation necessary in rule maintenance actions to achieve the common knowledge that there is a rule. Unanimity may be necessary in an abstract n-player coordination game to avoid common knowledge unravelling, but in practice majorities seem to serve just as well. More study is needed on the dynamics of achieving the degree of visible consensus necessary for actors to believe that there is a rule. It is also implausible that each actor counts equally. In this book I have focused on the decisions of two powerful states: the US and the UK. To what extent do powerful, or influential, actors matter in the creation of common knowledge? Can smaller or weaker states act as prime movers and start a cascade that leads to the creation or breakdown of an intersubjective understanding? Maybe there are sources of credibility other than military or economic power. It is possible that states can have a kind of reverse credibility. In a similar way that 'only Nixon could go to China' (Nixon's known anti-communist activities making accusations of being soft on communism less effective), maybe some states' reputations make them more effective at creating the impression of consensus on a rule. For example, China has been notorious for its anti-interventionist stance, especially as regards deploying peacekeeping troops. When it recently reversed this stance and started to contribute to peacekeeping missions, it is plausible that this created the impression that peacekeeping was now a consensus position. This and other questions are the sorts of lines of inquiry that are prompted by the findings in this book.

My arguments do have important implications for broader debates over the nature or sources of variation in which political entities are accorded recognition, that is, membership in the international community. In particular, 'recognition of states' is, for many purposes, not a homogenous concept.[6] The influences on state decisions to recognise may be found in the context of the norms of war or contingent dynamics of the institutional rules of peacemaking, rather than the rules specifically applying to membership in the international system. It is thus

206

problematic, and could lead to misleading conclusions, to treat each recognition decision as causally homogenous and divorced from the normative context. Further, the ubiquity of political considerations, which includes rule maintenance, indicates that a primarily legalistic approach, such as Crawford (2006), will miss a large part of what actually drives recognition decisions.

The nature of norms and the reality of rules

A constant underlying theme of this book has been that the nature of norms and rules is fluid, changing and manipulable, and yet they exercise considerable influence on the beliefs and decisions of individuals acting on behalf of states. This seemingly dual nature of norms, as both constructed and consequential, can seem incoherent and analysts often bracket one side in order to explain the other. The state of the field of IR has changed considerably since the early 1990s when arguments that norms matter at all were new and highly contested. Now it is much more common for empirical analyses to incorporate norms in some way or another. However, rigid conceptions of norms and their effects are widespread. For example, rationalist institutionalism, which is a highly prominent and influential research programme in IR, explicitly treats institutions and norms as behaviour in equilibrium.[7] Even work based on the conception of norms as something above and beyond behaviour often treats behaviour as binary: it is either in compliance with a norm or in violation of it. The findings of this book provide a convincing demonstration that foreign policy decision makers consider norms and rules as something separate from their own behaviour, and indeed separate from their own beliefs about what is right and appropriate. The cases studied reveal that there is often genuine uncertainty over whether a state's use of force 'counts' as aggression, and that actors strategically try to frame situations a certain way and legitimate actions to other states. Despite this uncertainty, and despite the seeming cynicism of politically expedient attempts to excuse the use of force, the results of these legitimation and framing contests can be significant. I submit that the concepts used in this book, particularly that common knowledge is created by public acts and declarations, can potentially lead to an explanation for the way in which once fluid and contested meanings can get 'fixed' and hence no longer easily changeable. If developed further and incorporated into research on norms and institutions in IR, this insight should dissolve many of the problems analysts currently face when trying to account for changes in normative and institutional structures.

The book also constitutes an attempt to take seriously Baldwin's (1985, 2000) exhortations to think about the multifarious uses, purposes and effects of sanctions. Baldwin's concern was primarily economic sanctions, but his insights apply a fortiori to primarily diplomatic sanctions, like non-recognition. One of the important questions about sanctions is: when are they imposed? This book suggests sources of variation in the imposition of collective sanctions, and provides a demonstration of the plausibility of some sources of variation. If a putative norm violation is deemed not to count as a rule violation, or if the members of the international community no longer see the value in perpetuating a norm or rule, then sanctions against a norm violator may not make strategic sense. Conversely, another question in the sanctions literature is why sanctions persist even when it is clear to many that they are not 'working' (inducing policy change in the target). Prior to this book, there was no satisfactory articulation of the rationale behind rule maintenance. Now the sanctions literature has another, seemingly abundant, mechanism to take into consideration and evaluate.

NOTES

1. League of Nations Official Journal (LNOJ). Referenced with the year and page number.
2. Kornprobst (2014) is one recent example.
3. This is the insight that Herbert Gintis, a passionate advocate for game theoretic analysis, credits for his turn towards the necessity of including norms into his work (2009: xiv).
4. A concept from Chwe (1998, 2001) who is employed in a political science department, used analytical methods from economics and published the work in sociology journals.
5. One manifestation of this is Kuran's idea of 'preference falsification' (1995) where people publicly tailor their choices to what appears to be socially acceptable.
6. Fabry (2010) also makes this point, highlighting the distinction between recognition requests from 'entities formed as a direct consequence of the threat or use of force by an external power across international boundaries' and those resulting from secession, dissolution or decolonisation (2010: 8).
7. Although some are moving away from this conception; see Greif and Kingston (2011) for a rationalist approach to institutions as rules rather than equilibria.

Bibliography

UNPUBLISHED PAPERS

Foreign and Commonwealth Office Archives, National Archives, Kew, *Military coup against President Makarios in Cyprus, 15 July 1974*, FCO 9/1894.

Foreign and Commonwealth Office Archives, National Archives, Kew, *Possible Unilateral Declaration of Independence by Turkish Federated State of Cyprus (TFSC)*, FCO 9/2168.

Foreign and Commonwealth Office Archives, National Archives, Kew, *International recognition of Bangla Desh*, FCO 37/902.

Foreign and Commonwealth Office Archives, National Archives, Kew, *International recognition of Bangla Desh*, FCO 37/1019.

Foreign and Commonwealth Office Archives, National Archives, Kew, *International recognition of Bangla Desh*, FCO 37/1020.

Henry L. Stimson, Diaries, 1931–2, Library of Congress.

Neville Chamberlain Diaries, 1938. *The Chamberlain Papers from University of Birmingham Library: The Papers of Neville Chamberlain. Diary Entries, February 19 and 27, 1938*.

Premier's Archives, National Archives, Kew, *Visit of Sheikh Mujib, Prime Minister of Bangladesh, to London: UK recognition of Bangladesh*, PREM 15/751.

War Office and Ministry of Defence Archives, National Archives, Kew, *Report on the Cyprus Emergency*, WO 386/21.

William R. Castle Diaries, 1918–1960 (MS Am 2021). Houghton Library, Harvard University.

GOVERNMENT AND INTERNATIONAL
ORGANISATION DOCUMENTS

Digital National Security Archive. 1975. *CSCE; Cyprus; China and Japan; Germany and Berlin; Emigration; SALT II, Secret, Memorandum of Conversation, February 16, 1975*, KT01499.

International Court of Justice Reports of Judgements, Advisory Opinions and Orders. 1995. *Case Concerning East Timor (Portugal v. Australia)*.

League of Nations. 1931. *Official Journal*, Geneva: League of Nations.

League of Nations. 1932. *Official Journal*, Geneva: League of Nations.

209

League of Nations. 1932. *Official Journal Special Supplement 101*, Geneva: League of Nations.

League of Nations. 1933. *Official Journal*, Geneva: League of Nations.

League of Nations. 1933. *Official Journal Special Supplement 111*, Geneva: League of Nations.

League of Nations, 1935. *Official Journal*. Geneva: League of Nations.

League of Nations. 1935. *Official Journal Special Supplement 138*, Geneva: League of Nations.

League of Nations. 1936. *Official Journal Special Supplement 151*, Geneva: League of Nations.

League of Nations. 1936. *Official Journal Special Supplement 155*, Geneva: League of Nations.

League of Nations. 1938. *Official Journal*, Geneva: League of Nations.

League of Nations. 1938. *Official Journal Special Supplement 138*, Geneva: League of Nations

UK Foreign and Commonwealth Office. 1960. *Documents on British Foreign Policy, 1919–1939*, Second Series. Vol. VIII. London: Her Majesty's Stationery Office.

UK Foreign and Commonwealth Office. 1965. *Documents on British Foreign Policy, 1919–1939*, Second Series. Vol. IX. London: Her Majesty's Stationery Office.

UK Foreign and Commonwealth Office. 1970. *Documents on British Foreign Policy, 1919–1939*, Second Series. Vol. XI. Far Eastern affairs October 1932 – June 1933, London: Her Majesty's Stationery Office.

UK Foreign and Commonwealth Office. 1976. *Documents on British Foreign Policy, 1919–1939*, Second Series. Vol. XIV. The Italo-Ethiopian dispute March 1934 – October 1935, London: Her Majesty's Stationery Office.

UK Foreign and Commonwealth Office. 1976. *Documents on British Foreign Policy, 1919–1939*, Second Series. Vol. XV. The Italo-Ethiopian war and German affairs October 1935 – February 1936, London: Her Majesty's Stationery Office.

UK Foreign and Commonwealth Office. 1977. *Documents on British Foreign Policy, 1919–1939*, Second Series. Vol. XVI. The Rhineland crisis and the ending of sanctions March – July 1936, London: Her Majesty's Stationery Office.

UK Foreign and Commonwealth Office. 1977. *Documents on British Foreign Policy, 1919–1939*, Second Series. Vol. XIX. European Affairs, July 1937 – August 1938, London: Her Majesty's Stationery Office.

UK Foreign and Commonwealth Office. 2006. eds. Keith A. Hamilton and Patrick Salmon, *Documents on British Policy Overseas, Series III, Volume V, The Southern Flank in Crisis, 1973–1976*, London: Routledge.

UK House of Commons, 1932. *Hansard, House of Commons Debates, 22 February 1932*, London: Her Majesty's Stationery Office.

UK House of Commons, 1932. *Hansard, House of Commons Debates, 14 March 1932*, London: Her Majesty's Stationery Office.

UK House of Commons, 1935. *Hansard, House of Commons Debates, 19 December 1935*, London: Her Majesty's Stationery Office.

UK House of Commons, 1936. *Hansard, House of Commons Debates, 26 March 1936*, London: Her Majesty's Stationery Office.

UK House of Commons, 1936. *Hansard, House of Commons Debates, 15 December 1936*, London: Her Majesty's Stationery Office.

UK House of Commons, 1938. *Hansard, House of Commons Debates, 11 May 1938*, London: Her Majesty's Stationery Office.

UK House of Commons, 1938. *Hansard, House of Commons Debates, 21 May 1938*, London: Her Majesty's Stationery Office.

UK House of Commons, 1938. *Hansard, House of Commons Debates, 29 June 1938*, London: Her Majesty's Stationery Office.

UK House of Commons, 1938. *Hansard, House of Commons Debates, 2 November 1938*, London: Her Majesty's Stationery Office.

UK House of Commons. 1983. *Hansard, House of Commons Debates, 15 November 1983*, London: Her Majesty's Stationery Office.

UK House of Commons. 1984. *Hansard, House of Commons Debates, 17 May 1984*, London: Her Majesty's Stationery Office.

UK House of Commons. 1987. *Foreign Affairs Committee, Third Report Session 1986–7, Cyprus: Report with an appendix, together with the Proceedings of the Committee, Minutes of Evidence and Appendices, 7 May 1987*, London: Her Majesty's Stationery Office.

UK House of Lords. 1983. *Hansard, House of Lords Debates, 16 November 1983*, London: Her Majesty's Stationery Office.

United Nations. 1974. *Yearbook 1974*. New York: United Nations.

United Nations Security Council. 1971. *Official Record 1971*, New York: United Nations.

United Nations Security Council. 1972. *Official Record 1972*, New York: United Nations.

United Nations Security Council. 1974. *Official Record 1974*, New York: United Nations.

United Nations Security Council. 1975. *Official Record 1975*, New York: United Nations.

United Nations Security Council. 1983. *Official Record 1983*, New York: United Nations.

United Nations Security Council. 2014. *Official Record 2014*, New York: United Nations.

US Department of State. 1943. 'Neutrality Act of August 31 1945', in Publication 1983, *Peace and War: United States Foreign Policy, 1931–1941*, Washington, DC: US Government Printing Office, pp. 265–71.

US Department of State. 1943. *Foreign Relations of the United States, Japan 1931–1941, vol. I*, Washington, DC: US Government Printing Office.

US Department of State. 1948. *Foreign Relations of the United States, 1932, vol. III*, Washington, DC: US Government Printing Office.

US Department of State. 1953. *Foreign Relations of the United States, 1936. The Near East and Africa, Volume III*, Washington, DC: US Government Printing Office.

US Department of State. 1954. *Foreign Relations of the United States, 1937. The British Commonwealth, Europe, Near East and Africa, Volume II*, Washington, DC: US Government Printing Office.

US Department of State. 2005. *Foreign Relations of the United States, 1969–1976, vol. XI, South Asia Crisis, 1971*, Washington, DC: US Government Printing Office.

US Department of State. 2005. *Foreign Relations of the United States, 1969–1976, vol. E-7, Documents on South Asia 1969–1972*, Washington, DC: US Government Printing Office.

US Department of State. 2007. *Foreign Relations of the United States, 1969–1976, vol. XXX, Greece; Cyprus; Turkey, 1973–1976*, Washington, DC: US Government Printing Office.

US House of Representatives. 1983. *Congressional Record*, 98th Cong. 1st sess., Washington, DC: US Government Printing Office.

US House of Representatives, Committee on Foreign Affairs. 1974. *Cyprus – 1974. Hearings before the Committee on Foreign Affairs and its Subcommittee on Europe*. 93d Cong., 2d sess. 19 and 20 August, Washington, DC: US Government Printing Office.

US House of Representatives, Committee on Foreign Affairs, Subcommittee on Europe and the Middle East. 1981. Ellen. B. Laipson (ed.), *Congressional-Executive Relations and the Turkish Arms Embargo*, Washington, DC: US Government Printing Office.

US Senate. 1983. *Congressional Record*, 98th Cong. 1st sess., Washington, DC: US Government Printing Office.

BOOKS AND JOURNAL ARTICLES

Abadi, Jacob. 1998. 'The Sino-Indian conflict of 1962–a test case for India's policy on non-alignment', *Journal of Third World Studies* 15(2): 11–29.

Agne, Hans, Jens Bartelson, Eva Erman, Thomas Lindemann, Benjamin Herborth, Oliver Kessler, Christine Chwaszcza, Mikulas Fabry and Stephen D. Krasner. 2013. 'Symposium "The politics of international recognition"', *International Theory* 5(1): 94–176.

Asmussen, Jan. 2008. *Cyprus at War: Diplomacy and Conflict during the 1974 Crisis*, New York: I. B. Tauris.

Baer, George W. 1967. *The Coming of the Italian-Ethiopian War*, Cambridge, MA: Harvard University Press.

Baer, George W. 1972. 'Sanctions and security: the League of Nations and the Italo-Ethiopian War, 1935–1936', *International Organization* 27(2): 165–79.

Baer, George W. 1976. *Test Case: Italy, Ethiopia, and the League of Nations*, Stanford University Press.

Baldwin, David A. 1985. *Economic Statecraft*, Princeton, NJ: Princeton University Press.

Baldwin, David A. 2000. 'The sanctions debate and the logic of choice', *International Security* 24(3): 80–107.

Barber, James. 1979, 'Sanctions as a policy instrument', *International Affairs* 55(3): 367–84.

Bassett, Reginald G. 1952. *Democracy and Foreign Policy: Case History of the Sino-Japanese Dispute, 1931–1933*, London: Longmans, Green and Co.

Bates, Robert H., Avner Greif, Margaret Levi, Jean-Laurent Rosenthal and Barry R. Weingast. 1998. *Analytic Narratives*, Princeton, NJ: Princeton University Press.

Beach, Derek and Rasmus Brun Pedersen. 2013. *Process-Tracing Methods: Foundations and Guidelines*, Ann Arbor, MI: University of Michigan Press.

Braddick, Henderson B. 1962. 'A new look at American Policy during the Italo-Ethiopian crisis: 1935-36', *The Journal of Modern History* 34(1): 64–73.

Briggs, Herbert W. 1940. 'Non-recognition of title by conquest and limitations on the doctrine', *Proceedings of the American Society of International Law* 34: 72–99.

Brownlie, Ian. 1963. *International Law and the Use of Force by States*, Oxford: Oxford University Press.

Burns, Richard D. and Edward M. Bennett. 1974. *Diplomats in Crisis: United States-Chinese-Japanese Relations, 1919–1941*, Santa Barbara, CA: ABC-Clio.

Caldwell, Dan. 1996. 'Flashpoint in the Gulf: Abu Musa and the Tunb Islands', *Middle East Policy* 4(3): 50–7.

Callaghan, James. 1987. *Time and Chance*, London: Collins.

Calvin, J. B. 1984. *The China-India Border War (1962)*, Quantico, VA: Marine Corps Command and Staff College.

Caspersen, Nina. 2012. *Unrecognized States: The Struggle for Sovereignty in the Modern International System*, Cambridge: Polity.

Caspersen, Nina and Gareth Stansfield. 2011. *Unrecognised States in the International System*, London: Routledge.

Checkel, Jeffrey T. 2005. 'International institutions and socialization in Europe: introduction and framework', *International Organization* 59(4): 801–26.

Chesterman, Simon and Beatrice Pouligny. 2003. Are sanctions meant to work? The politics of creating and implementing sanctions though the United Nations, *Global Governance* 9(4): 503–18.

Chwe, Michael Suk-Young. 1998. 'Culture, circles, and commercials: publicity, common knowledge, and social coordination', *Rationality and Society* 10(1): 47–75.

Chwe, Michael Suk-Young. 2001. *Rational Ritual: Culture, Coordination, and Common Knowledge*, Princeton, NJ: Princeton University Press.

Clark, Herbert H. and Charles R. Marshall. 1981. 'Definite reference and mutual knowledge', in Aravind Krishna Joshi, Bonnie Lynn Webber and Ivan A. Sag (eds), *Elements of Discourse Understanding*, Cambridge: Cambridge University Press, pp. 10–63.

Clausewitz, Carl von. [1832] 1976. *On War*, Michael Howard and Peter Paret (eds. and trans.), Princeton, NJ: Princeton University Press.

Coggins, Bridget. 2016. *Power Politics and State Formation in the Twentieth Century*, Cambridge: Cambridge University Press.

Cole, Wayne. 1990. 'American appeasement', in David F. Schmitz and Richard D. Challener (eds), *Appeasement in Europe: A Reassessment of US Policies*, Praeger, pp. 1–20.

Crawford, James R. 2006. *The Creation of States in International Law*, Oxford: Oxford University Press.

Crawford, Neta and Audie Klotz. 1999. *How Sanctions Work: South Africa in Comparative Perspective*, Basingstoke: Palgrave Macmillan.

Current, Richard N. 1954. 'The Stimson Doctrine and the Hoover Doctrine', *The American Historical Review* 59(3): 513–42.

Dallek, Robert. 2007. *Nixon and Kissinger: Partners in Power*, New York: HarperCollins.

Dart, Dorothy R. 1938. 'Chronicle of international events', *American Journal of International Law* 32(2): 355–68.

Das, Taraknath. (1949) 'The status of Hyderabad during and after British Rule in India', *American Journal of International Law* 43(1): 57–72.

213

Dasgupta, Punyapriya. 2000. 'Derecognition of Western Sahara: foreign policy volte-face', *Economic and Political Weekly* 35(33): 2914–17.

DeSilvio, David. 2008. 'The influence of domestic politics on foreign policy in the election of 1940', doctoral dissertation, Wayne State University.

Devereux, David R. 2009. 'The Sino-Indian War of 1962 in Anglo-American relations', *Journal of Contemporary History* 44(1): 71–87.

Dodd, Clement. 2010. *The History and Politics of the Cyprus Conflict*, New York: Palgrave Macmillan.

Doenecke, Justus. D. 1981. *The Diplomacy of Frustration: The Manchurian Crisis of 1931–1933 as Revealed in the Papers of Stanley K. Hornbeck*, Stanford, CA: Hoover Institution Press.

Doenecke, Justus. D. 1984. *When the Wicked Rise: American Opinion-Makers and the Manchurian Crisis of 1931–1933*, Lewisburg, PA: Bucknell University Press.

Dugard, John. 1970. 'South West Africa and the terrorist trial', *American Journal of International Law* 64: 19–41.

Durkheim, Emile. [1893] 1984. *The Division of Labor in Society*, L. A. Coser (trans.), New York: The Free Press.

Dutton, David. 1992. *Simon: A Political Biography of Sir John Simon*, London: Aurum Press.

Eagleton, Clyde. 1950. 'The case of Hyderabad before the Security Council', *American Journal of International Law* 44(2): 277–302.

Elster, Jon. 2007. *Explaining Social Behavior: More Nuts and Bolts for the Social Sciences*, Cambridge, MA: Cambridge University Press.

Fabry, Mikulas. 2010. *Recognizing States: International Society and the Establishment of New States since 1776*, Cambridge: Cambridge University Press.

Falk, Armin, Ernst Fehr and Urs Fischbacher. 2005. 'Driving forces behind informal sanctions', *Econometrica* 73(6): 2017–30.

Farnham, Barbara Rearden. 1997. *Roosevelt and the Munich Crisis: A Study of Political Decision-Making*, Princeton, NJ: Princeton University Press.

Feiling, Keith. 1970. *A Life of Neville Chamberlain*, London: Macmillan.

Ferrell, Robert H. 1957. *American Diplomacy in the Great Depression*, New Haven, CT: Yale University Press.

Finnemore, Martha and Kathryn Sikkink. 1998. 'International norm dynamics and political change', *International Organization* 52(4): 887–917.

Franck, Thomas M. 2002. *Recourse to Force: State Action Against Threats and Armed Attacks*, Cambridge: Cambridge University Press.

Galtung, Johan. 1967. 'On the effects of international economic sanctions: with examples from the case of Rhodesia', *World Politics* 19(3): 378–416.

Geanakoplos, John. 1992. 'Common knowledge', *Journal of Economic Perspectives* 6(4): 52–83.

George, Alexander L. and Andrew Bennett. (2005) *Case Studies and Theory Development in the Social Sciences*, Cambridge, MA: MIT Press.

Gibbons, Robert. 1992. *Game Theory for Applied Economists*, Princeton, NJ: Princeton University Press.

Gintis, Herbert. 2009. *The Bounds of Reason: Game Theory and the Unification of the Behavioral Sciences*, Princeton, NJ: Princeton University Press.

Giumelli, Francesco. 2011. *Coercing, Constraining and Signalling: Explaining UN and EU Aanctions after the Cold War*. Colchester: ECPR Press.

Goddard, Stacie E. 2015. 'The rhetoric of appeasement: Hitler's legitimation and British foreign policy, 1938–39', *Security Studies* 24(1): 95–130.

Goldman, Aaron L. 1974. 'Sir Robert Vansittart's search for Italian cooperation against Hitler, 1933-36', *Journal of Contemporary History* 9(3): 93–130.

Goldstein, Joshua. 2011. *Winning the War on War: The Decline of Armed Conflict Worldwide*, New York: Penguin.

Greif, Avner and Christopher Kingston. 2011. 'Institutions: rules or equilibria?', in Norman Schofield and Gonzalo Caballero (eds), *Political Economy of Institutions, Democracy and Voting*, Berlin and Heidelberg: Springer, pp. 13–43.

Hacking, Ian. 1999. *The Social Construction of What?* Cambridge, MA: Harvard University Press.

Haile, Semere. 1987. 'The origins and demise of the Ethiopia-Eritrea federation', *Issue: A Journal of Opinion* 15: 9–17.

Hamilton, Thomas Theodore. 1953. 'The impact of the Shanghai incident of 1932 upon the United States and the League of Nations', PhD dissertation, Duke University.

Hanhimaki, Jussi M. 2004. *Flawed Architect: Henry Kissinger and American Foreign Policy*, New York: Oxford University Press.

Hardie, Frank. 1974. *The Abyssinian Crisis*, Batsford: Archon.

Harris, Brice Jr. 1964. *The United States and the Italo-Ethiopian Crisis*, Stanford, CA: Stanford University Press.

Hart, Herbert L. A. 1994. *The Concept of Law*, Oxford: Oxford University Press.

Hecht, Robert A. 1969. 'Great Britain and the Stimson note of January 7, 1932', *The Pacific Historical Review* 38(2): 177–91.

Hicks, Sallie M. and Theodore Couloumbis. 1977. 'The "Greek lobby": illusion or reality?' in Abdul Aziz Said (ed.), *Ethnicity and U.S. Foreign Policy*, New York: Praeger, pp. 83–116.

Hovi, Jon, Robert Huseby and Detlef Sprinz. 2005. 'When do (imposed) economic sanctions work?' *World Politics* 57(4): 479–99.

Hull, Cordell. 1948. *The Memoirs of Cordell Hull, Vol. 1.* New York: Macmillan, p. 545.

Jackson, Patrick Thaddeus. 2006. *Civilizing the Enemy: German Reconstruction and the Invention of the West.* Ann Arbor, MI: University of Michigan Press.

Jackson, Patrick Thaddeus. 2010. *The Conduct of Inquiry in International Relations: Philosophy of Science and Its Implications for the Study of World Politics*, London: Routledge.

Jaeger, Hans-Martin. 2008. '"World Opinion" and the founding of the UN: governmentalizing international politics', *European Journal of International Relations* 14(4): 589-618.

Johnson, Gaynor. 2013. 'Philip Noel-Baker, the League of Nations, and the Abyssinian Crisis, 1935–1936', in G. B. Strang (ed.), *Collision of Empires: Italy's Invasion of Ethiopia and its International Impact*, London: Ashgate Publishing, Ltd, pp. 53–71.

Johnston, Alistair I. 2001. 'Treating international institutions as social environments', *International Studies Quarterly* 45(4): 487–515.

Kalha, R. S. (21 November 2012). 'What did China gain at the end of the fighting in November 1962?', Institute for Defence Studies and Analysis, <http://www.

idsa.in/idsacomments/WhatdidChinaGain%20attheEndoftheFighting_RSK-alha_211112> (last accessed 10 August 2017).

Katzenstein, Peter J., Robert O. Keohane and Stephen D. Krasner. 1998. 'International organization and the study of world politics', *International Organization*, 52(4): 645–85.

Kennedy, Paul. M. 1976. *The Rise and Fall of British Naval Mastery*, London: Allen Lane.

Ker-Lindsay, James. 2012. *The Foreign Policy of Counter-Secession: Preventing the Secession of Contested States*, Oxford: Oxford University Press.

Kier, Elizabeth and Jonathan Mercer. 1996. 'Setting precedents in anarchy: military intervention and weapons of mass destruction', *International Security* 20(4): 77–106.

Kissinger, Henry. 1979. *White House Years*, Boston, MA: Little, Brown and Co.

Kissinger, Henry. 1999. *Years of Renewal*, New York: Simon and Schuster.

Korbel, Josef. 1949. 'The Kashmir dispute and the United Nations', *International Organization* 3(2): 278–87.

Korbel, Josef. 1953. 'The Kashmir dispute after six years', *International Organization* 7(4): 498–510.

Korman, Sharon. 1996. *The Right of Conquest: The Acquisition of Territory by Force in International Law and Practice*, New York: Oxford University Press.

Kornprobst, Markus. 2014. 'From political judgements to public justifications (and vice versa): how communities generate reasons upon which to act', *European Journal of International Relations* 20(1): 192–216.

Kuran, Timur. 1995. *Private Truths, Public Lies: The Social Consequences of Preference Falsification*, Cambridge, MA: Harvard University Press.

Kux, Dennis. 1993. *Estranged Democracies: India and the United State 1941–1991*, Los Angeles, CA: Sage Publications.

Kux, Dennis. 2001. *Disenchanted Allies: The United States and Pakistan 1947-2000*, Washington, DC: Johns Hopkins University Press.

Langer, Robert. 1947. *Seizure of Territory: The Stimson Doctrine and Related Principles in Legal Theory and Diplomatic Practice*, Princeton, NJ: Princeton University Press.

Lauterpacht, Hersch. 1947. *Recognition in International Law*, Cambridge: Cambridge University Press.

Lindsay, James. 1986. 'Trade sanctions as policy instruments: a re-examination', *International Studies Quarterly* 30(2): 153–73.

Lippman, Walter and Allan Nevins. 1932. *Interpretations, 1931–1932*, New York: Macmillan.

Lowell, A. Lawrence. 1932. 'Manchuria, the League, and the United States', *Foreign Affairs* 10(3): 351–68.

Malawer, Stuart S. 1977. *Imposed Treaties and International Law*, Getzville, NY: William S. Hein & Co.

Maller, Tara. 2010. 'Diplomacy derailed: the consequences of diplomatic sanctions', *Washington Quarterly* 33(3): 61–79.

Mallinson, William. 2007. 'US interests, British acquiescence, and the invasion of Cyprus', *British Journal of Politics and International Relations* 9(3): 494–508.

McCarty, Nolan and Adam Meirowitz. 2009. *Political Game Theory: An Introduction*, Cambridge: Cambridge University Press.

Marks, Sally. 2003. *The Illusion of Peace*, London: Palgrave Macmillan.

Mercer, Jonathan. 1996. *Reputation and International Politics*, Ithaca, NY: Cornell University Press.

Mirbagheri, Farid. 1998. *Cyprus and International Peacemaking*, New York: Psychology Press.

Mitzen, Jennifer. 2011. 'Governing together: global governance as collective intention', in Markus Kornprobst and Corneliu Bjola (eds), *Arguing Global Governance: Agency, Lifeworld and Shared Reasoning*, London: Routledge.

Morgan, T. Clifton and Valerie L. Schwebach. 1997. 'Fools suffer gladly: the use of economic sanctions in international crises', *International Studies Quarterly* 41(1): 27–50.

Morgenthau, Hans J. 1939. 'The resurrection of neutrality in Europe', *American Political Science Review* 33(3): 473–86.

Mueller, John. 2004. *The Remnants of War*, Ithaca, NY: Cornell University Press.

Musson, Janice. 2008. 'Britain and the recognition of Bangladesh', *Diplomacy and Statecraft* 19(1): 125–44.

Mutsu, Munemitsu. 1982. *Kenkenroku: A Diplomatic Record of the Sino-Japanese War, 1894–5*, edited and translated by Gordon Mark Berger, Tokyo: University of Tokyo Press.

Myers, Denys P. 1939. 'The League of Nations Covenant – 1939 Model', *American Political Science Review* 33(2): 193–218.

Necatigil, Zaim M. 1989. *The Cyprus Question and the Turkish Position in International Law*, Oxford: Oxford University Press.

Nish, Ian H. 2002. *Japanese Foreign Policy in the Interwar Period*, Santa Barbara, CA: Greenwood Publishing Group.

Nossal, Kim R. 1989. 'International sanctions as international punishment', *International Organization* 43(2): 301–22.

Nossal, Kim R. 1991. 'The symbolic purposes of sanctions: Australian and Canadian reactions to Afghanistan', *Australian Journal of Political Science* 26(1): 29–50.

Offner, Arnold A. 1977. 'Appeasement revisited: the United States, Great Britain, and Germany, 1933–1940', *The Journal of American History* 64(2): 373–93.

O'Mahoney, Joseph 2014. 'Rule tensions and the dynamics of institutional change: from "to the victor go the spoils" to the Stimson doctrine', *European Journal of International Relations* 20(3): 834–57.

O'Mahoney, Joseph. 2015. 'Why did they do that?: the methodology of reasons for action', *International Theory* 7(2): 231–62.

Ostrom, Elinor. 1990. *Governing the Commons: The Evolution of Institutions for Collective Action*, Cambridge: Cambridge University Press.

Ostrower, Gary B. 1979. *Collective Insecurity: The United States and the League of Nations during the Early Thirties*, Lewisburg, PA: Bucknell University Press.

Pape, Robert A. 1997. 'Why economic sanctions do not work', *International Security* 22(2): 90–136.

Parker, R. A. C. 1974. 'Great Britain, France, and the Ethiopian crisis, 1935-1936', *The English Historical Review* 89(351): 293–332.

Parker, R. A. C. 1993. *Chamberlain and Appeasement: British Policy and the Coming of the Second World War*, Basingstoke: Macmillan Press.

Pegg, Scott.1998. *International Society and the De Facto State*, London: Ashgate Publishing.

Peterson, M. J. 1982. 'Political use of recognition: the influence of the international system', *World Politics* 34(3): 324–52.

Phillips, William. 1952. *Ventures in Diplomacy*, Boston, MA: Beacon Press.

Pinker, Steven. 2011. *The Better Angels of Our Nature*, New York: Viking.

Post, Gaines Jr. 1993. *Dilemmas of Appeasement: British Deterrence and Defense, 1934–1937*, Ithaca, NY: Cornell University Press.

Pratt, John T. 1971. *War and Politics in China*, Manchester, NH: Ayer Publishing.

Retzlaff, Ralph J. 1963. 'India: a year of stability and change', *Asian Survey* 3(2): 96–106.

Reus Smit, Christian. ed. 2004. *The Politics of International Law*, Cambridge: Cambridge University Press.

Ripsman, Norrin M. and Jack S. Levy. 2008. 'Wishful thinking or buying time? The logic of British appeasement in the 1930s', *International Security* 33(2): 148–81.

Roi, Michael L. 1994. '"A completely immoral and cowardly attitude": the British Foreign Office, American neutrality, and the Hoare–Laval Plan', *Canadian Journal of History* 29: 344–9.

Roi, Michael L. 1997. *Alternatives to Appeasement: Sir Robert Vansittart and Alliance Diplomacy, 1934–1937*, Westport, CT: Praeger.

Rosenne, Shabtai. ed. 1970. *The Law of Treaties: A Guide to the Legislative History of the Vienna Convention*. Leiden, the Netherlands: Brill Archive.

Rubinstein, Ariel. 1989. 'The electronic mail game: strategic behavior under "almost common knowledge"', *American Economic Review* 79(3): 385–91.

Rystad, Goren. 1987. 'Ethnicity and American foreign policy', *Scandia: Tidskrift for historisk forskning*, 53: 2.

Salerno, Reynolds. 2002. *Vital Crossroads: The Mediterranean Origins of the Second World War*, Ithaca, NY: Cornell University Press.

Saltford, John. 2000. 'UNTEA and UNRWI: United Nations involvement in West New Guinea during the 1960s', PhD thesis, University of Hull.

Sandholtz, Wayne. 2007. *Prohibiting Plunder: How Norms Change*, New York: Oxford University Press.

Sbacchi, Alberto. 1997. *Legacy of Bitterness: Ethiopia and Fascist Italy, 1935–1941*, Addis Ababa, Ethiopia: Red Sea Press.

Schelling, Thomas C. 1960. *The Strategy of Conflict*, Cambridge, MA: Harvard University Press.

Schimmelfennig, Frank. 2001. 'The community trap: liberal norms, rhetorical action, and the eastern enlargement of the European Union', *International Organization* 55(1): 47–80.

Searle, John. 1995. *The Social Construction of Reality*, London: Allen Lane.

Searle, John. 2010. *Making the Social World*, New York: Oxford University Press.

Self, Robert C. 2006. *Neville Chamberlain: A Biography*, London: Ashgate Publishing, Ltd.

Shannon, Vaughan P. 2000. 'Norms are what states make of them: the political psychology of norm violation', *International Studies Quarterly* 44(2): 293–316.

Sisson, Richard and Leo E. Rose. 1990. *War and Secession: Pakistan, India, and the Creation of Bangladesh*, Berkeley, CA: University of California Press.

218

Smith, Sara R. 1948. *The Manchurian Crisis, 1931–1932: A Tragedy in International Relations*, New York: Columbia University Press.

Steffek, Jens. 2003. 'The legitimation of international governance: a discourse approach', *European Journal of International Relations* 9(2): 249–75.

Steiner, Zara S. 2005. *The Lights that Failed: European International History, 1919–1933*, New York: Oxford University Press.

Steiner, Zara S. 2011. *The Triumph of the Dark: European International History, 1933–1939*, New York: Oxford University Press.

Stimson, Henry L. 1932. 'The pact of Paris: three years of development', *Foreign Affairs* 11(1): i–ix.

Stimson, Henry L. 1936. *The Far Eastern Crisis*, New York: Harper and Brothers.

Stimson, Henry L. and McGeorge Bundy. 1947. *On Active Service in Peace and War*, New York: Harper and Brothers.

Strang, G. B. ed. 2013. *Collision of Empires: Italy's Invasion of Ethiopia and its International Impact*, London: Ashgate Publishing, Ltd.

Swinhoe, Robert, 1861. *Narrative of the North China Campaign of 1860; Containing Personal Experiences of Chinese Character, and of the Moral and Social Condition of the Country; Together with a Description of the Interior of Pekin*, London: Smith, Elder and Co.

Talmon, Stefan. 1998. *Recognition of Governments in International Law: With Particular Reference to Governments in Exile*, Oxford: Oxford University Press.

Templewood, Samuel Hoare. 1954. *'Viscount.' Nine Troubled Years*, London: Collins.

Thompson, Alexander. 2009. 'The rational enforcement of international law: solving the sanctioners' dilemma', *International Theory* 1(2): 307–21.

Thorne, Christopher G. 1970. 'The Shanghai crisis of 1932: the basis of British policy', *The American Historical Review* 75(6): 1616–39.

Thorne, Christopher G. 1972. *The Limits of Foreign Policy: The West, the League and the Far Eastern Crisis of 1931–1933*, London: Hamish Hamilton.

Tostensen, Arne and Beate Bull. 2002. 'Are Smart sanctions feasible?', *World Politics* 54(3): 373–403.

Trinidad, Jamie. 2012. 'An evaluation of Morocco's claims to Spain's remaining territories in Africa', *International and Comparative Law Quarterly* 61(4): 961–75.

Tupper, Eleanor and George E. McReynolds. 1937. *Japan in American Public Opinion*, New York: Macmillan.

Turns, David. 2003. 'The Stimson doctrine of non-recognition: its historical genesis and influence on contemporary international law', *Chinese Journal of International Law* 2(1): 105–43.

Tyran, Jean-Robert and Lars P. Feld. 2006. 'Achieving compliance when legal sanctions are non-deterrent', *The Scandinavian Journal of Economics* 108(1): 135–56.

van Diepen, Remco. 2013. 'The former European neutrals, the Ethiopian crisis and its aftermath, 1935–1938', in G. B. Strang (ed.), *Collision of Empires: Italy's Invasion of Ethiopia and its International Impact*, London: Ashgate Publishing, Ltd, pp. 311–39.

van Ginneken, Anique H. M. 2006. *Historical Dictionary of the League of Nations*, Lanham, MD: Scarecrow Press.

Van Hollen, Christopher. 1980. 'The Tilt policy revisited: Nixon-Kissinger geopolitics and South Asia', *Asian Survey* 20(2): 339–61.

Waley, Daniel P. 1975. *British Public Opinion and the Abyssinian War, 1935–6*, London: Temple Smith.

Wallace, William V. 1962. 'Roosevelt and British appeasement in 1938', *Bulletin of the British Association for American Studies* (New series) 5: 4–30.

Walters, Francis Paul. 1962. *A History of the League of Nations*, Oxford: Oxford University Press.

Walters, Francis Paul. 1986. *A History of the League of Nations*, Westport, CT: Greenwood Press.

Watanabe, Paul Y. 1984. *Ethnic Groups, Congress, and American Foreign Policy: The Politics of the Turkish Arms Embargo*, Westport, CT: Greenwood Press.

Wendt, Alexander. 1999. *Social Theory of International Politics*, Cambridge: Cambridge University Press.

Wendt, Alexander. 2001. 'Driving with the rear-view mirror: on the rational science of institutional design', *International Organization* 55(4): 1019–49.

Whang, Taehee. 2011. 'Playing to the home crowd? Symbolic use of economic sanctions in the United States', *International Studies Quarterly* 55(3): 787–801.

Willoughby, Westel W. 1935. *The Sino-Japanese Controversy and the League of Nations*, Baltimore, MD: Johns Hopkins Press.

Wilson, Harold. 1979. *Final Term: The Labour Government, 1974–1976*, London: Weidenfeld and Nicholson.

Wright, Quincy. 1962. 'The Goa incident', *American Journal of International Law* 56(3): 617–32.

Zacher, Mark W. 2001. 'The territorial integrity norm: international boundaries and the use of force', *International Organization* 55(2): 215–50.

Newspaper Articles and Others

BBC. 2014. 'Ukraine crisis: "illegal" Crimean referendum condemned', 6 March, <http://www.bbc.co.uk/news/world-europe-26475508> (last accessed 27 July 2017).

Bernstein, Richard. 1983. 'Move by Cypriots rejected at U.N.: Council, 13 to 1, declares the action by Turks on island to be legally invalid', *The New York Times*, 6 November 1983.

Dews, Fred. 2014. 'NATO Secretary-General: Russia's annexation of Crimea is illegal and illegitimate', Brookings Institute, 19 March, <http://www.brookings.edu/blogs/brookings-now/posts/2014/03/nato-secretary-general-russia-annexation-crimea-illegal-illegitimate> (last accessed 23 January 2017).

Gelb, Lesli. 1976. 'The Kissinger legacy', *The New York Times Magazine*, 31 October.

Gwertzman, Bernard. 1974a. 'U.S. urges a cease-fire and resumption of talks', *The New York Times*, 15 August, p. 1, col. 6.

Gwertzman, Bernard. 1974b. 'Peking reports holding U.S. Aide: condition of observer for embassy, seized on island off Vietnam, isn't known', *The New York Times*, 26 January.

Harris, Louis and Associates. 1972. Harris Survey, Monday, 24 January 1972, <http://www.harrisinteractive.com/vault/Harris-Interactive-Poll-Research-LOYALTIES-DIVIDED-ON-INDIA-PAKISTAN-CONFLICT-1972-01.pdf > (last accessed 7 May 2012).

Harris, Peter. 2014. 'Is the "liberal international order" dying?', *The National Interest*, 25 September.

Ignatieff, Michael. 2014. 'The new world disorder', *The New York Review of Books*, 25 September.

James, Edwin L. 1932. 'The week abroad; Japan on her way: dangers of Shanghai Far Eastern developments will weigh heavily in Geneva Arms discussions. Reductions seem unlikely nations sure to contend that Chinese plight shows countries must depend on themselves', *The New York Times*, 31 January, E3.

Keesing's Record of World Events (formerly Keesing's Contemporary Archives). 1962. Volume 8, March, India, Portugal, Indian, p. 18659.

Keesing's Record of World Events. 1972. Volume 18, February, Bangladesh, Pakistan, Bangladesh, p. 25113.

Krastev, Ivan and Mark Leonard. 2015. 'Europe's shattered dream of order: how Putin is disrupting the Atlantic Alliance', *Foreign Affairs*, May/June.

Lowell, A. Lawrence. 1932. 'Dr. Lowell depicts crisis over Japan', *The New York Times*, 18 February, p. 17.

Markham, James M. 1974. 'Saigon reports clash with China', *The New York Times*, 19 January.

Rosenberg, Matthew. 2014. 'Breaking with the west, Afghan leader supports Russia's annexation of Crimea', *The New York Times*, 23 March, <http://www.nytimes.com/2014/03/24/world/asia/breaking-with-the-west-afghan-leader-supports-russias-annexation-of-crimea.html> (last accessed 23 January 2017).

Shevtsova, Lilia. 2014. 'Crowning a winner in the post-Crimea world', *The American Interest*, 16 June.

Streit, Clarence K. 1932. 'Resolution admonishes Japan', *New York Times*, 11 March, p. 1.

The Economist. 2014. 'The new world order', 22 March.

Index

EU representative:
Easy Access System Europe
Mustamäe tee 50, 10621 Tallinn, Estonia
Gpsr.requests@easproject.com

www.ingramcontent.com/pod-product-compliance
Lightning Source LLC
Chambersburg PA
CBHW050352270326
41926CB00016B/3704